The Island Acadians

Georges Arsenault

The Island Acadians

1720–1980

Translated by
Sally Ross

Ragweed Press
Charlottetown
1989

ISBN 0–920304–81–8

Cover and Graphic Design: Raymond Thériault and Cape Bear Associates
Book Design: Cape Bear Associates
Typesetting: Braemar Publishing Limited
Printing: Williams and Crue Ltd.

Ragweed Press
P.O. Box 2023
Charlottetown
Prince Edward Island
Canada C1A 7N7

Distributed in Canada by: University of Toronto Press

Originally published in French by
Les Editions d'Acadie, Moncton, N.B.
Canada E1C 8N8

With thanks to the Canada Council for its generous support.

Canadian Cataloguing in Publication Data

Arsenault, Georges, 1952–

The Island Acadians: 1720–1980

Translation of: Les Acadiens de l'Ile: 1720–1980.
ISBN 0–920304–81–8

1. Acadians — Prince Edward Island — History.
2. Prince Edward Island — History. I. Title.

FC2650.5.A77 1989 971.7'004114 C89-098509-X
F1049.7.A2A77 1989

à ma mère,
Aldine

CONTENTS

ILLUSTRATIONS

ILLUSTRATIONS

Maps

PREFACE

This book follows the evolution of the Acadian community on Prince Edward Island over a period of 260 years. The Acadians form approximately twelve percent of the Island population and are located mainly in Prince County on the western end of the Island. As a result of various demographic, sociological and political factors, more than half of the Acadians on the Island no longer speak French, the language of their ancestors. Nevertheless, many English-speaking Acadians still identify with the Acadian community.

I have attempted throughout this book to study the phenomenon of cultural and linguistic survival in relation to the general context in which the Island Acadians have evolved. Contrary to what one might expect, the history of the Acadians is not the same throughout the Maritime Provinces. Each province has specific features. I have examined the history of the Acadians particularly with regard to settlement patterns, religion, education, politics and the economy in the smallest of the three provinces.

The origin of this publication dates back to 1979 when, in the employ of the Saint Thomas Aquinas Society (the society for Acadians on Prince Edward Island), I was invited to direct a project on Acadian history and culture. The aim of the project was to publish learning materials that would help promote the Acadian identity in the classroom. This project stimulated a considerable amount of research and resulted in numerous publications, including six thematic booklets on Acadian history published by the Saint Thomas Aquinas Society. These booklets, revised and enlarged, form the basis of this book.

The Island Acadians could not have been published without the support and financial assistance of numerous institutions. I am particularly grateful to the Saint Thomas Aquinas Society, the Secretary of State of Canada, the provincial Department of Education, the University of Prince Edward Island and the Canada Council through its Explorations Program and its Translation Grants Program.

I wish to acknowledge the contribution of Cécile Gallant, Francine Desmeules and Patricia Baldwin toward the research for this book. I am also greatly indebted to Sally Ross for her meticulous editorial work on the original French manuscript and for her diligent work in translating *Les Acadiens de l'Île* into English. I would also like to thank Cathy Matthews at Ragweed Press for her methodical editing. To all these people and the many others who collaborated at various stages of the manuscript, my sincerest thanks.

Georges Arsenault

CHAPTER I

UNDER THE FRENCH REGIME

1720–1758

The Colonization Of Acadia

The shaping of a distinct Acadian people began more than a century before the first French colonists settled on Île Saint Jean, now called Prince Edward Island. The history of the Acadians on the Island cannot be examined without first mentioning those who colonized the mainland.

The boundaries of Acadia were never clearly defined. The two colonizing nations, France and England, could not come to an agreement as to the precise border of the disputed territory. For over a century France considered that Acadia included all of the territory which, in today's terms, comprises the Maritime Provinces, the south shore of the Gaspé Peninsula, the north shore of Maine and the Magdalen Islands. After the negotiations which led to the Treaty of Utrecht in 1713, in which France was forced to hand over Acadia to England, France maintained that Acadia included only the territory covered by what is now mainland Nova Scotia[1].

The first French settlement in America was founded on the Island of St. Croix in 1604. Approximately eighty men took part in the expedition led by Sieurs Pierre Du Gua de Monts, Samuel de Champlain and Jean de Poutrincourt. The first winter proved to be catastrophic for the tiny colony since almost half of the men perished from the cold and from scurvy. In the spring of 1605 the survivors settled in Port Royal, a more propitious site located on the mainland and one which was to become the capital of Acadia.

Fishermen from all the great maritime countries in Europe had been coming to the waters off this part of North America long before the first settlers arrived. They came every year to fish cod which proved to be extremely lucrative in their countries. These Europeans had dealings with the native people with whom they bartered for furs. Names on present-day maps attest to the presence of Basques, Portuguese and Spaniards who are known to have been in the Gulf of St. Lawrence as early as the mid-1400s. It should also be remembered that Jacques Cartier made his first great voyage in 1534.

Given the commercial interests of France, her early settlements were primarily devoted to the fur trade and the fishery. Nevertheless, they developed slowly due to financial difficulties and because the territory was also coveted by England. As a result, these trading stations

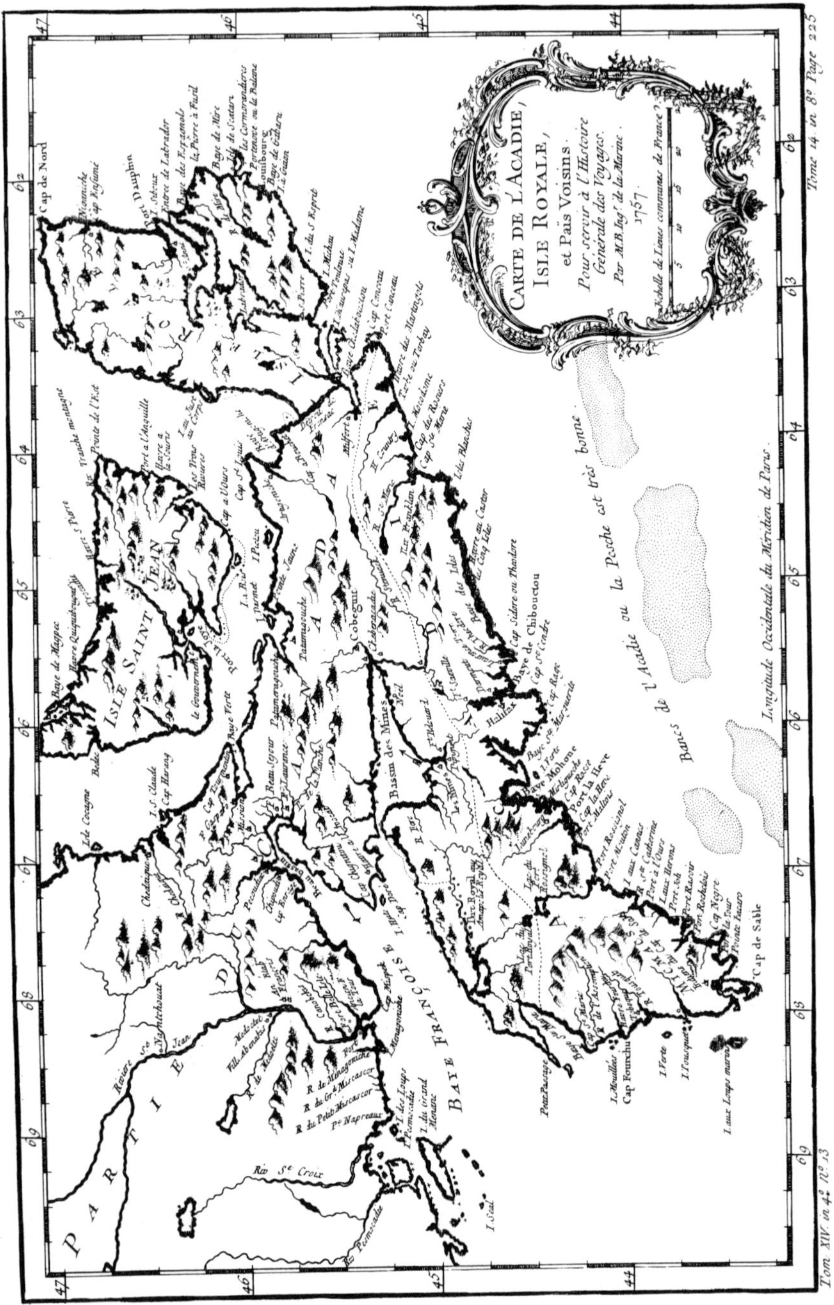
Carte de l'Acadie,
Isle Royale,
et Païs Voisins.
Pour servir à l'Histoire Générale des Voyages.
Par M.B. Ingr. de la Marine.
1757.
Isle Saint Jean
Baye Françoise
Bassin des Mines
Longitude Occidentale du Méridien de Paris.
Bancs de l'Acadie ou la Pesche est très bonne
Tome 14. in 8° Page 225
Tom XIV in 4°. N° 13

were attacked and destroyed on several occasions by British troops from New England.

It was not until after 1632 that the colonization of Acadia really began. With the Treaty of St. Germain en Laye, Acadia, conquered several years before, was given back to France. Cardinal Richelieu, prime minister under Louis XIII, devised an important plan for colonization which would strengthen France's position in America and exploit more advantageously the resources of the New World. Richelieu entrusted his cousin, Isaac de Razilly, with the colonization of Acadia in the name of the King of France.

Razilly and his successors attended to the recruitment of colonists, many of whom came from the province of Poitou in western France. They began by settling in the vicinity of Port Royal on the south side of the *Baie Française* (Bay of Fundy) along the vast salt marshes which they drained and dyked, thus enabling them to successfully farm the rich flood plains. Many of these pioneers had experience with the same type of terrain in their native French province[2].

As the number of settlers increased, the Acadian colony stretched out along the shoreline of the Bay of Fundy right up to the head of Cobequid Bay and Chignecto Bay. According to the first census in 1671 there were about four hundred inhabitants and by 1707 the population was estimated at approximately eighteen hundred[3].

The French colonists who settled in this part of North America soon formed a people with a distinct identity. Fundamentally a population of farmers, they developed a very intensive community life since the construction and upkeep of the dykes and *aboiteaux* required a strong spirit of co-operation. Many of the inhabitants not only came from the same regions in France but were also related. The homogeneity of the population was further strengthened by marriages that took place in Acadia.

There were other factors which helped foster the feeling of identity and independence amongst the Acadians. Established on a strategic territory that constituted a buffer state between New France and New England, the Acadians often found themselves victims of the struggles between France and England. In fact, Acadia changed hands nine times between 1604 and 1710 and was attacked about ten times by British troops. Never enjoying the political stability that characterized New France, the Acadians soon learned to rely on their own resources.

Consequently, they kept their distance from political conflicts, wanting to coexist as well as possible with the authorities in power in order to ensure some degree of security. On the other hand, the Acadians showed their independence even under French rule by trading with the neighbouring colonies in New England. The survival and economic development of Acadia depended on the growth of this maritime trade.

In 1710 the Acadian capital of Port Royal was captured by troops from New England. Three years later, with the Treaty of Utrecht which was concluded at the end of the War of the Spanish Succession, France ceded Hudson Bay, Acadia and Newfoundland to England. The treaty stipulated that within one year the Acadians had to leave the colony, henceforth called Nova Scotia, or remain on condition that they become British subjects. England guaranteed free exercise of the Catholic religion "insofar as the laws of Great Britain allowed."

Well-adapted on their land, the Acadians had no intention of relocating. Given the chronic political instability of the past hundred years, they had no reason to believe that this peace would be more lasting than previous ones. Although they refused to take the oath of allegiance to the British Crown in the form prescribed, the Acadians stated that they were willing to become British subjects provided they would not have to take up arms against France in the event of war. In addition, they wanted assurance that their Catholic faith would be respected.

Several English governors of Nova Scotia tried without success to force the Acadians to take an oath of unconditional allegiance to the monarch of Great Britain. The English threatened expulsion if they refused to obey; however, neutrality meant too much for the Acadians to be able to give in to such pressures.

This neutrality was put to the test during the 1740s when war broke out again between France and England. During the conflict, French troops stationed at Louisbourg tried in vain to recapture Acadia. Despite pressure from the military, most Acadians refused to join the ranks of the French army. A certain number did collaborate although nearly all of them stated afterwards that they had been forced to do so. These events prompted the British authorities to question the neutrality of the Acadians. In order to occupy her territory more efficiently England decided to send out Protestant colonists and build, in 1749, the fortress town of Halifax as a counterpoise to Louisbourg.

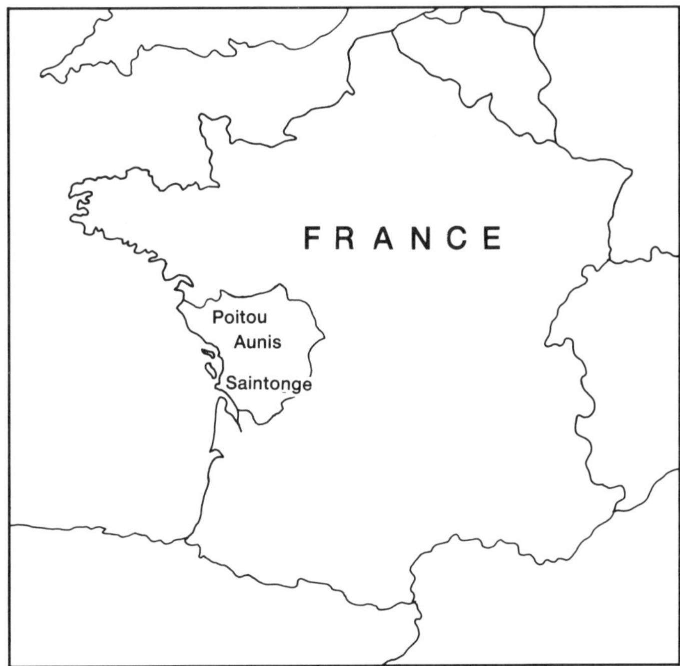

Most of the Acadian colonists came from this region of France.

Several years later, in 1755, Governor Charles Lawrence decided to force the Acadians, once and for all, to take the unconditional oath of allegiance. He expressed his intention to deport them from their homeland if they refused. The Acadians tried to change his mind, but to no avail. In the fall of 1755, Lawrence's troops, aided by those of Governor Shirley of Massachusetts, carried out the orders to expel the Acadians. Of the estimated ten thousand Acadian inhabitants about six thousand were exiled to the colonies of New England.

And so ends the first chapter in the history of the Acadians who colonized the mainland. The political instability of the colony, due partly to its strategic position, its isolation with regard to New France, the common geographic origin of the settlers and the way they adapted to their surroundings were all factors that contributed to the formation of a distinct people.

Île Saint Jean: The Beginnings of a Colony

France laid claim to Île Saint Jean long before she sent settlers there in 1720. As early as 1534, the French explorer Jacques Cartier had visited the Island briefly and had taken possession of it in the name of the King of France. While the first description of the Island can be found in his reports, it had long been frequented by the Micmac, especially in the summertime. They may even have established permanent settlements. The Micmac called the island *Abegweit* which means "cradled on the waves."

We do not know who named the island after Saint John nor when. We do know that the name was used by the Basques and Bretons who fished off the Island long before its first appearance on the map of New France drawn up by Samuel de Champlain in 1612[4].

The name Île Saint Jean appears in the text of royal concessions granted during the seventeenth century to certain shipowners and merchants who financed the cod fishery. Among the known holders of royal privileges we note the names of Nicolas Denys (1653), François Doublet (1663) and Gabriel Gautier (1686). However, it would seem that none of them ever founded a permanent settlement on the island.

After losing Acadia and Newfoundland in 1713, France wanted to colonize Île Saint Jean and Île Royale (Cape Breton). She recognized the need to strengthen her position along the Atlantic coast both to protect her colony in New France, which at the time included twenty thousand inhabitants, and to support the important codfish industry. In order to begin the colonization of Île Royale, France encouraged Acadians to move off the peninsula which now belonged to the British. French authorities wanted to profit from the Acadians' experience in order to quickly establish and develop a new colony. Recognizing the advantage which the Acadians represented, the Navy Board stated in 1717:

> These French Acadians are by nature industrious, they are born blacksmiths, joiners, coopers, carpenters, builders and they make the cloth and homespun for their own clothes. That is why in addition to clearing the land on Île Royale they would provide the colony with a considerable number of good workmen who would contribute much more to its settlement than people sent from France who would not be used to either the climate or the customs of the country. (TR)[5]

France began the construction of the fortress of Louisbourg in 1720 in order to protect the maritime approaches to her North American colonies. The location of Louisbourg was important because of the ice-free harbour. It was thought that the fortress could easily drive away any naval attack. However, there was a lack of arable land at this site on Île Royale and it was fog-bound and wind-swept for most of the year—drawbacks for a developing colony.

The shortage of agricultural land constituted a serious problem because it did not help to attract Acadian farmers and it meant that the fortress town had to be provisioned. For generations, the Acadians had been farming the fertile lands along the Bay of Fundy. At this particular time, nothing could induce them to give up their family farms in order to live in isolation on rocky and impoverished land.

Faced with this situation, the authorities in Louisbourg advocated colonizing Île Saint Jean where the soil seemed very fertile, thus more likely to appeal to Acadians. Moreover, its waters were teeming with fish and its forests constituted an excellent source of lumber.

In 1719 the Comte de Saint Pierre, first Equerry to the Duchesse d'Orléans, received from Louis XV a land grant for Île Saint Jean, Miscou Island and the Magdalen Islands in the Gulf of St. Lawrence "to establish inhabitants and a sedentary cod fishery" (TR)[6]. The letters patent stipulated that in order to retain his concession, the concessionaire must settle one hundred colonists the first year and fifty the following years.

The establishment of a colony and a fishery required large investments. Transport and fishing vessels had to be procured, the settlers' passage paid for, administrators hired and living quarters built along with places for worship, etc. In order to raise the necessary capital, the Comte de Saint Pierre founded the *Compagnie de l'Isle Saint Jean* which enabled him to attract several wealthy speculators[7]. He then recruited about three hundred colonists and fishermen who were willing to try their luck in the New World. On April 15, 1720, the expedition left Rochefort in three ships under the command of Gotteville de Bellisle, an employee of Saint Pierre's company. After a four-month-long crossing, the colonists landed at Port LaJoie on the 23rd of August, while the others, mainly fishermen, made their way to the north shore to Havre Saint Pierre (St. Peters) which was to become the main fishing centre and the most populated settlement in the colony. As early as the first year several Acadian families joined the colonists who had just arrived from France.

The efforts of the *Compagnie de l'Isle Saint Jean* were not very successful. The Comte de Saint Pierre (who never visited the Island) had hoped to recoup his investments with profits from the fishery, but he encountered innumerable obstacles. Although he had obtained exclusive fishing rights off his islands he was never able to make the fishermen from Île Royale respect his monopoly. Fiercely contested by the French merchants who employed the fishermen, they considered the monopoly to be against their interests and those of France. Deeply in debt and unable to make the colony pay for itself, the *Compagnie de l'Isle Saint Jean* ceased its activities at the end of 1724. The following year Louis XV revoked the Comte de Saint Pierre's fishing rights. The departure of the company prompted numerous settlers and fishermen to move to Île Royale or go back to France.

Colonization And Development: 1726–1745

After the departure of the *Compagnie de l'Isle Saint Jean*, France became concerned about the safety of the territory. According to rumours, the English were preparing to establish a foothold on the Island. Consequently the French government ordered the governor of Louisbourg to send over an armed detachment of about thirty naval fusiliers that would be responsible for confirming French sovereignty. This tiny company, under the command of Jacques d'Espiet de Pensens, landed on Île Saint Jean in the spring of 1726 and set up headquarters at Port LaJoie in the dilapidated buildings formerly occupied by the *Compagnie de l'Isle Saint Jean*. Jacques d'Espiet de Pensens was an experienced officer with years of service in the colonies of New France.

At this time the population was still sparse. In 1728 there were only 297 permanent residents and about 125 seasonal fishermen, in a total of 54 dwellings that housed 76 men, 51 women, 156 children and 14 servants[8].

French authorities still hoped to entice Acadians, and especially young couples, to settle on Île Saint Jean[9]. To this end Commandant de Pensens requested the approval and support of the Minister of the Navy in charge of French colonies. De Pensens felt that to attract

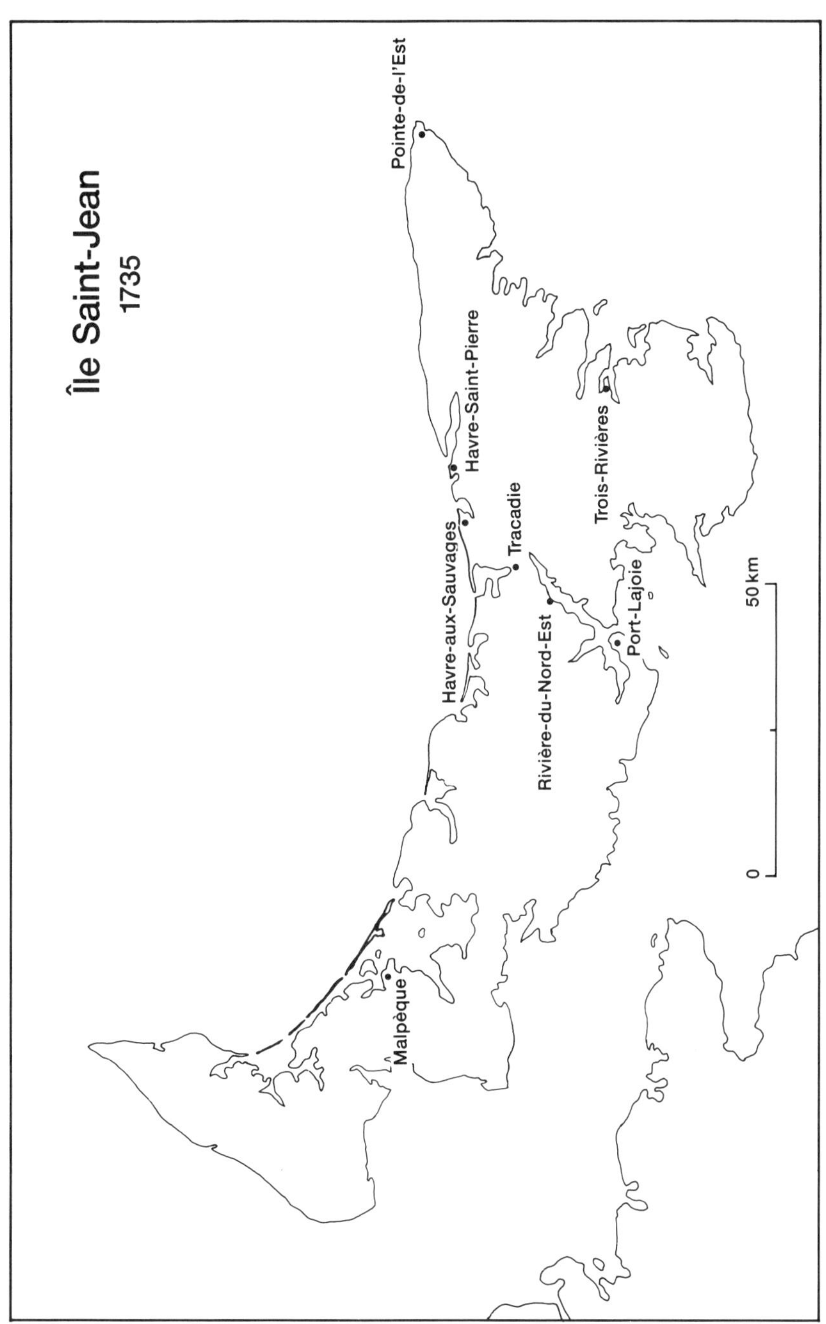
Île Saint-Jean
1735
Pointe-de-l'Est
Havre-Saint-Pierre
Havre-aux-Sauvages
Tracadie
Trois-Rivières
Rivière-du-Nord-Est
Port-Lajoie
Malpèque
0
50 km

Acadians they would have to be given financial help for the first few years while they cleared the land. He was convinced that an investment of this kind would be worthwhile to the extent that the island could eventually become the "storehouse" (TR) for Île Royale.

However, the Acadians hesitated to go over to the Island colony, particularly because they were afraid the *Compagnie de l'Isle Saint Jean* might exercise its rights and demand rent from the colonists. The inhabitants who were already established had similar concerns. De Pensens disclosed the following to the Minister in 1728:

> The inhabitants are extremely worried by the fact that I am giving them no guarantee for their lands. They have pressed me several times on this matter. I tried to reassure them as best I could by telling them they had nothing to fear from the Comte de Saint Pierre and that they could be sure that he would never bother them on Île Saint Jean. . .(TR)[10]

In order to give greater assurance to the Acadians, de Pensens and the governor of Île Royale, Saint Ovide de Brouillan, demanded that the French government revoke the letters patent of the Comte de Saint Pierre and that the Island become part of the Royal domain. This eventually took place in 1730. There was no large-scale immigration, in spite of the fact that the titles had been revoked. On the contrary, only a few Acadian families resettled and, even then, at a very slow rate.

The Acadians were profoundly attached to the properties which they had been farming for generations. They had succeeded in mastering their natural surroundings and were leading a relatively comfortable life. They produced enough not only to feed and clothe themselves, but also to export to New England and Louisbourg. So long as their life was not in danger, why would they abandon fertile soil to start from scratch in a land of uncertainties? Moreover, the move in itself presented definite problems since the transportation of furniture, personal belongings and often large herds of livestock had to be arranged. Financial help from France was not always available. For their part the English authorities governing Nova Scotia had no interest whatsoever in helping to populate the neighbouring French colonies, especially since the garrison and government located in Annapolis Royal depended on the Acadian farmers for supplies.

There was also a geographical factor that discouraged Acadian emigration to the Island. Unlike Acadia, Île Saint Jean had very few natural meadows. There were, however, beautiful forests. The Acadians would, with difficulty, clear these since they lacked proper experience and training. Besides, Acadians were undoubtedly deterred by the fact that in the early years of the Island colony, crops had been destroyed by plagues.

Despite all these obstacles, small groups of Acadians moved to the Island between 1720 and 1745. For example, six families came to settle in Port LaJoie in 1724 and about sixty Acadians originating from Beaubassin settled in various locations on the Island in 1730[11]. According to the census of the colony taken in 1735, out of 432 colonists, 162 (35.5%) were of Acadian origin[12]. The inhabitants were located at Port LaJoie, Havre Saint Pierre (St. Peter's), Tracadie, Havre aux Sauvages (Savage Harbour), Rivière du Nord Est (Hillsborough River), Malpeque, Trois Rivières (Brudenell Point) and Pointe de l'Est (East Point).

The settlement in Trois Rivières was unique in that it constituted an independent colony. In 1731 the King granted the *Compagnie de l'Est* a large tract of land at the mouth of what are known today as the Cardigan, Brudenell and Montague Rivers. The principal shareholder in the company was Jean-Pierre Roma, an energetic Parisian merchant who came to the Island in 1732 to administer his concession. Roma brought with him men to clear the forest, put up buildings and devote themselves to the fishery from which he hoped to make a profit. He also had facilities on the north coast at Havre Saint Pierre, the main fishing centre on the Island.

Roma undertook impressive projects to expand his business. For example, he had roads cut through the forest to link Trois Rivières, Havre Saint Pierre and Port LaJoie. His aim was to turn his settlement into an important trading centre. It should be noted, however, that Acadians avoided settling on the property of the *Compagnie de l'Est* because they refused to become tenants of a seigneur.

Jean-Pierre Roma was determined to make his enterprise succeed despite numerous obstacles. Unfortunately, fate would have it otherwise. All his endeavours soon collapsed: in 1745, during the War of the Austrian Succession, Trois Rivières was destroyed by a detachment of soldiers from New England[13].

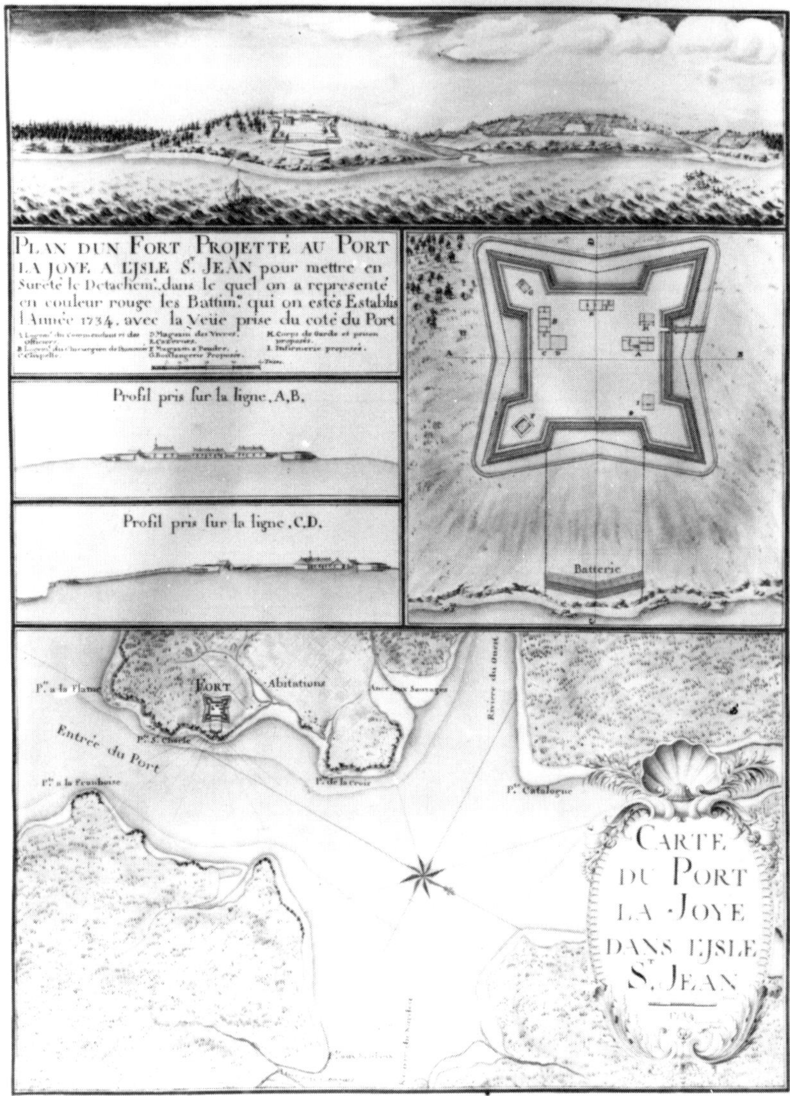

Plan of Port La Joye, 1734.

Original: Bibliothèque nationale, Paris, Cabinet des Estampes, Vd. 20a (f.42). Copy: Cartographic and Architectural Archives Division, Public Archives of Canada.

The British Siege: 1745–1748

The War of the Austrian Succession caused France and England to resume hostilities in 1744. The conflict affected their colonies on the other side of the Atlantic and in particular the Acadians whose neutrality was to be put to the test. As soon as news of the war reached Governor Duquesnel, who was in command at Louisbourg, he decided the time had come to carry out his plan to reconquer Acadia. Consequently, he sent an expeditionary corps under the leadership of François DuPont Duvivier with orders to capture Annapolis Royal (formerly Port Royal). The attempt failed for tactical reasons and a lack of reinforcements and supplies. Duvivier and Duquesnel had expected both the Acadians and the Micmac to rally to the cause. Much to their disappointment, however, with a few exceptions, the Acadians (as opposed to the Micmac) categorically refused to take part in the expedition. They feared reprisals from the English if the military venture were to fail. It was thus only with considerable difficulty that Duvivier managed to convince a few Acadians to help supply his soldiers with provisions[14].

It was not long before the New England colonies responded to the French attacks on Nova Scotia. In the spring of 1745 a squadron attacked and captured Louisbourg, a fortress the French considered impregnable. The siege was led by Commander Pepperel who encountered little resistance and forced Governor Duchambon to capitulate on June 17, 1745.

Several days before Louisbourg was captured, Pepperel sent a reconnaissance party to Île Saint Jean. A detachment marched on Trois Rivières where, as we have seen, they destroyed Jean-Pierre Roma's establishment. The seigneur and his family were able to make their way to Havre Saint Pierre and then to Quebec, never to return to Île Saint Jean. The remainder of Pepperel's men marched on Port LaJoie where they set fire to the fort and other buildings. The tiny garrison of about twenty men, under the command of Dupont Duvivier, proceeded up the Northeast River with the English hot on their heels. With the support of a group of Micmac, Duvivier's soldiers were able to turn around and attack the English, forcing them back to the sea. The English left behind twenty-eight who were either killed, wounded or made prisoner following the skirmish[15].

With the conquest of Louisbourg, Île Saint Jean also fell into the hands of the English since it depended on the fortress for protection. According to the terms of an agreement signed in Louisbourg, in exchange for the liberation of six hostages, the British authorities promised not to disturb the inhabitants of Île Saint Jean and gave them one year to leave the Island[16].

After the Island was conquered, the Acadian colonists began to fear the looming spectre of expulsion. According to rumours, the English were preparing to deport the Acadians. The plan, in fact, was not carried out partly because they lacked the material facilities and partly because they did not regard these colonists as a real threat[17].

A military expedition was being prepared in New France with the aim of reconquering Acadia, Île Royale and Île Saint Jean. De Ramezay left Quebec in 1746 at the head of an expeditionary corps of seven hundred men. A detachment of these soldiers, led by Montesson and accompanied by Micmac, attacked an English ship in the Northeast River. The English suffered a few casualties and several soldiers were taken prisoner[18].

De Ramezay's expedition, like Duvivier's, was a failure. Neither was successful in winning over the Acadians to the Royal army. The few Acadians who did join the ranks of the Canadian corps declared later that they had been forced to do so.

Despite these setbacks, Louisbourg and the settlements dependent upon her were returned to France by the Treaty of Aix la Chapelle in 1748. In this document, England agreed to give back these Atlantic colonies to France in exchange for the Indian state of Madras. Thus, three years after the fall of Louisbourg, and as a result of dealings over another colony on the opposite side of the world, Île Royale and Île Saint Jean became French colonies once again.

The Administration And Protection Of The Colony

As we have already seen, Port LaJoie was chosen as the administrative centre of Île Saint Jean at the time of Gotteville de Bellisle's settlement in 1720. From then until the British conquest in 1745 Île Saint Jean was under the administrative jurisdiction of the government of Louisbourg.

In 1726, two years after the departure of the employees of the *Compagnie de l'Isle Saint Jean*, the French government appointed Jacques d'Espiet de Pensens as Commandant of the Island. He was serving on Île Royale at the time of his appointment and was not particularly pleased about his transfer. Elderly and in delicate health, he had no desire to abandon the comfort of his apartments in Louisbourg for an isolated and sparsely populated colony. Nevertheless, he obeyed and made his way to Port LaJoie with about thirty soldiers, a chaplain and a surgeon. In his eleven years as commanding officer on the Island, de Pensens did not spend much time at Port LaJoie. He preferred to spend the winter in the comfort of Louisbourg rather than in the old headquarters of the *Compagnie de l'Isle Saint Jean*. The living conditions were rather appalling, as he wrote to the Minister of the Navy in 1728:

> I have the honour of bringing to your attention, Sire, the impossibility of staying on Île Saint Jean unless, in the future, your Highness has the kindness to order the construction of some dwellings. Since the casemates left by the Comte de Saint Pierre's company are in total disrepair, the soldiers and I constantly run the risk of being crushed by the buildings in which we are lodged and which I have had repaired so that they could last until now. (TR)[19]

No doubt the complaints of the Commandant were justified: his colony received very little help from the government. In 1729, he complained that he had been refused the boat and the shallop required for his own transportation around the Island and for the transport of the effects belonging to the garrison[20]. In November 1730, he informed his minister that more than half of the rifles of the garrison were defective and that the hospital was lacking in virtually everything, even firewood[21].

During a visit to France in 1732, de Pensens put pressure on government authorities. He became the King's Lieutenant, an appointment he had been coveting for a long time. He was promised funds for the construction of new quarters for himself and his troops, and a new Royal storehouse. De Pensens made futile requests that the garrison at Port LaJoie be augmented[22]. It was not until after his departure in 1737 that a reinforcement of forty soldiers was sent[23].

Louis Duchambon replaced de Pensens. He was chosen because of his popularity among the Acadians whom the authorities were still

Soldier, Compagnies franches de la Marine.
Environment Canada, Parks.

trying to entice to Île Saint Jean. As soon as he arrived, Duchambon criticized the choice of Port LaJoie as a capital. He felt that it was not a good centre for either farming or fishing and was too far away from Havre Saint Pierre where most of the trading took place. He wrote on October 2, 1737:

> With regard to inhabitants, although I shall do my best to attract as many as I can, there is no point talking about the ones at Port LaJoie because, with the exception of the Gallans who make up four households, there are none left. They have, or are now deserting the settlement because they are dying of hunger. I cannot understand why this location was chosen as the principal settlement since it is truly the most infertile part of this [island] and where no one can fish... (TR)[24]

Duchambon left Île Saint Jean in 1744 to become governor of Île

Royale. In 1749, at the end of the British siege, he was replaced by Commandant Claude Denis de Bonnaventure. In 1754, Officer Rousseau de Villejoin was the last person to fill the position.

The administration of Ile Saint Jean at the local level was not left entirely to the King's Lieutenant. When the *Compagnie de l'Isle Saint Jean* was operating, an assistant deputy of the Intendant of New France was sent by the French government to attend to the administration of justice. Subsequently, his duties included the running of the Royal storehouse, census-taking and the distribution of rations to the soldiers and the inhabitants[25]. The first assistant deputy, Robert Poitier Dubuisson, occupied the position from 1722 to 1744. His successor, François-Marie Degoutin, did not take up his functions until 1749 after the Island had been given back to France. He remained in office until 1752.

Acadian Immigration: 1748–1755

By 1748 the population of the Island was still relatively small: approximately 735 inhabitants[26]. However, a sudden change in England's policy with regard to Nova Scotia triggered a wave of immigration. The question of the oath was becoming increasingly problematic. English authorities still wanted the Acadians to become British subjects. This was made clear to the new governor, Edward Cornwallis, who proved to be far less tolerant than his predecessor, the French Protestant, Paul Mascarène. Cornwallis demanded that the Acadians take the unconditional oath of allegiance or else be deported. They refused.

France, on the other hand, doubled her efforts to attract Acadians to her territory. Authorities in Quebec and Louisbourg, with the disinterested support of the missionary Jean-Louis Leloutre, urged the Acadians to move to the French territory north of the Missaguash River (on the Isthmus of Chignecto), the supposed border separating the French and English possessions. Acadians were also encouraged to go over to Île Saint Jean and Île Royale.

This is why France hurriedly began the reconstruction of Port LaJoie, which had been reduced to ashes during the English siege. The new governor, Commandant Claude Denis de Bonnaventure, was responsible for welcoming, housing and provisioning the Acadian immigrants. Immigration increased beginning in 1749: 151 people in 1749, 860 in 1750, 326 in 1751 and 27 in 1752[27]. Newly arrived Acadians settled amongst the earlier colonists but they also founded numerous other settlements including Pointe Prime (Point Prim), Anse à Pinette (Pinette), Grande Anse (Orwell Bay), Bedeque, Rivière des Blonds (Tryon), and Rivière à la Fortune (Fortune River)[28].

As a result of the sudden immigration, the population of the Island tripled within the space of four years which gave rise to serious problems. On the one hand, administrators were unable to house and feed all of the immigrants properly; on the other hand, because there was no surveyor the colonists could not obtain titles for their properties. They felt insecure not only because of their lands, but also with regard to the effectiveness of the military protection. Located in Port LaJoie, the garrison was in fact too distant from the main settlements. To make matters worse, the French government forced the colonists to devote themselves exclusively to farming. Only the inhabitants of Havre Saint Pierre and Tracadie retained their fishing rights. This policy was aimed at turning Île Saint Jean into a granary for Louisbourg.

In 1751, the engineer Louis Franquet arrived on Île Saint Jean to study the situation of the colony with a view to drawing plans for fortifications. Over the course of his visit he had the opportunity to hear grievances from a large number of settlers. Franquet's recommendations to the French authorities provide information about the concerns of the Island inhabitants. He recommended in particular: 1) that the principal ports on the Island be protected by a garrison and that land communications be improved; 2) that three new religious parishes be created; 3) that the inhabitants be allowed to fish, although without neglecting farming; 4) that a surveyor be sent to the Island in order to finally settle the problem of the land grants; 5) that the administration of the Island be independent of Louisbourg; 6) and, finally, that direct communication be established between Île Saint Jean and France[29]. Unfortunately, Franquet's report attracted little attention since the tiny colony did not constitute a priority for the French government.

A flood of Acadian immigrants arrived in the fall of 1755. Indeed, it was at this time that Governor Charles Lawrence decided to carry out the expulsion of the Acadians of Nova Scotia who still refused to take the unconditional oath of allegiance to the British sovereign. This decision followed the capture of Fort Beauséjour which had been built by the French on the Isthmus of Chignecto, north of the Missaguash River, in territory claimed by France. When Charles Lawrence captured the fort, with the help of troops from Massachusetts, he encountered two hundred Acadians. They swore they had been forced, under pain of death, to take up arms on the side of the French, thus violating their neutrality. Highly suspicious, Lawrence decided to obtain total allegiance from the Acadians or deport them. In his view, the Acadians constituted a real threat.

In 1755 there were about ten thousand Acadians in Nova Scotia of whom approximately six thousand were deported to the colonies in New England. Lawrence's troops burned the villages, destroyed the crops and loaded the inhabitants on board ships under very unpleasant conditions. About half of the four thousand Acadians who managed to escape took refuge on Île Saint Jean. By 1756, there were over 4,400 inhabitants on the Island[30]. Lieutenant-Governor Vaudreuil of Quebec came to the rescue of these refugees. But in writing to the Minister of the Navy on August 7, 1756, he stated that the situation on Île Saint Jean was deplorable.

> There is great misery on Île Saint Jean, most of the inhabitants are without bread. Mr. de Villejoin has been feeding 1,257 refugees since the autumn. He received 230 people from Cocagne this spring, but was obliged to send several families on to Quebec on the orders of Mr. de Drucourt and, following my instructions, he got rid of the less industrious ones. (TR)[31]

And so ends, on a tragic note, the great wave of immigration to Île Saint Jean. Within eight years the population increased from 735 to 4,400 inhabitants. Now begins the painful depopulation of the Island.

The Deportation Of 1758

The Acadian refugees' stay on Île Saint Jean was short-lived. In 1758, the fortress of Louisbourg was once again attacked by British troops. The French capitulated on July 26, thereby forfeiting Île Saint Jean as well. General Amherst sent Lord Rollo and a contingent of

Expulsion of the Acadians from Île Saint Jean.
Environment Canada, Parks; Lewis Parker.

five hundred men to the Island with an order to round up and deport the inhabitants and to burn their settlements. When the people on the Island learned of their conquerors' plans, they went in a delegation to ask Lord Rollo to allow them to remain on their lands. Lord Rollo replied that he was obliged to obey orders from his superiors, but he gave Fathers Cassiet and Biscaret permission to take their parishioners' request to General Amherst in Louisbourg. Their appeal was rejected, and in October English soldiers began transporting Acadians by ship to France. It is estimated that over three thousand people were deported from Île Saint Jean[32]. The other inhabitants fled to the Bay of

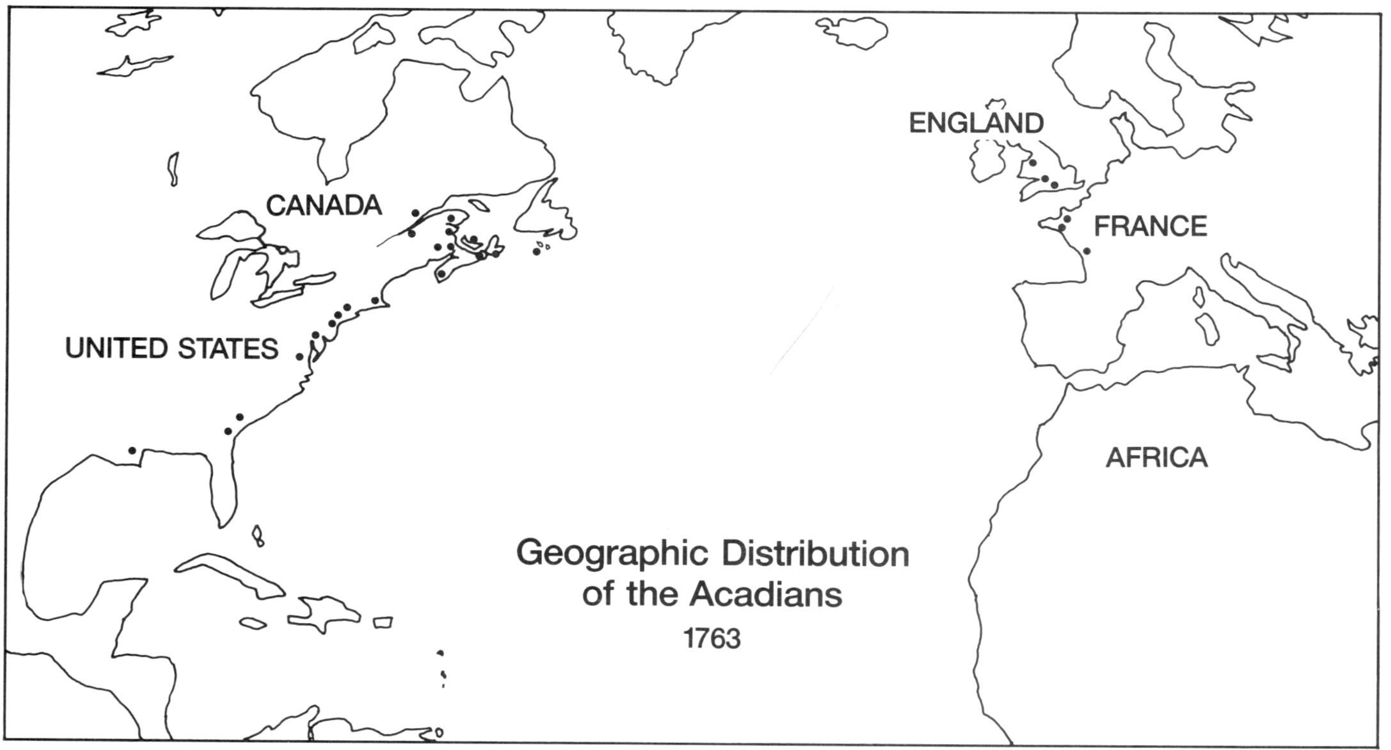
ENGLAND
CANADA
FRANCE
UNITED STATES
AFRICA
Geographic Distribution
of the Acadians
1763

Chaleur and Quebec in their own boats or on French vessels that came to their rescue. Some families managed to hide from the enemy and stay on the Island.

What was the fate of the estimated three thousand deportees? Approximately seven hundred of them were crowded on board the *Duke William* and the *Violet* and perished during the transatlantic crossing when both vessels sank during a storm. Many others died on board ship. The survivors were disembarked in French ports. France welcomed them and gave them pensions until they were able to resettle with the help of the State.

The Acadians did not feel at home in France. It was of course the land of their ancestors, but for the majority of them it was not their birthplace. Their homeland was Acadia, that seacoast their forefathers had colonized a century before and where they had developed over several generations a way of life that was very different from that in France. Within a short time most of the Acadians wanted to return to Acadia or to settle in the new French colonies, rather than stay in France.

In the twenty-five years that followed the expulsion, these exiled Acadians were forced to move numerous times. In addition to several relocations within France, where some families settled permanently[33], many Acadians crossed the ocean again in search of their lost country. A certain number returned to Acadia, others sailed to the West Indies and some as far as the Falkland Islands. Many of these attempts to resettle failed. These wandering Acadians went back to France but in the 1780s quite a large number left for Louisiana.

The Fishery

Throughout the French regime the life of the inhabitants of Île Saint Jean revolved mainly around fishing and farming. As we have mentioned, the Comte de Saint Pierre was interested above all in the codfish industry which constituted a very important part of the French economy in the eighteenth century. Cod was highly valued commercially, especially in Portugal, Spain and Italy[34]. At the beginning of the eighteenth century, French fishermen fished mainly on the Grand Banks off Newfoundland, a territory controlled by France. Without establishing any permanent settlements the French fishermen dried and salted their fish along the shores of Newfoundland. When France lost Newfoundland and Acadia by virtue of the Treaty of Utrecht in 1713, her economy was seriously jeopardized. One can see why Île Royale, Île Saint Jean and Labrador became important[35].

The fisheries in North America played a dual role. France, like England, relied on her fishing industry as a source of sailors. Young men between sixteen and eighteen years of age were introduced to ships and the sea, then recruited as crew for the Royal Navy. During the eighteenth century a powerful and well-trained navy represented an essential component of the strength of a nation[36].

While France ensured the training of her sailors and the protection of her fisheries, she also wanted to assert her sovereignty in her distant possessions by establishing colonies. But this was a costly and unprofitable venture in the short run, unlike the fishing industry. Like all colonialist nations of the period, France resorted to concessions. In other words, she conceded a territory by granting exclusive fishing rights to an individual or a company who, in turn, was required to settle the land granted and to assume the costs of the settlement[37]. It was under these circumstances that the Comte de Saint Pierre and his *Compagnie de l'Isle Saint Jean* were obliged to colonize the Island in order to retain the monopoly of fishing in the area.

As we have seen, the company soon went bankrupt. By 1722, only two years after the colony was founded, the Comte de Saint Pierre was preparing to abandon his settlement. Competition from fishermen out of Île Royale and France resulted in financial problems for the *Compagnie de l'Isle Saint Jean* which had already invested over 8,000 pounds for the establishment of the colony. According to the directors, the success of the colony could be guaranteed only if they had the monopoly of cod and seal fisheries[38]. Consequently, the admiral of France was called upon to protect the company's fishing rights against "the greed and envy of the neighbouring fishermen on these coasts" (TR)[39]. Unfortunately, there was not enough support from France and the Comte was forced to abandon his settlement in the Gulf of St. Lawrence[40].

Throughout the French regime, Havre Saint Pierre remained the most populated settlement in the colony and the main fishing centre. The families of thirty-three fishermen were living there in 1734. These fishermen were born in France, usually originating from the provinces of Normandy, Brittany, Saintonge and Gascony. In addition to the fishermen who had settled permanently on the Island, there were also sailors and other fishermen who would go back to France after the fishing season was over. According to the census of 1734, there were 163 of these men in Havre Saint Pierre alone. The settlement also included three ploughmen, a blacksmith, a surgeon and a carpenter. Six of the permanent fishermen were also farming the land[41]. Only a few Acadians lived in Havre Saint Pierre. The Acadians, who were primarily farmers, established their own communities elsewhere on the Island.

Relations were often tense among the people of Havre Saint Pierre. Indeed, the Commandant de Pensens or one of his officers frequently had to settle differences between the merchants, the inhabitants and the fishermen[42]. De Pensens wrote that the fishermen on the north coast were "people without discipline" (TR)[43] and "a people who avoided only too easily obedience and discipline (TR)[44].

It should be said that the French government did not do much to encourage the expansion of the fishery on Île Saint Jean. In fact the development of this tiny colony never constituted a priority during the French regime. The authorities were concerned mainly that the colony on Île Royale, and the fortress of Louisbourg, located there be strong enough to defend the French colonies in North America. Despite this policy, the fishermen living on Île Saint Jean succeeded in catching codfish, but not without difficulties. Some of them were employed by local merchants, while others were independent and sold their catches to merchants from Louisbourg or France.

Vessels came from both these places to fish off the Island. They also took the opportunity to trade with the inhabitants. In 1731, Robert Poitier Dubuisson, the assistant deputy of the intendant, stated in a letter to the Minister of the Colonies that "two ships of about one hundred tons had come directly from France to this island for two years in succession, last year from Granville and this year from Bordeaux, to fish for cod and to trade with the inhabitants" (TR)[45]. We learn from a letter, the following year by Lenormant de Mezy from Louisbourg that a ship commanded by Captain Mathé went to Havre Saint Pierre to pick up the cod caught by the employees on the ten shallops belonging to Jean-Pierre Roma[46].

In 1728, the fishery was more successful on Île Saint Jean than on Île Royale, even though its growth was constantly hindered by a shortage of equipment[47]. In fact, it would appear that the greatest problem encountered by the fishermen was obtaining fishing gear, food and clothing at a fair price. Either they had to lose days by going to Louisbourg, or buy directly from French boats at exorbitant prices. De Pensens describes these problems in a letter dated March 5, 1732 addressed to the Minister of the Colonies:

> Although fishing is good and much less costly than on Île Royale, nevertheless until now the fishermen have had considerable difficulty in coping for lack of fishing gear. For the past two years a boat has been coming to this port [Havre Saint Pierre]: prompted by necessity, the inhabitants often paid half as much again for their provisions as in Louisbourg, which meant that they were incapable of paying their debts and even of having the foodstuffs to feed their families during the winter. (TR)[48].

Twenty years later the situation had changed very little. In his census of 1752, Sieur de la Roque noted that while the fishermen on the Island were paying excessive prices for provisions, they were not receiving much for their cod and were thus almost always in debt. De la Roque recommended that the fishermen increase their farming activities in order to be more self-sufficient in food. Then they would only have to buy salt, fish-hooks and a few other items from the merchants[49]. Most of the fishermen raised a few animals and owned land that was partially cleared. De la Roque described one of these fishermen who was typical of the inhabitants of Havre Saint Pierre:

> Guillaume Patris, fisherman and ploughman, native of Saint Brieux, 38 years of age, has been in the country for 20 years, married to Françoise Chiasson, widow of the late Guillaume Gallet, she is a native of Acadia and 46 years old.
>
> They have 6 children: 4 boys and 2 girls.
> Guillaume Gallet, aged 22.
> François Gallet, aged 12.
> Georges Patris, aged 8.
> Paul, aged 5.
> Françoise, aged 15.
> Angélique, aged 7.
>
> Their livestock consists of: 2 oxen, 2 cows, 1 calf, 6 sheep, 1 pig, 2 geese, and 8 turkeys.

Drying cod.
From the Traité général des pêches *by Duhamel du Monceau.*

> The land on which they are settled was formally granted to them by Messieurs Aubert and Dubuisson in 1723, but they were not able to farm it because it was burned in the fire of 1724. They made a clearing where they sowed 3 bushels of wheat, and they have enough fallow land left to seed 37 bushels. (TR)[50]

In mentioning Tracadie, de la Roque pointed out that it was a favourable place for both fishing and farming. He noted that the eight families who had settled there were doing well in both occupations[51]. It should be remembered that since 1749 only the inhabitants of Tracadie and Havre Saint Pierre were allowed to fish. The French authorities were so anxious that the Island become the granary of Louisbourg that they decided to restrict fishing to ensure that the inhabitants devote all their energy to agricultural production.

De la Roque criticized strongly the policy of forbidding fishing everywhere except Havre Saint Pierre and Tracadie. In his opinion it was contrary to the interests of the population, which was often on the verge of starvation due to poor crops. Fishing would help the inhabitants survive. Taking the example of Havre Saint Pierre and Tracadie he insisted that the two occupations were compatible:

> ...believing that inhabitants who fish neglect to farm the land is a prejudice into which we have stumbled because of a lack of experience, Havre Saint Pierre and Tracadie are obvious and definite proof of the contrary. The inhabitants have made large clearings there and I dare say that fishing is an undeniable way of helping with farming. It enables people to have servants and cattle without which the land would never be ploughed. (TR)[52]

Farming

The Acadians who emigrated to Île Saint Jean devoted themselves mainly to agriculture. When they arrived, they tried to settle on land that was similar to that which they had left in Acadia. The few existing natural meadows along the rivers and bays were taken up quickly since they provided a ready source of hay for the winter[53]. These meadows were later cultivated by the Acadians, and dyked if necessary. During his inspection tour of 1751 the engineer Franquet noted that all the settlements on the Island

> ...are located along, or crossed by, rivers and streams, most of which are bordered by meadows, the inhabitants preferring those areas to any others because it would cost them hardship and labour to create meadows; besides, the fishing there always provides them with means of survival, and the soil is of the same quality as in the interior of the island. (TR)[54]

Gradually, as the population grew and all the natural meadows were taken up the colonists had to cut and clear the forest to increase the size of their farms. This arduous and painful task did not appeal to the Acadians who were more accustomed to building dykes and draining marshlands. The clearing process resulted in disastrous forest fires which on several occasions destroyed the crops in some communities. According to the settlement patterns of the Acadians on the Island, it was customary for at least part of the farm to have access to a waterway. They did not, therefore, venture very far inland[55].

Wheat and peas were the principal crops of the colony. They were the main ingredients for the bread and soup which constituted the basic diet of the population. In 1739, about 670 bushels of wheat and 150 bushels of peas were planted. Sieur de la Roque's census of 1752 gives us a very good idea of the types of crops at the time. As a matter of fact, the inhabitants had sown 1,490 bushels of wheat, 129 of oats, 181 of peas, 8 of barley, 8 of rye, 1 bushel of flax and 1 of buckwheat[56].

According to the same census, one thousand acres of land had been cleared in the colony, but only six or seven hundred acres had been seeded[57] due to a lack of seed. In previous years, a large portion of the crops had been destroyed by natural disasters. Thus the settlers had to look elsewhere for their seed, namely in Louisbourg where it was not always available.

Île Saint Jean was never able to fulfill its role as a supply colony for Louisbourg during the French regime. Because of the disasters that struck their tiny colony, the inhabitants often depended on help from Louisbourg to survive. There were several good years but the crops could only feed the local population. In fact, at no point did the Island export wheat or peas, even to Louisbourg[58].

The colony suffered various types of plagues: field mice, grasshoppers, rust and forest fires which destroyed the crops of a single community one moment and of the whole colony the next. The area around Malpeque Bay was particularly hard hit between 1749 and 1751. Sieur de la Roque describes these catastrophic years:

> ...the first one was brought on by field mice, [...] as soon as they had totally devoured the countryside, they scurried into the water and drowned...
>
> The second one was brought on by countless swarms of grasshoppers that were of phenomenal size, and so voracious that they ravaged the grain and all the vegetables, and even the hay and the buds on the trees; during the last one their wheat was completely shrivelled. (TR)[59]

The colonists were quite successful with their vegetable gardens. In 1753, Intendant Prévost reported that the inhabitants produced a large enough crop of vegetables to be able to export some to Louisbourg[60]. One particular settler, for example, managed to sell five hogshead of turnips to Louisbourg[61]. It should be noted that the Acadians did not grow potatoes at this time.

The agricultural practices of the early settlers do not appear to have been particularly effective since they depleted the soil. It is for this reason that Intendant Prévost recommended that the inhabitants be taught to fertilize their lands and to let them lie fallow at least every third year[62].

Herds were still relatively large on Île Saint Jean. In 1735, although there were only 432 settlers, there were 433 head of cattle and 190 sheep[63]. Unfortunately the census that provides these details does not give any statistics pertaining to other animals. We can assume that pigs and poultry were also raised at the time. The census of 1740 is more detailed but mentions neither pigs nor poultry. Thus, for a population of 440 people there were 166 oxen, 337 cows, 402 sheep and 14 horses[64]. The increase in population and livestock between the two enumerations is attributed mainly to the immigration of Acadians. The extremely detailed census of 1752 provides us with information on livestock holdings towards the end of the French regime. As a result of the arrival of many Acadians by 1749, the population had grown to 2,223[65]. Livestock numbers had also increased considerably. In round numbers, there were 100 horses, 800 oxen, 1,300 other cattle, 1,200 sheep, 1,300 pigs, 2,300 hens, 300 geese, 100 turkeys, and 12 ducks[66]. However, an average family like that of Joseph Arsenault and Marguerite Boudrot who had been living in Malpeque for twenty-three years only owned two oxen, one cow, four ewes, one ram, three pigs and six hens[67]. In the winter prior to this census, the inhabitants on the island had lost 414 head of cattle through sickness and lack of fodder[68].

The preferred meats were pork, chicken and, less frequently, mutton. Cattle were rarely slaughtered for meat. Oxen were used mainly as draft animals for clearing the land and ploughing. Veal calves were kept exclusively for export to Louisbourg.

In conclusion, the years were rare when the population of the colony was self-sufficient. Île Saint Jean never experienced agricultural prosperity under the French regime due to the various disasters that destroyed the crops, to the lack of seed and to the accelerated influx of Acadian refugees. The tiny colony often had to appeal to Louisbourg for food.

The Spiritual Framework

Virtually all the French immigrants who came to settle in Acadia in the seventeenth century belonged to the Catholic religion. Indeed, they left a country where Catholicism was the state religion and where the Church had considerable political power. Among the most influential ministers of the King at the time was Cardinal de Richelieu who, in 1627, limited the colony in New France to Catholic immigrants only[69]. Thus the Acadians, like the French Canadians generally, were destined to form a very homogeneous people from a religious point of view.

When a French colony was founded, the recruitment of a priest was always a priority. The *Compagnie de l'Isle Saint Jean*, responsible for the first settlement on the Island, called upon Father Charles-René de Breslay. He was a sixty-two-year-old Sulpician priest who had a long career as a missionary in the New World, and served for many years in the Montreal region. Given his age and his ill-health, he was accompanied by a young Sulpician, Father Marie-Anselme Métivier, who also had several years' experience in New France[70]. It is thought that both priests arrived with the approximately three hundred colonists who left France for Île Saint Jean in the spring of 1720.

Father de Breslay and Father Métivier only stayed on the Island for three years. When they accepted the mission they had planned to found a seminary that would serve the Maritime region. They soon realized, however, that such a project was hardly feasible at this stage in the colonization, especially given the fact that the *Compagnie de l'Isle Saint Jean*, on which they depended financially, did not appear to be having much success in its commercial ventures[71].

After the two Sulpician priests left, the Island mission was handed over to the Recollects, mendicant friars who came over to found a convent in Louisbourg. Supporting these priests promised to be much less of a burden for the *Compagnie de l'Isle Saint Jean*. Thus, for almost thirty years the Recollects alone attended to the spiritual needs of the settlers on the Island. The priests replaced each other at fairly regular intervals, given that about twenty different Recollects ministered on the Island between 1723 and 1754[72].

The priests served the inhabitants on the Island from Port LaJoie where the *Compagnie de l'Isle Saint Jean* built a small chapel dedicated to Saint John the Evangelist. Like most of the buildings in Port LaJoie this structure was very poorly maintained after the departure of the company in 1725. Commandant de Pensens complained in 1733 that 'there was no chapel.

> There is a chaplain with a few adornments for a chapel, but no chapel; we are using a wretched house which is the only remaining part of the old company. As many things are lacking for the daily celebration of the divine service, particularly candles, I have the honour to address to Monseigneur a memorandum which the former chaplain sent me when he left the chapel. (TR)[73]

The priest in Port LaJoie, whose expenses were paid for by the State, served as chaplain for the King's garrison. He also ministered to the settlers in the vicinity of the fort and in the other communities on the Island. The missionary's work consisted of administering the Sacraments to the colonists, teaching religion to the young people, evangelizing the Micmac, and sometimes fulfilling the role of notary or judge to settle differences between settlers or to write official documents[74]. The priest exercised these functions under very difficult circumstances: in order to reach his parishioners, he had to travel by foot, canoe or boat.

According to certain evidence of the time, the settlers on Île Saint Jean were strongly attached to their religion. As we have seen, the engineer Franquet made an inspection tour of the Island in 1751.

He noted that the settlers were "zealous with regard to religion and even a bit superstitious" (TR)[75]. His observations proved that the presence of a priest was of prime importance to the inhabitants. Everywhere he went, they begged him to obtain a priest for them. Despite the fact that the colonists were scattered in several settlements, a single missionary somehow managed to serve them all. But after 1749, the accelerated immigration altered the situation considerably. The new arrivals joined the other settlers in asking France to provide them with priests since one missionary was no longer sufficient.

When Franquet arrived the parishes were just being created. The people in Havre Saint Pierre had a church since the beginning of the 1740s[76], the Acadians in Pointe Prime had built a chapel at their own expense and another one was underway in Rivière du Nord Est. In fact, it was Franquet who helped solve the problem of a site for the church. He made the following remarks in his report:

> On the 13th, most of the senior inhabitants having gone to the said Sieur Gauthier's, we discussed the type of church they wanted. The cost of construction posed no difficulties; they even stated that all the wood was ready and that everyone would contribute without protest; but opinions were divided concernings its location, and it became apparent that each would benefit if it were on his side of the river. . .(TR)[77]

Franquet's report appears to have borne fruit because Father Peronnel arrived from France in 1752 to take charge of the parish of Saint Louis du Nord Est. Due to his ill-health, he was unable to stay long. The same year, Father Girard settled in Pointe Prime with his former parishioners from Cobequid (Truro) who had immigrated to the Island several years before. Three other priests arrived in 1753: Fathers de Biscaret, Cassiet and Dosque. The colony now had five parishes served by priests: Father Girard at Pointe Prime, Father Cassiet at Saint Louis du Nord Est, Father de Biscaret at Saint Pierre du Nord and Father Dosque in Malpeque where a little church was built and named after the Holy Family[78]. The Recollect priest, Ambroise Aubré, served as the chaplain at Port LaJoie.

The colony was in a state of extreme poverty: there was a shortage of seed, crops were poor and the majority of the settlers had just arrived. The French government was thus obliged to attend to the missionaries' needs until the inhabitants were able to pay their tithes.

In 1753, for example, the Intendant Prévost asked the Minister of Colonies to help the settlers furnish their churches and to send them four bells[79]. A memorandum presented to the King's Court pointed out that three churches on the Island lacked articles of worship including "a chalice, a vestment of each colour, a missal, an Antiphonal and Gradual, an altar chart, an alb, a cincture, a surplice, an altar stone, a ciborium and a box for the holy oils" (TR)[80].

The expulsion of the settlers from the Island, after the fall of Louisbourg, put an end to the development of the new parishes. Their growth, already precarious during the years that preceded the "great upheaval", was to be of short duration. Consequently, it is difficult to measure with certainty the role of the Church and the importance of religion for Acadians on the Island under the French regime. There were many factors that made parish life very difficult to organize: the colony was isolated from the religious structures of New France, the settlers were scattered throughout the Island, the influx of refugees took place suddenly and the overall state of the economy was poor.

CHAPTER II

THE FIRST CENTURY AFTER THE EXPULSION

1758–1860

RETURNING TO THE ISLAND

The expulsion of the settlers signalled the end of the French regime on Île Saint Jean. Fort Amherst was built by the British near the remains of the fortifications of Port LaJoie. A garrison of 190 men ensured the protection of the new British territory until the end of the Seven Years War and the signing of the Treaty of Paris in 1763. Several years later the garrison was withdrawn and the fort abandoned for good.

As already mentioned, many Acadians were able to escape deportation from the Island by taking refuge on the mainland. A few families managed to remain hidden on the Island. An examination of the history and genealogy of the principal Acadian families living on the Island today shows that most of them experienced at least a few years of exile. This confirms what the Bishop of Quebec, Monseigneur Joseph-Octave Plessis, wrote in his diary on the occasion of his pastoral visit in 1812:

> Most of them abandoned their lands for two or three years, others only came back after the peace of 1763. Still others, having settled elsewhere, forgot their former homeland and never returned. (TR)[1]

The first statistics that provide information on the Island Acadians after 1758 are those of the surveyor, Samuel Holland. He reported in 1764 that he discovered approximately thirty Acadian families whom the British authorities at Fort Amherst considered prisoners of war[2]. Samuel Holland gives the following description of the pitiful circumstances in which they were living:

> They are extremely poor, and maintain themselves by their industry in gardening, fishing, fowling, etc. [. . .] The Acadians now have recourse to little cabins or huts in the woods, where they are screened from the violence of the weather, and at the same time have the convenience of wood for fuel. Here they live on the fish they have cured in the summer, and game which they frequently kill, as hares and partridges, lynxes or wild cats, otters, martins, or musk rats,—none of which they refuse to eat, as necessity presses them.[3]

Four years later another surveyor, Alexander Morris, enumerated the Island population. He counted sixty-eight Englishmen, almost all of whom were employed in the fishery, and 203 Acadians. The latter, he noted, were all hired to fish for the British. There were thirteen families at St. Peters, five in Rustico, ten in Tracadie, one family in Bay Fortune and ten in Malpeque[4].

A number of Acadian families must have settled on the Island between the census of 1768 and 1798. According to the enumerator, Robert Fox, there were 115 Acadian families or 675 individuals located in three communities: Malpeque, Rustico and Bay Fortune[5]. Their family names are common amongst the Acadian population living on the Island today.

Some of the families that returned after the expulsion had been among the first inhabitants of the colony in 1720. The main family names in this group were: Blanchard, DesRoches, Cheverie, Gallant, Arsenault and Martin. Other families had lived on the Island for several years as refugees during the period that preceded the deportation of 1758; their names were Gauthier, Poirier, Chiasson, Doiron, Buote, Pitre and Bourque. Lastly, there is another group of family names that were not present on the Island before the deportation, but that appear in the census of 1798: Blaquière, Pineau and LeBrun. However, these more recent arrivals can be linked to the early Acadian families by their wives.

The Acadian families who settled on St. John's Island after the British Conquest had come from several places: New Brunswick, Nova Scotia, the Magdalen Islands and the Island of Miquelon. Some of them had even spent time in France following their deportation. To give a better idea of their wanderings let us look at four representative cases.

Jean-Baptiste Gallant was born in Port LaJoie in 1750. His grandfather, Michel Haché-Gallant, was one of the first Acadian settlers there. At the time of the deportation of 1758, Jean-Baptiste fled with his parents to the mainland. Records show that in 1760 they were in Ristigouche on the Gaspé Peninsula. Fifteen years later, at the age of twenty-five, Jean-Baptiste was on the Island of Miscou from whence he came to settle in Malpeque[6].

Jean-Baptiste Arsenault was born in Malpeque in 1750 where his father had been living since he had left Beaubassin in 1741. To avoid being deported, Jean-Baptiste and his parents moved to the Bay of Chaleur region. He married in Miscou in 1773 and later returned to his birthplace, Malpeque[7].

CENSUS OF 1798
Acadian Families

Malpeque	**Rustico**	**Bay Fortune**
15 Arsenault	12 Gallant	6 Chiasson
10 Gallant	6 Martin	6 Bourque
6 Poirier	5 Pitre	4 Pitre
4 Bernard	3 Doiron	3 Cheverie
3 Doucette	2 Blanchard	3 Longuépée
3 Gaudet	2 Doucette	1 Michel
2 Chiasson	1 Chiasson	1 Landry
2 Richard	1 Gautreau	
1 Bourque	1 LeBrun	
1 DesRoches	1 Muise	
1 Downing	1 Buote	
1 Aucoin	1 Gaudet	
1 Roussel	1 Pineau	
1 St-Jean	1 LeClair	
	1 Blaquière	
	1 Gauthier	

The travels of Alexis Doiron's family lasted longer and were more dramatic. Born in Acadie in 1723, Alexis Doiron moved with his parents to Île Saint Jean in 1750 to settle in Grande Anse, near Point Prim. He and his family were deported to France in 1758, but he returned to the Island to settle in Rustico, probably during the 1770s[8].

Louis Blaquière was born in France in 1760 where his family had landed following deportation from Louisbourg. His father brought him out to Miquelon around 1763. Records show that Louis was married in Miquelon and that he lived there until about 1792 when he fled with other Acadians who refused to take an oath under the new constitution adopted after the French Revolution. Louis Blaquière finally arrived in Rustico via the Magdalen Islands and Cape Breton Island[9].

The Acadians who decided to resettle on St. John's Island were obligated to swear an oath of loyalty to the King of England. According to the census of 1768, except for fishermen at sea most of the 203 Acadians did so[10]. In his diary, Monseigneur Joseph-Octave Plessis describes the confusion that appears to have prevailed with regard to this oath:

> ...because of a religious misunderstanding, some of them believed that they could not, in good conscience, swear an oath of loyalty to a heretic prince; and others that did foolishly convinced themselves that such an oath was not binding, consequently they broke it and joined the French armies again. (TR)[11]

Up until the end of the eighteenth century, the governing authorities on the Island appear to have questioned the loyalty of some Acadians. During the American Revolution, the acting governor, Phillips Callbeck, wrote to the Privy Council in London that Acadians were not obedient, and that they all had hunting rifles (but fortunately no ammunition). In his opinion, if the Acadians had the means they would eliminate the English population[12]. Callbeck had undoubtedly heard about a group of Acadians in south east New Brunswick who had taken up arms in support of American rebels against British soldiers[13].

An incident that took place in Rustico in 1794 shows that the loyalty of certain Acadians was still in doubt. The inhabitants of Grand Rustico refused to gather on the order of the captain of the militia. As a result, Governor Edmund Fanning went to Rustico accompanied by a troop of soldiers and several civil officials. He rounded up the members of the population suspected of disloyalty and made them take the oath of allegiance. It could well be that these were the people who had come from Miquelon and who had already refused to take an oath under the French constitution. Whatever the case, the event took place without incident and the governor was pleased to have acted in a decisive manner and to have solved once and for all the problem of civil disobedience amongst the Acadians in Rustico[14].

The main Acadian families, often interrelated, were thus established on the Island by the end of the eighteenth century and were located, as we have seen, in Malpeque, Rustico and Bay Fortune. Almost all the Island Acadians today can trace their ancestry back to these families.

LAND OWNERSHIP PROBLEMS

The resettlement of the Acadians on the Island did not take place without problems, since it was soon discovered that the entire colony had been turned over to "deserving" Englishmen. Thus, in order to stay on the Island, Acadians had to accept tenant status.

After the Treaty of Paris (1763) Île Saint Jean became St. John's Island, and then Prince Edward Island in 1799. At first the colony was under the administrative jurisdiction of Nova Scotia. In 1764, Captain Samuel Holland was appointed to survey the Island. He divided it into sixty-seven lots or townships, each covering about twenty-thousand acres. In the meantime, the Commissioners of Trade and Plantations, the British governing body in charge of colonies, began receiving petitions for large land grants on the Island. The Commissioners thus conceived a system (a type of lottery) by which the lots were distributed to a number of prominent Englishmen. There were, however, several conditions attached to the grants. In effect each grantee was to undertake the settlement of his land within ten years at the rate of one person per two hundred acres; to introduce only Protestant settlers recruited in Europe or in the British North American colonies; and to pay annual quit-rents of between 20 and 60 pounds to the Royal Treasury.

The distribution of the lots soon proved to be a failure. The grantees did not take the conditions of the grants seriously and many of them seized the first opportunity to sell their Island property. Within two years, one quarter of the lots had changed ownership and ten years after the lottery, forty-nine of the sixty-seven lots still remained uninhabited[15]. Most proprietors preferred to entrust their affairs to agents rather than actually live on their land amidst their tenants. In the final analysis, the land grants on the Island resulted in a muddled and complex system of absentee landlords. A source of considerable discontent and serious problems, this system was to mark the history of the Island until it entered Confederation in 1873.

This "seigneurial system" significantly affected the Acadians. From the very beginning, it caused hardship among the families who had resettled on the Island. Some of the proprietors or their agents exploited the families unscrupulously. William Cooper, a very popular politician and champion of the tenants, gave a clear summary of how the Acadians served the interest of the proprietors. He wrote in 1844:

> The remnant of the Acadian French were allowed to take the Oath of Allegiance; were encouraged to settle themselves, on the promise of protection in person and property by British Officers then in command. The Acadians were left undisturbed until British Emigrants arrived, when the Grantees ordered the Acadians to pay rent or give up their improvements, because they were not Foreign Protestants. They chose the latter, and bought unimproved land from another grantee. Thus both grantees gained by the transfer; the one gained the value of the Acadian's improvements, and an annual rent for his land, and the other grantee gained a number of settlers, a high price for his land, and interest upon the purchase money[16].

Some Acadians who were deeply in debt left their land and moved to another lot. A few years after re-establishing themselves, they had to either give in to an agent's demands or move on and start clearing land again elsewhere. Such was the fate of numerous families.

There was some question as to whether the Acadians were legally entitled to settle on the Island after the British conquest. The Anglophone opponents of the absentee landlords, who were sitting in the Legislative Assembly of the Island in 1850, stated that the French colonists did have the right to settle. In a memorandum to the Queen of England the members pointed out that the Treaty of Paris (1763) had stipulated that the inhabitants of the former French colonies would not be dispossessed. According to the members of the Legislature, only the rights of the Acadians on the Island had not been respected. When the Island was granted to the proprietors the Acadians had not been taken into account. The authors of the memorandum requested that Her Majesty consider this injustice and redress the wrong perpetrated on the Acadians by granting them Crown land on generous terms.

The Island Legislative Assembly was providing a liberal interpretation of the Treaty of Paris with regard to the Acadians. In fact, the Treaty only stated that the French inhabitants of Canada (Quebec) should retain ownership of their properties. The Acadians do not appear to have been included in this stipulation. In 1764, however, the Board of Trade in London allowed the Acadians to resettle in the Maritimes on condition that they swear an oath of allegiance[18]. Apparently the Acadians in Bay Fortune did this around 1764. They took

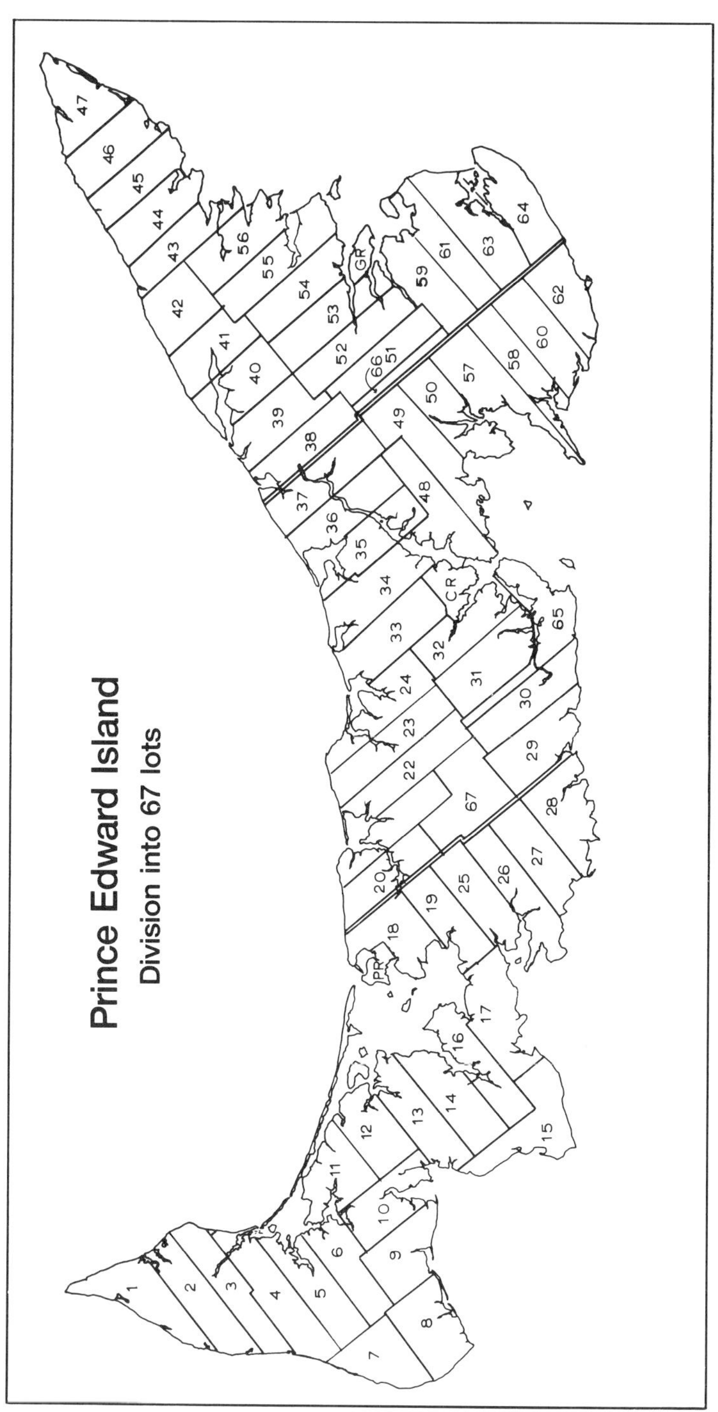
Prince Edward Island
Division into 67 lots

the oath in the presence of a British naval commander who handed over an official document confirming their land ownership, conditional upon their remaining loyal British subjects[19].

BAY FORTUNE

Unfortunately the land titles that the people of Bay Fortune received from the British officer proved to be worthless. Around 1770, David Higgins, the agent for the proprietor of Lot 43, demanded rent for the lands occupied by Acadians[20]. Without the means to defend their rights, the Acadians complied unwillingly to his request. Higgins promised them leases, but without ever asking them to sign anything. The Acadians continued clearing and farming their land, despite their precarious situation.

Following Higgins' death in 1783, a group of Acadians from Bay Fortune who still had reservations about their future on St. John's Island, were trying to resettle in Cape Breton where the likelihood of obtaining free Crown land was much greater. In 1784 a group went there on a survey expedition. A few years later, in 1786 and 1787, a number of families moved to Cape Breton, including about a dozen to Cheticamp[21].

In June of 1787, thirteen men from Bay Fortune presented a petition to the new governor of the Island, Edmund Fanning, in the hope of securing titles for the lands they and their families were occupying. They pointed out that ever since the death of David Higgins they had no idea who they were dealing with and, in addition, they were afraid they might have to give up their land to outsiders armed with valid titles. Moreover, they had reluctantly just given away the salt marshes that constituted their hay supply to a group of Loyalists. Governor Fanning was sympathetic to the Acadians' petition and consequently the Executive Council on the Island recommended that their request be granted[22]. The Governor himself distributed ownership titles to a number of Acadians in Bay Fortune[23].

However, the request does not appear to have been approved by the Board of Trade in England since the deeds the Acadians received from Fanning were revoked. Confronted with this sudden reversal, in the spring of 1788 the heads of seventeen households in Bay Fortune asked the governor of Cape Breton to grant them lands in the Margaree area. They informed the governor of Cape Breton that Governor Fanning would like to have granted them lands free of charge, but that he was not authorized to do so since Crown land on St. John's Island had to be sold[24]. Yet, around the same time an exception was made for the Loyalists who received free grants.

Not all the Acadian families in Bay Fortune moved to Cape Breton. The inhabitants who thought they possessed valid titles stayed on their lands, at the risk of having to face another landlord. In 1798, William Townsend and Edas Summers together bought Lots 17 and 43. They demanded that the occupants pay several years of back rents. The Acadians who considered themselves landlords took the matter to court, but by clever manoeuvring on the part of the proprietor Townsend and the legal system, they lost their case[25].

Confronted with this defeat, more Acadians decided to join the families already established in Cape Breton. Others bought fifty acre farms from John Cambridge in the adjacent lot (Lot 44) where they moved in 1801 and 1802. These Acadians thus became the first settlers in the parish of Rollo Bay[26].

RUSTICO

The Acadians who settled in Rustico (Lot 24) likewise had to face the absentee landlords' agents. It is not known whether the original proprietors of the Lot, Charles Lee and Francis MacLean, made the Acadians sign leases. Whatever the case, in 1787, sixteen Acadian families were obliged to sign perpetual leases, thus recognizing the authority of Alexander Fletcher as the agent of the new landlord Isaac Todd[27].

Lot 24 changed ownership several times at the beginning of the nineteenth century. The Acadians came to terms with each of their new landlords although that did not mean that their situation improved. Reduced to extreme poverty they were barely able to pay their annual rent. Given this impasse, the only solution was to seek a better life elsewhere. Like their compatriots from Bay Fortune these Acadians made their way to Cape Breton. The missionary, Joseph-Etienne Cécile, was worried that Rustico would be entirely deserted. He wrote of his concern in a letter to his bishop dated January 22, 1822:

> Rustico, where I reside, is on the verge of being abandoned by the Acadians. I am sure that [. . .] in no time at all the inhabitants will be forced to leave the place. Rather than decreasing, the rent that they are now unable to pay only increases. By this spring, most of them will be obliged to go to Labrador [Lake Bras d'Or] in Cape Breton where Mr. Gaulin assured them they would find Crown land. Finding themselves surrounded and interspersed with peoples from different nations, those who do stay will follow the same course as the others. (TR)[28]

In early September of the same year, Father Cécile informed Bishop Plessis in another letter that thirty-six families were preparing to go over to Cape Breton[29]. This outflow appears to have lasted for several years, since we know that another five families resettled in Cape Breton in 1829[30].

Despite the fears of Father Cécile, the bulk of the population in Rustico did not move. A few privileged people managed to buy their lands while the majority remained tenants, often indebted to their landlord. The circumstances worsened with each generation. As the lands were divided up to make room for the younger families, the farms became smaller and smaller. As a result it was extremely difficult to make a decent living on the land. Around 1860 the situation became very critical in Rustico. Father George-Antoine Belcourt's arrival in the parish in 1859 was to be providential.

MALPEQUE

It is not known exactly where on Malpeque Bay the Acadians resettled after the expulsion. It might have been in Lot 18, near the present-day village of Malpeque. In fact there were Acadian families there in 1770 since in that year they gave shelter to the shipwrecked Scottish immigrants from the *Annabella*[31]. This was the same year the first governor, Walter Patterson, arrived on the Island. He was joint owner of Lot 19 and also became the agent for the proprietor of Lot 17[32]. He therefore invited Acadians, probably living in Lot 18 and elsewhere, to relocate to the Lots in which he had interests[33]. Later on, many Acadian families did settle in Lot 16 along the shores of Malpeque Bay. It is not known under what conditions the Acadians took up residence in these Lots, but it is quite possible that they became tenants almost immediately[34].

At the time of the 1798 census, the Acadian population of Malpeque was concentrated mainly in Lot 17 which William Townsend and Edas Summers purchased in 1798 when they also acquired Lot 43 in Bay Fortune. Once again they demanded several years of back rent from the Acadian farmers[35]. Their demands resulted in the departure of numerous families who moved from Malpeque to Lots 1 and 2 where they founded the settlement of Tignish in 1799, and to Lot 5 where they founded Cascumpec in 1801.

Lot 17 did not remain in the hands of the associates Townsend and Summers for long. Colonel Harry Compton became the new landlord in 1804. He was so interested in his acquisition that he actually left England. In the beginning it would appear that he got along well with his tenant farmers, as Father Angus B. MacEachern explained in 1805:

> A Lt. Col. Compton has bought the French Settlement of Malpeque, is very good to the people, and has let lands to them on very reasonable terms. He is a good friend to our Religion.[36]

However, this understanding appears to have deteriorated. Tensions increased between the Acadians and their landlord and their English neighbours. Perhaps in an effort to solve the problems with his Acadian tenants, Compton offered in 1812 to sell them the lands they were occupying at the rate of one pound per acre[37]. The Acadians felt this price was too high, given the fact that they had cleared the land. Beginning in the fall of 1812 the Acadians gradually started leaving Compton's estate and moving to Lot 15, still uninhabited, where they founded the settlements of "La Roche" (Egmont Bay) and "Grand Ruisseau" (Mont Carmel). In 1813, Father MacEachern wrote the following about this move:

> I am very sorry to hear that the poor Acadians of Lot 17 are to move to Egmont Bay, Lot 15. It is said that their neighbours are troublesome to them in temporals and spirituals where they are.[38]

A ballad telling the story of the departure from Malpeque and the arrival at Egmont Bay has been handed down by oral tradition. The song was composed by Julitte Arsenault, one of the pioneer women of the parish, and gives a good description of these people's

ROYAL GAZETTE.

Charlottetown, Monday, May 3, 1852

CROWN LANDS.

THE Government will sell to the Acadian French, who may require the same for actual settlement, Tracts of the Crown Lands of 50 acres each, on Township No. 15, at the price of Four Shillings per Acre, to be paid in three instalments.

Enquire at the Office of the Keeper of Plans, at Charlottetown.

W. SWABEY, Keeper of Plans.

April 5, 1852.

lamentable struggle with their landlord. The first two verses enable us to capture the mood of the pioneers:

> Who were the ones who drove us here?
> Twas the wicked people in our land.
> A whole crew they were
> Agin the Acadians
> And all together
> Living off our goods.
>
> Scarcely do we pick a grain of wheat
> When we have to run to them with it.
> Those barbarians
> Without charity
> Care not one bit
> For our poverty. (TR)[39]

Despite letters from Father MacEachern, Bishop Plessis does not seem to have sympathized with the Acadians from Malpeque in their dealings with Colonel Compton. He had heard about the serious dispute between the landlord and tenants during his pastoral visit to the Island in 1812. He also knew about the offer Colonel Compton had made to the Acadians for the sale of their lands. On the other hand, Bishop Plessis had pleasant memories of the warm welcome Compton had given him. In his opinion the Acadians should have accepted their landlord's offer because, by leaving their lands to re-establish elsewhere on the Island, they were likely to find themselves in the same situation again. He expressed his position to Father Beaubien in 1815:

> I am sorry that the blunder of their refusing Mr. Compton's offers in 1812 resulted in the inhabitants of Malpec being expelled from their lands. They should have expected it. At least when they left they should have taken Crown lands in New Brunswick or Cape Breton. I fear that as a result of their miscalculations, they will take lands in some other lot on Île Saint Jean, from which they will be evicted once again. (TR)[40]

In 1816, Colonel Compton and the Acadians still living in Lot 17 finally came to an agreement. For the sum of 625 pounds the colonel sold them a section of six thousand acres most of which was made up of lowland and swamps[41]. About fifteen families moved to the newly acquired land. The new settlement was called *Belle Alliance*, perhaps in honour of the agreement with Colonel Compton. This was how the parish of Miscouche came to be founded in 1817 and why the Acadian settlement in Malpeque disappeared.

TIGNISH AND CASCUMPEC

The land problem was not solved by the Acadians when they left the Malpeque settlement for Tignish[42] and Cascumpec to avoid having to pay rent. The Lots (principally 1, 2 and 5) were uninhabited when they arrived, but after fifteen or twenty years the pioneers of Cascumpeque and several families from Tignish were urged by the merchant John Hill to recognize him as their landlord. A letter from Father Beaubien to Bishop Plessis in 1817 refers to the problem:

> The last news I had from Cashcompeck was not good. It would appear that these people, along with a portion of those from Tignish, were being harassed by Mr. Hill. (TR)[43]

Bishop Plessis was not surprised in the least by the difficulties the people from Cascumpec and Tignish were having. He replied by saying that "it was merely a repetition of what happened in Malpec" (TR). He even added: "It is with dread that I foresee the day when the poor Acadians will be completely [dispossessed] and shoulder their foolish bid based on false confidence" (TR)[44].

In the fall of 1821[45] some of these Acadian pioneers decided to sign leases on terms that were far beyond their means. Father MacEachern noted in 1828 that the Acadians in Tignish and Cascumpec feared for their future because they were unable to pay the outrageous rents[46]. Once again, some Acadians who either were unable to honour their lease or who refused to become tenants abandoned the land that had been improved with many years of hard labour. Consequently, they looked elsewhere for a place to settle, always hoping to find a piece of land they could actually own. It should be said that the landlords were not always sorry to see them leave because cleared land could, after all, be leased or sold for a good price.

During the 1830s the Acadian tenant farmers in Lots 1, 2 and 5 learned that they had new landlords. Townships 2 and 5 were bought by the great financier, Samuel Cunard, while Township 1 was transferred to Edward Palmer. Around 1835 Cunard sent an agent to make the occupants of his estate sign leases. Through threats and bribery, the agent succeeded in making numerous Acadians accede so that for the first time in thirty years they became tenants. The agent even forced them to pay arrears. Nicholas Conroy described this case to the Land Commission of 1860 which was established to inquire into the unique land problems on Prince Edward Island. He gave the following description:

> The leases were for a term of 999 years, and at 1 shilling sterling an acre. In addition to this, they signed notes of hand for 10 pounds, to be paid up to the 25th March, then last past. Your Honours will remember that another year's rent was then nearly due, so that by the coming 25th of March, which was about one month hence, they were involved in 15 pounds arrears. Now, some who signed those notes of hand, were very poor, and for them to make good their notes was impossible. In the meantime, the proprietor pressed and threatened them, so that the greater number left their farms from sheer inability to pay these arrears.[47]

The Acadians who abandoned their farms resettled on new woodlots for which they signed leases. The farms they had lost were then sold, usually to more well-to-do English farmers. Many Acadians had to move away from their farms situated along the coast to the interior of the Island where land was often low-lying and less productive.

After 1840 the situation in the Tignish area became more and more critical. On the whole, the tenant farmers were so indebted they could not pay their rents. Over a period of three years a resistance movement was organized against the proprietor and his agents[48]. The farmers refused to pay rent and protected each other from foreclosures. The matter came to a head during the winter of 1844 when the entire population decided to resist the agent who wanted to seize their properties. When the sheriff, accompanied by several peace officers, arrived in Tignish to carry out the foreclosures and arrest the leaders of the resistance, he was confronted by a population ready to defend itself. Approximately five hundred men, determined to prevent them from executing their plans and armed with sticks and rifles, gathered in front of the officers of the law[49]. The attempt appears to have failed because *The Royal Gazette* published, on July 9 1844, a list of thirty-four individuals from Lot 1 whose lands had been seized[50].

As was the case in Rustico, several years were to pass before the land question was finally resolved in this part of the Island.

EGMONT BAY AND MONT CARMEL

The Acadians from Malpeque who settled on Lot 15 from 1815 and onwards had better luck than all of their other compatriots. In 1817, the Island government confiscated this Lot because the proprietor had done nothing with it. The Acadians were thus able to buy the land from the government for the sum of 4 pounds 10 shillings per hundred acre. The rate was later increased to 100 pounds for the same acreage[51]—which posed problems for those who did not have the means to pay for such highly priced land. In 1850 and 1852, the Legislative Assembly intervened on behalf of the Acadians (whose rights, it was recognized, had been infringed upon) in order to lower the price of land in Lot 15[52]. In 1852 the government offered the Acadians the possibility of obtaining fifty acres in Lot 15 for the modest sum of 10 pounds (4 shillings an acre)[53].

This sale affected the inhabitants of the parish of Mont Carmel and part of the parish of Egmont Bay. The other part of the latter parish was located in Lots 14 and 16. By 1814 the Acadians resettled in Lot 16 had already signed leases for the proprietor, Stephen Sullivan, as had those living in Lot 14 when Samuel Cunard became the proprietor. Once again the Acadians found themselves victims of a type of feudal system that was to last until the 1870s.

In conclusion, the Acadians adapted very badly to the absentee landlord system. Impoverished people with neither economic nor political power and almost entirely devoid of educated leaders, they were highly vulnerable to exploitation by the proprietors or their agents. The traditionally independent nature of the Acadians forever compelled them to seek a "country" where they could live in peace, away from proprietors and people who were hostile to their culture and their values.

People Of The Sea

While the Acadians were essentially farmers before the expulsion, they were forced by circumstance to become fishermen after they returned. The transformation was so profound that the French historian, Edme Rameau de Saint-Père, noted in 1859 that a large proportion of the Acadian population made their living from the sea and had lost interest in farming. He made the following observations:

> ...the ocean has become their friend, their foster parent, their refuge, their homeland, as it were. Thus their settlements are always located along the coastline; they even seem to mistrust land-based trades, and it is not without reluctance that they ever agree to settle inland with no view of the shore. (TR)[54]

During the stormy years of the deportation, the Acadian refugees along the Atlantic were able to survive to a large extent from hunting and fishing. After the Treaty of Paris, the men were recruited in large numbers by British fishing companies. These Acadians were therefore guaranteed some measure of protection and means of survival. This was a common situation throughout the region. At the time of the 1768 census the heads of the forty-one Acadian families on Île Saint Jean, enumerated in five different localities, all fished for Englishmen who owned most of the fishing vessels. The Acadians did, however, own two schooners, five shallops and one sloop[55].

Several months after his arrival in 1770, Walter Patterson, the first governor of the Island, observed that the Acadians had been hired by several British subjects to fish during the summer. They were paid with clothing, rum, flour, gunpowder and rifle bullets[56]. They were also employed in boat-building.

In the years following the conquest, British investors were mainly attracted to the Island by the fishing industry. The products were exported to Quebec, Halifax and Boston[57]: codfish, and oil and skins from seals and walruses. This trade was curtailed, if not eliminated, during the 1770s by the American Revolution. Indeed, the Island was in such a state of economic disarray that all commercial activity of importance came to a halt in the fishing industry during this period. Henceforth, clearing and farming the land became a priority for both the proprietors and the colonial administrators. It was not until the middle of nineteenth century that the fisheries regained a degree of significance in the Island economy. Meanwhile, it was largely the Americans who were profiting from the abundance of fish in the waters off the Island where, by around 1807, they had 938 fishing boats[58]. Even during the 1830s the Americans still dominated the scene. Islanders barely had twenty vessels involved in commercial fishing[59].

The Acadians did not totally abandon the sea even after the departure of the English businessmen who had hired them. While devoting more and more energy to farming, they did not give up saltwater fishing. In fact, the Acadians lead a diversified life from an economic point of view because in addition to fishing and farming they practised their skills as lumberjacks, navigators and boat builders. In 1803, Lord Selkirk noted that it was above all the Acadians who were fishing and who owned most of the seventy boats being used for the export trade. He wrote:

> ...none of the [English] Settlers follow it—the French on the North Coast do—and own nine tenths of the Schooners, which are the only shipping boats belonging to the Island. They are not however regular fishermen, but follow it at intervals of their agricultural business...[60]

Lord Selkirk added that the Acadians' schooners, with a tonnage between thirty and forty, were generally poorly equipped. He stated, however, that the Acadians rarely had mishaps since they were good sailors: they predicted the weather judiciously and could navigate over great distances without a compass. As coastal traders they sailed chiefly to Halifax and Newfoundland[61].

At the beginning of the nineteenth century, the importance of seafaring activities varied from one Acadian community to another. For example, according to John McGregor's observations, people in Rustico would not prosper because they did not devote themselves entirely to fishing. He stated that "at one time they are employed in building vessels, at another for a few weeks farming, then fishing, and again cutting timber. It follows that they are poor, while the Acadians in other parts of the island [...] acquire what renders their condition independent"[62]. During the 1830s S.S. Hill made similar remarks with regard to the inhabitants of Rustico[63].

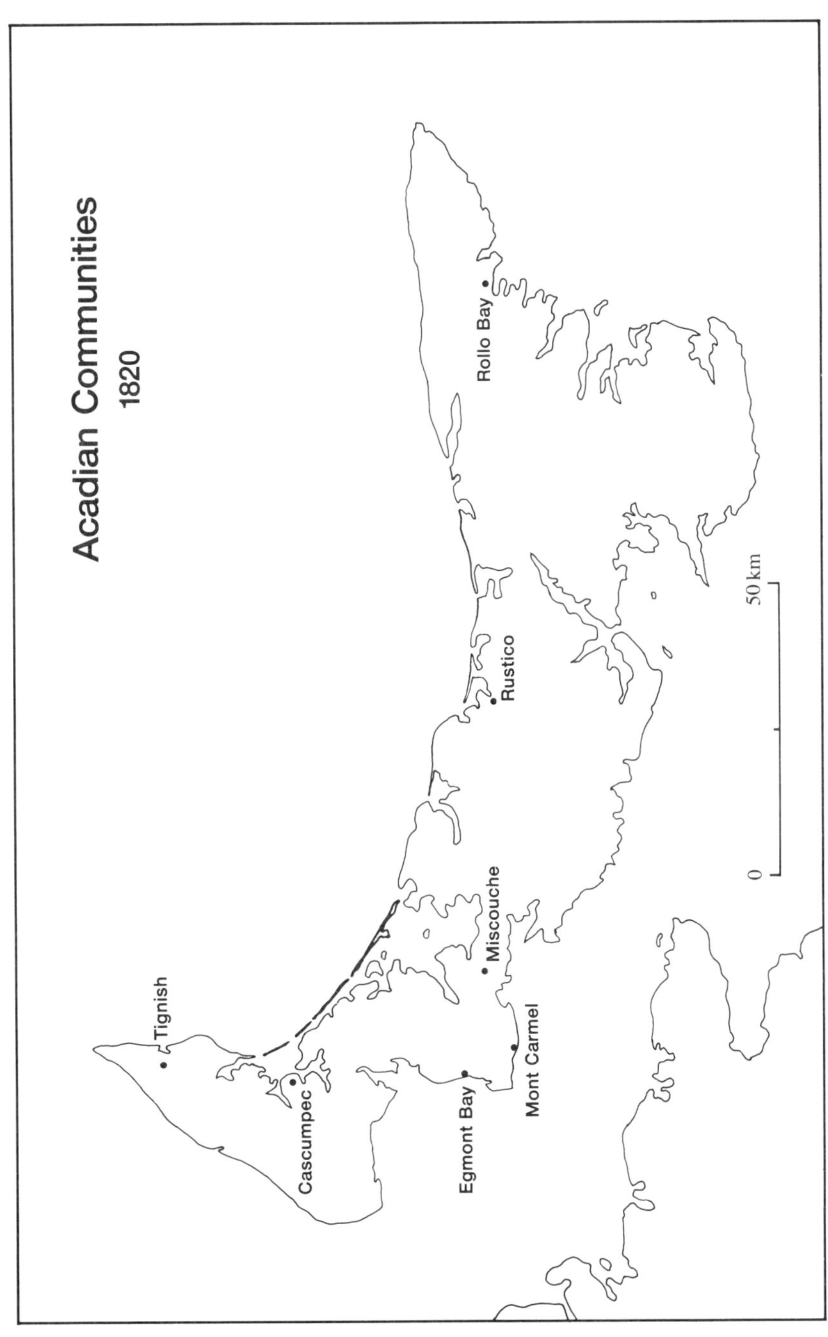
Acadian Communities
1820
Rollo Bay
Rustico
Miscouche
Tignish
Cascumpec
Egmont Bay
Mont Carmel
0
50 km

As for Cascumpec, Hill noted that the Acadians were not involved in fishing but rather in cutting timber and in farming[64]. In Tignish they devoted themselves exclusively to farming for which they were praised by Mr. Hill. He deemed their position to be better than that of their compatriots in Rustico and Cascumpec[65].

In Egmont Bay, Mont Carmel and Miscouche, agriculture constituted the chief occupation at the beginning of the century. There was some fishing but it was essentially for home consumption. In 1825, Célestin Robichaud, an Acadian from St. Mary's Bay in Nova Scotia, noted that herring, trout and mackerel were caught in Egmont Bay but codfish did not frequent the waters off that shore[66].

Distressed by the American control of the fisheries, around 1830 the Island government decided that it was time to stimulate the industry. As an incentive, the Legislature passed an act which awarded a bounty on fishing vessels and on codfish exported from the Island.

While the Acadians around Tignish and Cascumpec were not very involved in fishing during the early decades of the nineteenth century, the situation was to change considerably in the ensuing years. It was there, in fact, that the recovery of the Island fisheries was to take place. Although John Hill and his sons founded an establishment in Alberton at the beginning of the century, no Acadians appear to have been involved.

The industry began expanding in the Tignish area with the arrival in 1845 of merchants like Frank Arsenault and Thomas J. Caie who traded farm and fish products for imported goods. In 1850 the American W.B. Dean and Captain Hubbard from Charlottetown founded an important fishing and commercial establishment near the present village of Tignish[67]—the first large-scale one in the colony. The impact of this business soon became apparent because in 1852 Tignish was exporting more fish products than any other port on the Island: 244 barrels of gaspereaux, 2113 quintals of cod, 115 barrels of herring and 21 barrels of fish oil. The entire amount was shipped to the other British colonies in North America and to foreign countries[68].

During the 1850s the fishing industry played an increasingly important role in the Island economy. Expansion took place after the signing of the Reciprocity Treaty between Britain and the United States in 1854. The treaty, which remained in effect until 1866, eliminated customs tariffs on certain raw materials and gave the Americans the right to fish off the coast of the British colonies in North America. They were even permitted to come ashore to dry their nets and salt their fish.

After 1858 Americans were authorized to buy land on the Island. As a result of this new policy the fishing industry benefited from substantial American investments. With the help of this capital, numerous fishing companies sprang up in the colony. While there were only five businesses of this type in 1850, by 1855 there were thirty-seven and eighty-nine in 1861[69]. Among the American investors were Isaac C. Hall and James H. Myrick who founded the fishery in "Tignish Run"[70]. The Myrick establishment was to become the most important one in the region. Furthermore, the Myrick family played a prominent role for a long time in the fishing industry and in the economy as a whole.

Skilled fishermen and workers were available on the spot for the new companies that were set up in Acadian localities. The regrowth in the fisheries took place just around the time when the Acadians were experiencing difficulties finding land for the younger generation. The expansion provided both employment and the opportunity for Acadian farmers to fish in order to pay their rents to the proprietors[71].

After approximately sixty years of moving and quarrelling as a result of the land question, the growth of the fisheries pointed to a more promising future for the Acadians. After the middle of the nineteenth century, all the maritime colonies enjoyed some degree of prosperity. To a certain extent the Island Acadians were to benefit from this prosperity.

People Of The Land

The Acadians on the Island after the deportation years tried to keep vegetable gardens. But as we have seen they had to turn to the sea for a living. Agricultural endeavours were thus very limited. The first governor of the Island, Walter Patterson, noted that the Acadians did not grow any grain whatsoever in 1770[72].

Gradually the Acadians began to apply themselves more earnestly to clearing the land and cultivating the soil. In 1782, a petition submitted to government officials of the time by the Acadians in Rustico shows that farming constituted their principal means of subsistence. The petitioners in this document were requesting help from the government because their grain crop had been completely destroyed by mice and they feared their roots or tubers would suffer the same fate[73]. Several years later when the inhabitants of Rustico signed their lease with the proprietor, Isaac Todd, they were all identified as farmers[74].

John McGregor pointed out at the beginning of the century that a large number of Acadians on the Island were involved almost entirely in farming which, he wrote, made them fairly independent economically. Nevertheless, it was difficult for families to make their farms pay since they were reduced to poverty as a result of exorbitant rents and disputes over land titles. Furthermore, constant relocation was not conducive to agricultural development.

John McGregor concurred with other observers of the time in stating that Acadians were not as successful as other Island farmers, be they English, Scottish, Loyalist or Irish[75]. It should be noted, however, that agricultural practices on the whole left a great deal to be desired; documents of the period deplore the primitive farming techniques in use. Newly cleared lands remained relatively productive for several years but were soon exhausted due to farmers' ignorance of how to maintain soil fertility. Few farmers rotated their crops or fertilized the land. Manure was scarce because the small number of farm animals roamed the woods instead of being contained in pastures. Farmers were not yet exploiting the readily available fertilizers from the sea such as mussel mud, fish and seaweed.

The fifth lieutenant-governor of the colony, Colonel John Ready, who arrived on the Island in 1824, was interested in promoting agriculture and encouraged the formation of the Central Agricultural Society in 1827[76]. Thirteen regional societies were created between 1827 and 1842, including one in Cascumpec in 1840 and another in Tignish in 1842[77]. Although both these societies were situated in areas with a sizeable Acadian population, the farmers of French origin do not appear to have participated in the movement which was organized and run by the more affluent English-speaking farmers.

The improvements that took place in agriculture during the first half of the nineteenth century can be attributed to the development of agricultural societies and particularly to the arrival of some settlers who already had experience in farming. According to John McGregor the latter included a number of Loyalists and Englishmen and a few Scots[78]. The majority knew very little about cultivating the soil and some of the settlers were farming for the first time in their lives.

Very little information is available pertaining to the agricultural practices of the Acadians of the time. John McGregor and other observers reported that the Acadians were using rudimentary and backward methods and unfortunately were not following the example of their more successful neighbours[79]. The Acadians persisted in keeping their one-handled plough while other farmers were using a more efficient Scottish-type plough with two handles and a cast-iron mould-board[80].

The Acadian community remained for a long time at the pioneering stage. They had better luck with freshly cleared land than with land that had run out as a result of planting the same crops for several years in succession[81]. During his visit to Egmont Bay in 1825, Célestin Robichaud noted that farmers grew potatoes the first year in new ground, then beautiful wheat the second and third years, and oats the fourth year[82].

CROPS

As we have seen, the main crops on Île Saint Jean during the French regime were wheat and peas. In the century that followed the expulsion, the Acadians continued to prefer wheat to any other cereal. At the beginning of the century, Acadian tenant farmers in Colonel Compton's Lot 17 all paid ten bushels of good wheat as part of their annual rent[83]. In 1856, the parishioners in Tignish contributed in one day one thousand bushels of wheat to finance the construction of a new church[84]. Other Island inhabitants like the Scots and the Irish favoured the production of oats[85].

It was British settlers who introduced the potato to the Island. Acadians adopted it quickly since it was easy to grow and the yield was good. Potatoes were planted in newly cleared ground, even around stumps. According to Célestin Robichaud's account of his visit to Egmont Bay, potatoes grew quite well, namely "one hundred bushels to a thousand" (TR) or, in other words, one hundred bushels to one thousand seed potatoes. Wheat yielded twenty to twenty-five bushels per bushel of seed, and grass (hay) produced one or two tons per acre, a yield considered to be satisfactory. Célestin Robichaud also reported that Acadians grew flax, corn, peas, string beans and broad beans, cabbage, cucumber and various types of grain and tubers[86]. Thanks to Joseph Bouchette we know that at the beginning of the century wheat, barley and potatoes were being produced in Tignish in reasonable quantities[87].

As of 1845 Island farmers were hard-hit by plagues that reduced crop yields. Potatoes were attacked by a blight and wheat was damaged by rust and insects, all of which meant hard times for the population.

LIVESTOCK

The livestock on the Island at the beginning of the British regime was comprised of animals originating mainly from the old Acadian stock[88]. In 1764 the surveyor, Samuel Holland, recorded that the approximately thirty Acadian families living on the Island owned about a hundred head of cattle. However, they were not permitted to dispose of them at their will since the British officer in charge at Fort Amherst regarded these escapees of the expulsion as prisoners of war and laid claim to all their belongings[89]. John McGregor reported that for several years after the expulsion, a considerable number of horses were roaming free on the eastern part of the Island. They were later domesticated again and made good saddle and harness horses[90].

Most of the bloodlines of livestock owned by the Acadian farmers and even by the early British settlers went back to the French regime. In general the animals were of poor stock and badly cared for, especially if the farmers did not manage to store enough hay and oats in order to winter them properly. In this case they were fed straw for part of the winter[91].

In the description of his travels, Célestin Robichaud writes that people kept horses, beef, cows, pigs, and two breeds of sheep, one of which produced up to fifteen or sixteen pounds of wool[92]. The census carried out on the Island in 1833 indicates that the population, numbering 32,292, owned thirty thousand head of cattle, fifty thousand sheep, twenty thousand pigs, and six thousand horses[93]. A careful examination of this census shows that the Acadians favoured horses over oxen—contrary to preferences in some parts of the Island[94]. Finally, we should add that Acadian farmers who were tenants of Colonel Compton in Malpeque at the turn of the century had to include one sheep as part of their annual rent[95].

To conclude, Acadians of this period were carrying out subsistence farming since they barely produced enough to feed their large families. While poverty prevailed in most households, people were content with the bare minimum and apparently were healthy. John Lawson pointed out around 1850 that the Acadians were capable of raising a large family on what would be scarcely enough for one English-speaking man to live on[96]. In the years when crops were bad and when there was not enough flour to make bread or other basic foods, it was possible to avoid starvation thanks to hunting and fishing. A strong community spirit lead people to help each other and often to share their resources. This mutual help was particularly obvious on Candelmas Day. Indeed, on the 2nd of February young men went from door to door distributing the produce they had collected for the needy in their village. People usually contributed flour, potatoes, meat and other basic food items[97].

An Impoverished Church

The Treaty of Paris in 1763 guaranteed Acadians and other French settlers the right to practice the Catholic religion but only within the context of the laws of Great Britain[98]. However, the rights of Catholics in Britain at the time were very limited; they were excluded from the House of Parliament, deprived of the right to vote and the right to purchase or inherit real estate[99]. These restrictions and others were enforced by the governments put in place by the English after the conquest, including the government formed on the Island in 1770[100]. The constraints were gradually lifted in order to allow Catholics to enjoy more civil rights. An amendment to the law in 1786 on Prince Edward Island granted Catholics the right to own land; it was not until 1830, however, that they gained the right to vote and to sit in the Legislature[101].

During the French regime, Acadian Catholics were under the jurisdiction of the Diocese of Quebec, the only See in North America—a situation which was not altered by the conquest. When Monseigneur de Pontbriand died in 1760 six years elapsed before the British au-

Monseigneur Jean-Olivier Briand
National Archives of Quebec, Initiale Collection.

Father de Calonne

Father Jean-Louis Beaubien

Father Sylvain-Ephrem Poirier

thorities accepted a successor, Monseigneur Olivier Briand who was appointed by the Holy See[102]. The Island remained under the spiritual responsibility of Quebec until 1819 at which time the Diocese of Charlottetown was created as suffragan diocese of Quebec. Ten years later, in 1829, it became completely independent[103].

As soon as he was installed in his new functions, Monseigneur Briand was asked to appoint a priest to minister to the Acadians on Prince Edward Island. Following this request the bishop addressed his first pastoral letter to the Acadians and to their compatriots established elsewhere. In his message, dated March 15, 1766, he expressed his sympathy to the Acadians and praised them for their loyalty to the Catholic faith despite the absence of religious services.

Nevertheless, the prelate's principal message related to the loyalty which the Acadians owed to the King of England. He told them that it was their religious duty to obey the royal power. Bishop Briand was expressing the official position of the Church in this document:

> Rejoice then, dear Brethren; after so many trials and tribulations, after so much unhappiness, it would seem that God has at last willed an end to it all. Prepare yourselves to show Him your gratitude by a constant and sacred loyalty to His holy law and all His wishes: but it is not enough to thank God for what you owe Him; you have the same obligation towards our gracious sovereign... (TR)[104]

Finally, Bishop Briand promised his distant congregation that he would find them a priest for the following year. This proved to be a difficult task since the number of priests had greatly diminished since the conquest: both the recruitment and training of new priests were complicated by restrictions imposed by the British administration; the Jesuit College had been closed down and the Quebec Seminary destroyed during the war[105]. Nevertheless, the bishop first succeeded in sending Father Charles-François Bailly de Messein, and then the Jesuit priest, Father Jean-Baptiste de la Brosse to the Acadians in the Maritimes. It would appear, however, that neither one ever went to St. John's Island.

Four years later, the Bishop of Quebec addressed a second pastoral letter to the Acadians on the Island. Monseigneur Briand told them that he was sorry that neither missionary had ministered to them yet even though he had instructed them to do so. He also wrote that he had tried without success to get a priest from France, but that there was no money to pay his passage. He recommended several steps for them to take in order to obtain the services of either Father Bailly, residing in Halifax, or of Father de la Brosse who had to travel as far as the Bay of Chaleur. He warned them clearly, however, that before inviting any missionary to visit them, prior authorization from the Governor of Halifax was absolutely essential. In the same missive Bishop Briand announced that he was having four Acadians educated in France, two of whom would soon be ordained. He gave them hope: "Perhaps, you will have a resident who will even be of your own nation" (TR)[106]. Monseigneur Briand declared that he was most sensitive to their spiritual needs and implored them to lead a wholesome life:

> Many of your young people have never seen the celebration of the Blessed Sacrament of the Holy Mass, have never been to confession, have never received the Holy Sacrament of the Eucharist, and consequently only know their religion through their imagination and words. This is very little, indeed too little, to create invincible ties to the religion that we admire with great satisfaction in the ancient Acadians. [...] Since you cannot go to confession and you are likely to die without sacraments, look after yourselves well. Those considerations must, I think, make a strong impression on you. (TR)[107]

The Acadians had to wait until 1770 before they were able to welcome their first priest, Father James MacDonald, who arrived with a group of Scottish families fleeing religious persecution in their own country. Monseigneur Briand made haste to grant the necessary powers to this member of the clergy. He spoke several languages and would be able to work not only amongst his Scottish compatriots, but also the Acadians on the Island.

The premature death of Father James MacDonald in 1785 created a hiatus in the Catholic community on the Island since the Canadian episcopate still did not have the means to send a resident priest. To fill the gap the bishop authorized Jean Doucet, an Acadian from Rustico, to baptize and receive marriage vows anywhere on the Island when no missionary was available.[108].

In the meantime, the Acadians in the Maritimes welcomed the first priest of Acadian origin, Father Joseph-Mathurin Bourg, who was educated in France and ordained in Quebec City by Monseigneur Briand in 1772. The following year he began his ministry as Vicar

General of the eastern missions. He thus was required to travel throughout the Maritime region and only visited St. John's Island on rare occasions[109].

From 1785 to 1790, with the exception of a few visits from Father Bourg, the Island Acadians had to be content with the services of missionaries from Arichat (Cape Breton), Saint Mary's Bay (Nova Scotia) and Memramcook (New Brunswick)[110]. It was not until 1790 that the Island received its second resident priest: Father Angus Bernard MacEachern, a Scot who was to become the first bishop of the Diocese of Charlottetown after thirty-one years of Apostolic service. Father MacEachern had some knowledge of French and devoted considerable energy to the Acadian missions, much to the displeasure of the Scots who often found themselves without a priest and who felt the Acadians were not contributing enough towards his maintenance[111]. On several occasions Father MacEachern and his compatriots expressed their disappointment with the meager support provided by the Bishop of Quebec for the Acadians in particular and the Catholic community on the Island in general. In fact, the problem was a delicate one for the prelate whose inadequate resources could not fulfil the constant demands of the numerous missions throughout his vast diocese. In addition, he was obliged to show a certain discretion in sending priests into colonies which were under the jurisdiction of Protestant governors.

In 1798, another Acadian delegation from St. John's Island went to the bishop's palace in Quebec to request a French-language priest. Monseigneur Joseph-Octave Plessis promised to undertake the necessary steps, since he appears to have had Governor Fanning's backing in order to bring out an *émigré* priest from revolutionary France[112]. As a result, in 1799 two French priests arrived on the Island via England: Father Jacques-Ladislas-Joseph de Calonne and Father Amable Pichard. Like many other priests they had fled France during the Revolution.

These priests discovered on their arrival that the scattered Catholic population on the Island was comprised of Micmac, Acadians, Scots and Irish. Father de Calonne wrote that "the French are the ones to whom we can be most useful but whose need for our services is the least pressing" (TR)[113]. He noted that they were very well grounded in their religion and carried out their duties faithfully. These French priests thus shared the ministry with Father MacEachern.

Father Pichard resided in Rustico and took charge of the three Acadian missions of Malpeque, Rustico and Bay Fortune, while Father de Calonne, who spoke English, served the Catholics in Charlottetown[114].

Father Pichard served only four years on the Island because he was transferred to Tracadie, Nova Scotia—evidently due to a disagreement he had with the people of Rustico[115]. Father de Calonne took over in Rustico but his stay on the Island was cut short in 1804. Once again, the Acadians found themselves without a French-speaking priest. Father MacEachern remained the only Catholic missionary on the Island. This situation lasted until 1812 when Monseigneur Plessis brought with him on his pastoral visit a young twenty-five-year-old priest, Father Jean-Louis Beaubien, whom he posted in Rustico.

Father Beaubien's stay on the Island came at the end of the great wave of migrations caused by the land question. The number of Acadian communities had thus multiplied which meant that the young missionary had to travel from one end of the Island to the other in order to meet with his congregation. In addition, he was also asked by his bishop to serve the Magdalen Islands and the Micmac on Lennox Island. Normally he would visit each mission on Prince Edward Island twice a year and spend several weeks in the summer on the Magdalen Islands[116].

Father Beaubien returned to Quebec after six years. He was replaced by the young abbé Joseph-Etienne Cécile who ministered to more than two thousand faithful until 1822. On the request of the bishop he took a census of his missions that were comprised mainly of Acadians, but also of Micmac, Scots and Irish[117]. This Catholic population was distributed in the following way: Rustico: 608; Miscouche: 202; *la Roche* (Egmont Bay and Mont Carmel): 312; Cascumpec: 194; Tignish: 270; Rollo Bay: 228; Lennox Island: 186.

THE FIRST ACADIAN PRIEST

Shortly after his arrival on the Island, Father Cécile met a young Acadian from Tignish who was interested in the priesthood. The young man in question was Sylvain Poirier and was the first Acadian from the Island to become a priest. Father Cécile's letter to Monseigneur Plessis gives a clear picture of the young man:

Drawing of the first church in Tignish, built in 1801.
L'Impartial Illustré.

> A young Acadian (Silvain Poirier by name) expressed a desire to continue his studies, thinking of the Ecclesiastical estate. He is a little old, being in his seventeenth or eighteenth year.
>
> He has only average skills; however he will be able to pass, I have taught him for about a month, he is up to the Prepositions, having done the Verbs quite well. Above all, he is virtuous, and resolutely good. I request that your Lordship put him in the College that you deem appropriate, he has but 30 pounds and I hope to secure the same amount for him next year. (TR)[118]

The Bishop of Quebec received this candidate for the priesthood and enrolled him in the Seminary in Nicolet, even though the amount of money Father Cécile had sent was not enough to cover the cost of his first year. Financing the studies of the young seminarian proved to be a problem since the impoverished parishioners refused to contribute towards his education without a specific order from the bishop. On the other hand, Monseigneur Plessis would not allow Father Cécile to tax the parishioners of Tignish and warned him not to send students without financial resources[119]. Nevertheless, the young Acadian was able to continue his studies with the help of a Quebec priest, who knew the Poirier family, and with small contributions from Father Cécile[120].

Father Sylvain-Ephrem Poirier (or Perrey, as he usually signed his name) was ordained on Prince Edward Island by Bishop Angus Bernard MacEachern on June 28, 1828. He exercised his ministry for fifty years until age and blindness forced him to retire. In the beginning, he was in charge of all the Acadian missions in Prince County: Tignish, Cascumpec, Mont Carmel, Egmont Bay, Miscouche, etc. In 1843 his territory was limited to the parishes of Miscouche, Egmont Bay and Mont Carmel. From 1869 up to the time of his retirement in 1879 he was the parish priest for Mont Carmel only. He died in 1887 in Egmont Bay where he was buried[121].

For many years Father Poirier remained the only French-language priest in the province. We should mention, however, that during the reign of Bishop Bernard Donald MacDonald who succeeded Bishop MacEachern in 1837 and who established his residence in Rustico, several French-language priests did work in that parish in their capacity as bishop's aides[122]. Moreover, anglophone priests working on the Island at the time usually had quite a good knowledge of French because, for the most part, they had been trained in seminaries in Quebec.

But the diocese was still experiencing a shortage of priests. In 1857, Bishop MacDonald asked the Montreal diocese to send him a priest to assist the Island clergy whose mission was becoming more and more onerous[123]. For that purpose, therefore, Father Fortunat Aubry arrived in Rustico in May 1858. The following are Father Aubry's initial comments:

> On Sunday I preached in Rustico where Bishop MacDonald resides. It has been almost a year since the Acadians, who form five-sixths of the population, have heard a sermon in French; the priest living with the Bishop does not understand French, not even enough to be able to hear confessions, and Monseigneur has difficulty speaking, he coughs so much. (TR)[124]

In the end, Father Aubry only stayed on the Island for one year. After his departure, three more priests from Quebec were sent by the bishop of Montreal at the request of his colleague on the Island. They were: Fathers George-Antoine Belcourt, Joseph Quévillon and André Roy. These priests were to play an important role in the Acadian parishes.

A DIFFICULT MINISTRY

The prolonged absence of priests amongst the Acadians during the period that followed the expulsion definitely affected the way they practiced their religion. Even if several missionaries were on the Island the territory to be served was so vast that each mission was only visited two or three times a year, and then only for about two weeks at a time. Given these circumstances, the layman was called upon to play an important role, replacing the priest for certain duties normally reserved for the clergy. Thus, on Sundays and Feast Days people went to church, even if there was no priest, and would celebrate "White Mass" and Vespers. There would be no consecration, but one of the more educated and respected men in the parish would preside over the reading of the prayers for Mass. It was almost a routine occurence at the time to be without a priest for the baptism of the new-born. The Church authorized laymen to give private baptism to infants who were in danger of dying rather than waiting for solemn Baptism to be performed by a priest. This might not be for another ten or twelve months. We have already noted that circumstances forced the Bishop of Quebec to grant Jean Doucet from Rustico the power to baptize and receive marriage vows when there were no priests.

If there was a missionary located in a nearby community, people did not hesitate to go and find him in order to receive the sacraments. The inhabitants of Tignish would often travel as far as Rustico, over a distance of about 160 kilometres, in order to have their marriage blessed or to have one of their children baptized.

The missionary had a very demanding ministry which he carried out in isolation, far away from his ecclesiastical superiors: he would administer the sacraments, teach catechism, organize schools and instruction, direct the worldly business of the parish, often serve as justice of the peace, combat social problems such as drunkenness, and more! He was responsible for these in all of his missions.

Given the circumstances in which the Acadians of the time were living, the missionaries found it difficult to enforce some of the regulations of the Church. A couple wishing to marry, for example, but who were related or connected somehow, had to obtain a special dispensation from the bishop and also pay him a certain sum which varied according to the degree of kinship. Considering the limited number of Acadians on the Island and the fact that they were concentrated in a few small communities, one could hardly be surprised by the blood ties. Missionaries were often faced with this problem. Father de Calonne described the special circumstances of his congregation to Bishop Plessis in 1800, asking him for leniency with regard to dispensations:

> I have already had the honour, I believe, to remark to your Lordship that there are three Acadian settlements, one in Malpeque, another in Rasticot and the third in Bay Fortune. In each case the settlements were formed by two or three families who produced many offspring, but without ever marrying anyone else, so that in each of the localities you will find that everyone is more or less related. Since they have not been established for more than forty years, the degree of cousinship is still very close. I cannot disapprove of the aversion they have for marrying their neighbours (the English, the Scots or the Irish) because it has meant that they have kept their faith, their customs and their piety intact. They can scarcely intermarry between the three settlements because they are too far apart to know each other. The result is that all the marriages are between relatives, and until I arrived third cousins were being married without any difficulty. Either the early missionaries had the power to do it, or thought they did. In any case I caused a great stir last year when I refused. (TR)[125]

The problem was further complicated by the fact that people did not always have the means to pay the fees established by the bishopric. In response to the difficulties Father de Calonne described, Monseigneur Plessis recommended flexibility under the circumstances in order to eliminate the risk of union between Acadians and people of some other religion. Monseigneur Plessis also suggested that he not be too demanding with regard to the dispensation fees in cases of extreme poverty. He also informed him that it was customary in the diocese to demand a few prayers or charity work from people who were incapable of paying[126].

Missionaries often had a hard time getting their parishioners, who had been deprived of priests for a long time, to change some of their deeply rooted customs. Monseigneur Plessis did not approve of the habit of giving all newborn a private baptism without determining whether the state of their health warranted it. Nor did he approve of the function being performed by laymen. However, his missionary Father Beaubien did not find it easy to make people give up this practice so firmly entrenched in tradition. He wrote the following in

October 1812, shortly after his arrival on the Island:

> Another thing is the baptism of sound children which your Lordship forbids; everybody protests. The women say they cannot live like that, knowing a child might die unnoticed. As for me, I shall do as your Lordship orders. But if a child were to die like that, I think I would grieve for the rest of my life. (TR)[127]

The extreme poverty of the people was another problem that had to be taken into consideration by the missionaries. The situation was such in Rustico that in 1818 the parishioners were not even able to take care of the sanctuary lamp, therefore they could not keep the Blessed Sacrament in the church permanently[128]. Given these economic circumstances, parochial organization proved to be difficult. The construction of churches, the tithes, and the sale of pews gave rise to serious problems for parishioners and missionaries alike.

Education Of The Island Acadians

The Acadians on Prince Edward Island did not receive any formal education until the beginning of the nineteenth century. There do not appear to have been any educational institutions on the Island during the French regime. Some settlers could read and write, but most of the farmers and fishermen were illiterate[129]—not an unusual phenomenon for the period, since the peasantry in both Europe and the colonies in America had little education.

In the fifty years that followed the deportation, the members of the clergy were about the only people to attend to the education of the Acadians on the Island. Despite the fact that the early priests had a very heavy load and visited communities sporadically, they taught the fundamentals and concentrated on religious education. The first attempt to establish a school for the Island Acadians failed. Indeed, Father de Calonne put forward a proposal to the government for a French school in Charlottetown in 1799. But his project did not receive the approval of the British authorities in London who continued to adhere to their policy of allowing the French language to die out gradually in their colonies[130].

The first truly Acadian school was opened around 1815 in Rustico, thanks to the initiative of a young missionary from Quebec, Father

Jean-Louis Beaubien. In the autumn of 1814 he informed his bishop that he intended to open a school in order to educate the youth. He wrote:

> I believe that a sure way of bringing up young people in piety is to educate them as much as possible. That is why I am going to undertake to have a school built and, since I do not have a schoolmaster as I would like, I shall use my boy who can read quite well, is starting to write and is doing Arithmetic; following that, I shall do my best to keep an eye on the school myself. (TR)[131]

The boy mentioned in the letter was François Buote, a young man from Rustico who lived with Father Beaubien. On January 3, 1816, Father Beaubien wrote to his bishop a second time, saying simply: "My school is open. There are not many pupils yet. We shall have more towards the spring." (TR)[132]

Nothing is known concerning the fate of this school. It could have been in operation for several years. It is known, however, that François Buote took up teaching as a career and is considered to be the first Acadian teacher on the Island. After Rustico he taught in Miscouche and then in Tignish where he retired around 1857 after many years of valuable service to his fellow citizens[133].

Another Acadian school was opened around the same time as the one in Rustico. In 1816 a young man from Brittany by the name of Dominique Charles Auffray settled in the Tignish area where he taught for three years[134].

Despite the efforts of a few individuals, the majority of Acadians remained illiterate for a long time. John McGregor, a former member of the Legislative Assembly, wrote around 1830 that the Acadians had virtually no schooling. He also noted that most of the men understood English, but that in his opinion French would continue to be their mother tongue for a long time to come[135]. It should be mentioned that settlers, be they Acadian, Scottish, English or Irish, were not particularly concerned about the education of their children. Life was difficult during those years of pioneering; what counted above all was manual labour. Besides, as long as the upkeep of the schools and the teachers' salaries depended entirely on the parents, education would remain a luxury.

A SCHOOL SYSTEM TAKES SHAPE

The few schools that did exist on the Island were run without financial help from the government until 1825 at which time the Legislature of the colony voted an amount of money designed to encourage the establishment of schools[136]. From that year onward the Island government became increasingly interested in the education of its citizens. In 1830 it created a Board of Education, composed of five members responsible for issuing teaching certificates, and alloted 590 pounds for the upkeep of schools[137]. The following year the Public Treasury contributed towards the operational costs of three grammar schools and fourteen district schools[138].

The School Act of 1834 laid down the terms of the system of instruction which was to develop in the colony. This law established three categories of teachers for the district schools. The so-called "first class" teachers were to be sufficiently qualified to be able to teach English, Reading, Writing and Practical Arithmetic; "second class" teachers were to be capable of also teaching Geometry, Trigonometry, Mensuration, Surveying and English Grammar. Finally, in addition to all these subjects, the "third class" teacher had to have a good knowledge of the Classics and the highest branches of Mathematics and Geography. He also had to be familiar with globes and be able to use them in class. In order to obtain one of these certificates the teacher had to pass the examinations set by the Board of Education in the required subjects[139].

In 1837 John McNeill was appointed as the first school inspector. His initial report is interesting because it shows that education was spreading throughout the Island: there were now fifty-one schools and 1,169 school children. The population of the Island at the time was approximately forty-seven thousand. McNeill's remarks pertaining to the quality of the teaching were less encouraging:

> I regret to have it to state, from recent personal observation, that the system of instruction pursued in many of the county schools throughout the Island is extremely defective, and consequently but little really useful and substantial knowledge is acquired by the children attending them.[140]

The government subsidies to the schools were not large; they paid for a portion of the teachers' salaries. The remainder came out

Petition written in 1816 by Placide Arsenault, one of the rare Acadians of the time who was able to write. The Acadians in Lot 15 request that Samuel Green of St. Eleanors petition the government for a road between Abram's Village and Miscouche.

Public Archives of P.E.I.

of the district school taxes or the enrolment fees which the teachers were allowed to charge their pupils. It was estimated that in 1842 the government contribution only covered one-fifth of the teacher's salary[141]. The responsibility for the construction and the maintenance of the school lay entirely with the parents.

In 1852 important changes took place in the colony with regard to education. The newly elected Liberal government passed a bill making education more accessible to the general public. This legislation lead to the levying of a school tax on all the property owners in a district which either had or wanted a public school. This locally collected tax was only to be used for the construction, furnishing and upkeep of school buildings[142]. The government took over the responsibility of the salaries although they could be supplemented according to the generosity of the ratepayers. Under the terms of the new law school teachers could no longer charge tuition fees. Within two years of the enactment of the law, the number of school children doubled on the Island[143]. We should mention, however, that school attendance was not always compulsory and many parents kept their children at home.

ACADIAN SCHOOLS

By 1830 Acadians were benefiting from the government subsidies directed toward education. Joseph Arsenault from Egmont Bay received a contribution of 7 pounds 10 shillings for his teaching that year[144]. The following year the government voted for the first time a sum of 36 pounds designated specifically for "worthy" teachers in Acadian establishments. The act stipulated that no teacher could receive more than 6 pounds from this grant[145]. The sum was later reduced to 5 pounds per teacher which was less than the amount paid to teachers in English schools in rural areas of the colony. In fact government authorities regarded teachers in Acadian schools and the schools themselves as both different and inferior because almost all the teaching was done in French. In order to teach in this category of schools a teacher did not have to have a certificate from the Board of Education. Over the years, some schools run by Acadian teachers were promoted to the level of first class schools if the teacher was deemed to be qualified to teach English properly and if a significant number of his pupils were studying it.

There were six Acadian schools operating in the early 1830s when the government first began subsidizing education. Here is a list of the schoolmasters: John Richard Bott, Rustico; Jacques Pitre, Wheatly River (Rustico); Placide Arsenault, Abram's Village; François Buote, Belle Alliance (Miscouche); Pierre Dollard, Tignish; J. Arsenault (Magitte), St. Joseph (St. Chrysostome)[146]. Of these men, John Richard Bott and probably Pierre Dollard were from Europe whereas the others were native Islanders[147]. The number of French schools remained virtually the same for about twenty years.

According to the reports of the Superintendent of Schools, the Acadians still refused to educate their children in English. Referring to the Acadian Schools in the Tignish area, Inspector John McNeill made the following remarks in 1845:

> In these, as in all the Acadian Schools on the Island, except that on Lot 17 [Miscouche], above alluded to, instruction is principally, or altogether, conveyed in the French language. A few read English, learning it through the medium of translations; they are useful Schools, being the only class which this part of the population support, who still retain a prejudice against educating their children at a mere English school.[148]

The inspector was impressed by the effective teaching of Joseph F. Gaudet, holder of a first class certificate, at the school in Miscouche. The inspector noted that, in addition to French, Joseph F. Gaudet taught Mathematics and English Grammar on a regular basis. Mr. McNeill also ascertained that three of the pupils in the school were preparing for a career in teaching. Since Gaudet was carrying out the teaching duties required for a district school and an Acadian school, the inspector suggested that he was entitled to receive the combined allowance for both types of school[149].

An important amendment was made to the School Act in 1847 which was designed to place a stricter control on the competence of Acadian schoolmasters. Until this time few regulations had existed[150]. The amendment stipulated that teachers in Acadian schools had to be Catholic and obtain their teaching certificate from their local priest. He had to be able to certify that, among other things, the candidate was capable of teaching French effectively, and of teaching reading and writing in the English language, and that he was of good moral character[151]. No doubt the clergy were entrusted with this responsibility because the members of the Board of Education were not in a position to evaluate the candidates' proficiency in French. In the same amendment the government increased to 10 pounds its annual contribution towards the salary of the Acadian schoolmaster. Despite this, he still earned less than teachers qualified to teach in first and second class schools. According to the new clause, the latter now received 15 and 20 pounds respectively.

Gradually English was taught more and more in the Acadian schools, which, in Inspector McNeill's view, rendered them much more useful institutions. He was happy to note in his report of 1847 that Acadians were becoming much more interested in learning the language of the country:

> These Schools are giving evidence of improvement and increased usefulness; the prejudices which formerly existed against instruction in any other than their own vernacular, are gradually giving way among this portion of the population. English reading is now regularly taught in almost all their schools. When the Acadian commences learning to read the language, the meaning of the English words in the lesson is told him in the language which he understands, and in that manner is soon able, not only to read, but to speak English, he will thus acquire a knowledge of both languages as well as the other elementary branches, in a period of time very little longer than he would require for the acquisition of French alone.[152]

For a long time there was no law forcing schoolmasters to teach English in Acadian schools. In 1854, however, an amendment to the School Act required teachers to give their classes in Reading, Writing and Arithmetic in English. Otherwise they would lose their salary from the Public Treasury[153]. According to the school inspector's reports for the ensuing years, these subjects were taught principally in the higher grades.

When the integration of English into the curriculum became compulsory, there were thirteen Acadian schools on the Island. In Abram's Village, for example, the school was deemed satisfactory in the eyes of the inspector: of the fifty-two pupils enrolled in the register, forty-one were present at the time of his visit. He noted that all the pupils were learning to read, eighteen of them in English. He found their proficiency in that area passable, and their spelling excellent. In the other subjects, fifteen were learning to write and eight were studying Grammar, seven of the latter were studying French Grammar. The inspector did not indicate the number who were taking Arithmetic but he did note that their knowledge in this field was praiseworthy. Last of all, he wrote that this French school was becoming more and more useful as it was gradually being turned into an English school[154]. Usefulness, in this case, probably meant adopting the curriculum taught in English schools.

The clergy exercised a strong influence in the Acadian schools both with regard to the subjects taught and the choice of teachers. In Tignish, for example, the parish priest, Father Peter McIntyre, kept a close eye on the operation of the French-language schools. Since he wanted the Acadian schools to be classified eventually as district or first class schools, he gradually introduced more English[155].

The content of the textbooks used in the Acadian schools was generally of a religious nature. The books ordered by the priests through the archdiocese of Quebec give an indication of the subjects taught during this period. In 1845, Father Sylvain-Ephrem Poirier asked Monseigneur Charles-Félix Cazeau, the archbishop's secretary, for copies of the *Alphabets Français* and *Abrégés de l'histoire sainte* (compendium of Bible history)[156]. Several years later, the bishop of Charlottetown (residing in Rustico) Monseigneur Bernard-Donald MacDonald, also ordered textbooks from Monseigneur Cazeau for the Acadian schools. He asked for several copies of the *Syllabaire*, one copy of the *Nouveau Traité des devoirs du Chrétien* being used by the Christian Brothers, one dozen short French Grammar books, and two dozen short Geography books[157].

There were not many schoolbooks at this time and it was not uncommon for a school to have only one copy. Father Poirier referred to this shortage of books when he wrote to Monseigneur Cazeau in 1846:

> I was about to write you concerning my books, eagerly awaited since the arrival of spring. I was very pleased to know that they were on their way to the Island, and I will be even more so when they arrive, considering how badly our schools need them. (TR)[158]

SCHOOL ATTENDANCE

Only 150 children were attending Acadian schools in 1843, although the Acadian population on the Island was approximately five thousand[159]. The number of school children increased considerably after the School Act of 1852 which made public education more accessible. Thus in 1855, there were 781 Acadian boys and girls enrolled in school[160].

During the first half of the nineteenth century poor school attendance was attributed mainly to the settlers' circumstances. Due to their extreme poverty they were not able to contribute to the upkeep of a school, no matter how modest. The main priority of these pioneers was to survive; their children's education would come later. The scarcity of food in 1849 resulting from the loss of crops forced several Acadian schools to close down simply because the ratepayers could not collect enough money to pay their portion of the teachers' meager salaries[161].

For the entire Island population, the average age of school children during this difficult period was very low. Normally children would start school when they were seven or eight years old, but would rarely continue their studies once they reached thirteen or fourteen[162]. Attendance was also a serious problem. Inspector John McNeill wrote in 1843 that an average of thirteen out of twenty children attended school regularly. He observed that parents had no compunction about keeping their children at home if they needed them, particularly at planting and harvest time (from May until October)[163]. Teachers had considerable difficulty respecting a regular curriculum in such unstable conditions.

SCHOOL TEACHERS

To a certain extent the quality of education in these little schools depended on the skills of the teachers. They were almost always male and too often had insufficient training. Even if they were trained teachers, the working conditions did not make their task any easier. In fact teaching materials were scarce, schools were poorly maintained, attendance was unreliable, parents' interest was limited and, finally, salaries were very low. As a rule, the teacher was the least remunerated and the least esteemed of all public servants[164].

Due to a shortage of funds in the early days, people in the district took turns providing teachers with room and board. This practice was not likely to enhance the public image of this important profession, as Inspector John McNeill explains:

> I must also mention another practice which is too prevalent in the country, and which I conceive to be exceedingly injurious to the respectability of the teacher in the eyes of his pupils, and consequently hurtful to his usefulness—that is, receiving his board by going from house to house, in which case, he is regarded, both by parents and children, as little better than a common menial. . .[165]

The overall situation of teachers in Acadian schools was perhaps even more lamentable. Obviously qualified teachers were hard to find since there was no institution where Acadian teachers could receive training in French. Therefore ratepayers had to be content with people who could reasonably manage the basic skills of reading, writing, grammar and arithmetic.

A Separate People

In the course of the fifty years that followed the deportation, Acadians sought to rebuild a homeland and reunite a society scattered throughout the world. Those who came back to establish themselves on Île Saint Jean suffered innumerable hardships caused by the land tenure system and were forced to resettle several times. The Acadian population was thus split into small groups scattered over the Island and the mainland. The moves from one area to another weakened the demographic and geographic concentration of the Acadian community which was gradually surrounded by, and even intermingled with, people of another culture and another language.

However, cultural and linguistic assimilation was not yet a reality. Until the middle of the nineteenth century the entire Acadian population on the Island succeeded quite well in closing itself off from outside cultural influences, despite the fact that it was broken up into small communities relatively isolated from one another. These people held on doggedly to their language and apparently were not interested in having their children learn English at school. In the 1810s, they had their own system of primary education in which the English language occupied a very minor position[166]. As devout Catholics, the Acadians entrusted their educational system to the clergy in whom they obviously had great confidence.

The Acadians could be distinguished visually from the other Island settlers by the way they dressed. They were deeply attached to their traditional costume, a legacy from France. In addition, the social control exercised in their villages prevented changes in clothing styles or other customs, as witnessed by the English writer, John McGregor, who lived for several years in the colony:

> The dread of being exposed to the derision of the rest, for attempting to imitate the English inhabitants, and the want of an education that would conquer prejudices, are the principal causes that prevent individuals among them, who would willingly alter their dress and habits, from doing so.[167]

We have already seen how attached the Acadians were to their traditional farming practices. Consequently, they hesitated a long time before adopting the more advanced agricultural methods of their English, Scottish or other neighbours.

Their values were profoundly different from those of Anglo-Protestants who not only respected work and wealth but regarded them as priorities, while leisure activities played a minor part in their society. The Acadians were practising Catholics and conscientiously observed their numerous religious holidays. One can understand, therefore, why they were severely criticized by English observers like S.S. Hill who wrote in the 1830s:

> They are in fact a careless and light-hearted people, with the improvidence of Indians, ever preferring the passing enjoyments of the hour, to the solid pursuits of industry; so that, reckoning saints' days, on every one of which they make holyday, and the time they occupy in shooting and other amusements, they probably lose about a fifth of the year.[168]

The author hastened to add, however, that the Acadians were happy people and content with their lot. He also noted that they had plenty of all the necessities of life[169]. Others wrote that the French on the Island were eager workers and hard to outdo, but that they did not manage to prosper because they were involved in too many kinds of activities[170]. It was also mentioned that the Acadians did not try to climb the social ladder, preferring to remain ordinary farmers[171]. This was perfectly compatible with their lifestyle as characterized by a strong feeling of communal solidarity that honoured mutual help rather than personal gain.

For a long time Acadian communities remained relatively isolated and self-sufficient, apparently seeking a certain independence as indicated in a petition signed by the inhabitants of Rustico in 1792. They asked the governor of the Island for permission not to contribute to the public assistance program because they were taking care of their own poor people.

It is not surprising that the Acadians preferred to handle their own affairs and avoid the colonial administration since memories of the expulsion and the way they had been mistreated by the English remained vivid for several generations. The absentee landlord system, as we have seen, did not help to reassure them that the period of the Great Upheaval had come to an end. The Acadians did not, however, show any hostility either toward the British administrators or their neighbours from a different culture. They adapted to the system while at the same time keeping their distance. When Governor Edmund Fanning left the Island in 1804 he praised the Acadians for their "orderly, peaceable and meritorious" behaviour, for their "constant obedience to government" and their "unshaken loyalty to the King"[173]. Despite everything, feelings of independence and suspicion were still strong amongst the Acadians on the Island at the end of the 1860s. This is clearly indicated in a letter by an Acadian published in *The Summerside Progress*:

> Although British subjects, the Acadians in this Island are in reality a separate people, holding themselves aloof in most of the social affairs of life from their fellow-colonists who speak a different language from their own, and who are too often apt to look upon them as an ignorant and antiquated class of people. The Acadians, on the other hand, while they look upon their more conceited fellow-colonists as their superiors in learning and wealth, are repelled from proper sympathy with them by the remembrance of the sufferings their fathers endured at the time of the conquest of these Provinces by the English, and subsequently.[174]

Until 1830, Catholics on the Island could neither vote nor sit in the Legislature. From then on, Acadians ventured timidly into the political arena. They elected their first member of the Legislative Assembly in 1854: Stanislas-F. Poirier, or Perry, as he preferred to sign his name. In the meantime more than one politician took advantage of the Acadian vote, and not always honestly.

The election of an Acadian to the Legislature marked the beginning of an important transformation in the Acadian community on the Island. It began to move out of its century-old isolation and to open up to the English-speaking world that surrounded it.

CHAPTER III

A PERIOD OF TRANSITION

1860–1890

Changing Cultural Values

Important changes took place in the Acadian community on Prince Edward Island between 1860 and 1890. These years coincide with a period of Acadian renewal which expressed itself throughout the Maritime Provinces. Saint Joseph College, the first Acadian post-secondary institution, was founded in Memramcook (New Brunswick) in 1864, and the *Moniteur Acadien*, the first French-language newspaper was published in Shediac (New Brunswick) in 1867. In the years that followed, other Acadian newspapers and colleges were founded, as well as several convents. It was during this period that Acadians gradually began to enter politics, business and the professions. In 1880, the Acadian patriot, Pascal Poirier, described the awakening of the Acadians in the following manner:

> If, until now, they have played an insignificant role in the political life of the country, it is because they were isolated and had no higher education whatsoever; now that they have educational establishments, they can learn their history; now that they are getting to know themselves, they are rising from the lower ranks and advancing boldly toward the higher ones. (TR)[1]

The first three national conventions of the Acadians also took place during this period: in Memramcook (1881), Miscouche (1884) and Church Point (1890). These important conventions dealt with ways to promote the advancement of the Acadian people and the preservation of their culture.

On Prince Edward Island during these years a small, relatively well-educated Acadian governing class was developing under the strong influence of the Catholic clergy. The leaders of this new generation no longer accepted that the Acadian people remain isolated and disadvantaged. Hence they took on the task of elevating Acadians to the same rank held by English-speaking Islanders in social, economic and political spheres. In 1870, an Acadian from Tignish writing in *The Summerside Journal* in French made a vibrant appeal to his compatriots for the revival of the Acadian "race":

> Sirs,—I have been considering for some time our position in relation to the other races on the Island and I note that we lag behind in many respects. As the oldest inhabitants of the Island, we do not occupy the position in society that we should. We have to borrow from others almost all our public figures.

> Most of our legislators and magistrates, all our doctors and lawyers, and even our priests are of foreign races, and if there are any small positions vacant in Acadian parishes, they are immediately filled by Englishmen. [. . .]
>
> One of the main reasons we are still behind is the lack of education resulting from the unfair treatment of our forefathers. But, Sirs, it is now time to rise up. . . (TR)[2]

The young leaders of the time realized that a recovery meant that they would have to break through the cultural isolation that had been reinforced by previous generations. But how could Acadians be encouraged to move out of their isolation into the dominant anglophone culture and society, and at the same time not lose their own language and culture?

This question appears to have divided the members of the Acadian governing class on the Island. Some maintained that a certain degree of anglicization was necessary in order for the Acadian people to catch up with the rest of the Island population[3]. Others, without opposing the idea of learning English as a means of social advancement, insisted that the French language and culture be preserved intact.

These divergent positions are typical of this period in Acadian history. As a matter of fact, it was at this time that a strong current of Acadian nationalism was developing on Prince Edward Island and elsewhere in the Maritime Provinces. However, this nationalism which obviously stressed the value of Acadian culture came up against the growing anglicization of French-speaking Islanders. In fact it was during these last decades of the nineteenth century that the Acadians lost control of their French-language educational system. This explains to a great extent the trend towards anglicization. It was a gradual process. First the government forced Acadian schoolteachers to obtain a teacher's certificate in English, and then it proceeded to almost totally anglicize the curriculum in Acadian schools.

The training in English which was forced upon Acadian teachers undoubtedly influenced the conduct of many members of the Acadian elite. It should be pointed out that on the whole these leaders were teachers or former teachers who had moved on to better paid and often much more influential careers. Some had become merchants, civil servants, politicians, lawyers or priests. A few of these educated men had married English-speaking women, much to the disapproval of their more nationalistic compatriots[4]. In some Acadian localities,

LE MONITEUR ACADIEN

ORGANE DES POPULATIONS FRANÇAISES

DES PROVINCES MARITIMES.

"NOTRE LANGUE, NOTRE RELIGION ET NOS COUTUMES."

Shédiac, Nouveau-Brunswick.—Jeudi, 9 Octobre 1873.

FEUILLETON

LE

COUREUR DES GREVES.

XII

Suite.

teachers and educated people were frequently accused of preferring to speak English[5].

The Catholic clergy, who had considerable influence over this lay elite, did not form a unified group. The clergy included priests of Québécois, Irish and Scottish descent who were far from agreeing on the Acadian question. Their attitude with regard to the Acadian culture and the French language varied greatly. Therefore, the influence of the clergy on Acadian leaders was not consistent. So it was under the direction and influence of a rather varied leadership with differing opinions that the Acadian community began to emerge from its cultural isolation.

In order to hasten the evolution of their people, Acadian leaders advocated changing some of the popular values of the time. In their opinion, the development of the Acadians was being hindered by certain traditional values. Consequently, they conducted a propaganda campaign in an attempt to prove to Acadians that they would probably benefit if they modified their attitudes and abandoned some of their old customs. Needless to say, this elite stressed the importance of education. One of the most stirring pleas in defence of change appeared on the front page of *The Summerside Progress* in 1868. The author who identified himself merely as "An Acadian" entitled his article: *Manners and Customs of the French Acadians in P.E. Island.—Reform*. He wrote with conviction that if the Acadians did not change their lifestyle, they were likely to remain an insignificant people:

> Acadians! You deserve praise for your virtues; but to remain in your present condition, wedded to traditions of the past, holding in reverence antiquated notions of exclusiveness, and hugging to your breast old manners and customs, will not conduce to your material prosperity, respectibility or happiness! [. . .]
>
> If you do not avail yourselves of the advantages of education,—if you do not assimiliate [sic] your manners and customs to those prevailing around you,—and if your women do not conform in some near degree to the fashions in dress, and become more *susceptible du poli* [sic], you will continue a separate, and, as a matter of necessity, an insignificant people.
>
> Think of it, Acadians, and wake up![6]

This anonymous writer urged Acadian women to abandon their traditional costume in order to conform to the fashions of the day. He does not appear to have been the only person to advocate this change, because within a few years most Acadian women on the Island

Young Acadian from Rustico
Robert Harris, published in 1882 in Picturesque Canada: the Country As It Was and Is.

no longer wore the so-called "French frock" (TR). After all, by wearing the traditional dress, Acadian women did stand out from other women on the Island. In 1880, according to an Island correspondent for the newspaper *Le Moniteur Acadien*, the other ethnic groups made fun of this traditional costume:

> A few years ago our women used to wear the old-fashioned dress our mothers brought from Acadia. They were very fond of it. It is hard to imagine why for it is neither pretty nor practical. Because of it we were mocked and ridiculed by other nationalities. To avoid disgrace, we persuaded our women to adopt the present-day fashion and today the majority of them are dressed like the

> women of other peoples. They are not any the worse off for it and Acadian men are much better off. (TR)[7]

The cultural isolation of the Acadians was broken down for good between 1860 and 1890. They became more and more interested in education, they were more willing to learn English (in fact, they were eventually compelled to do so by the government), their farmers began to try new agricultural methods, and generally people took a greater interest in public life. However, becoming more open also meant becoming anglicized—a trend that was particularly apparent in communities such as Rollo Bay, Miscouche, Cascumpec and Tignish where Acadians lived amongst an English-speaking population.

It was estimated that in 1860 the Acadian population of the Island was approximately nine thousand[8]. At the time of the 1881 federal census, the first to enumerate people of French origin as a specific group, Acadians accounted for 9.9 percent of the population of the province—in other words 10,751 inhabitants[9].

The Clergy Leads The Way

Bishop Peter McIntyre directed the Catholic Church on the Island throughout the period we are examining. He was consecrated in 1860, after Bishop Bernard Donald MacDonald's death, and served as prelate of the diocese until 1891. Before being called to the episcopal See he was the parish priest in Tignish, a predominantly Acadian township. The diocese of Charlottetown, which at the time included the Magdalen Islands, expanded considerably during his reign; new parishes were founded, magnificent churches built, convents opened and numerous priests recruited[10].

During the early years of his episcopate, Bishop McIntyre, like his predecessor, had to rely on the Montreal diocese for resident priests. Thus several priests from Quebec[11] and two from the Magdalens came to serve on the Island[12]. Even one priest from France and another from Belgium spent several years among the Acadians[13]. The first Acadian priest from the Island, Father Sylvain-Ephrem Poirier, retired in 1879, one year before the second Acadian was ordained. This was Father Jean Chiasson from Tignish. In 1884, Father François-Xavier

Gallant from Rustico was next to enter the priesthood. It should be pointed out that during this period several priests of Scottish origin, usually perfectly bilingual, were posted in predominantly Acadian parishes[14].

Many of these priests made outstanding contributions to the development of the Acadian communities. They played a crucial role in the Acadian revival, thanks to their privileged position in society, their energy and their organizational and leadership skills.

We have already mentioned that for a long time the priest was the only person in the community with a formal education. As a result, the Acadians regarded him as a person they could trust and who would protect them from any hostile element. Looked upon as an earthly representative of God, the priest was the symbol of authority and justice. In 1868, an Acadian wrote in *The Summerside Progress*:

> The Acadians are peaceable in character, and strongly attached to the religion of their forefathers—which is the Roman Catholic. They have great reverence for their clergy, in whom they place an almost unbounded confidence.[15]

For a long time the Church praised this unlimited respect for the priest. Indeed, this period of Acadian renewal coincides with the rise of ultramontanism in the Catholic Church of French Canada. This was a very conservative doctrine that extolled the submission of the faithful to all forms of authority, including the clergy. According to this doctrine, the Church, through its divine mission, had authority not only over spiritual matters but also over all earthly matters in life. Ultramontanism favoured traditional rural life, as opposed to urbanization and industrialization which were seen as threats to religion. Thus, ultramontanism stressed the merits of farming and colonization. The proponents of this doctrine made a strong connection between French-Canadian culture and the Catholic religion, hence the expression "he who loses his language, loses his faith" (TR).

The ultramontane ideology had a profound influence on the Acadians since they were served by a clergy trained in this school of thought. Given his special status in the community, the priest could exercise tremendous power. Acadians seemed to exhibit almost irreproachable dedication and obedience to their spiritual leader. Before undertaking any project likely to have an impact on the collective life, the faithful would first seek the support of the clergy; otherwise nothing would happen. Writing to the French historian, Edme Rameau de Saint-Père, in 1867, Israël Landry made the following comments:

> ...our good Acadians are Catholic and would not do anything against their priests' wishes. If they have a priest who cares for their well-being, you will see them support him wholeheartedly in anything he undertakes on their behalf; take for example Rustico, Miscouche, Memramcook, etc. (TR)[16]

For most people, the priest was virtually untouchable. Even if he did have faults and even if he did misuse his power, no one was permitted to criticize him. The following story illustrates this mentality. At the beginning of the twentieth century, a pedlar from Shediac visiting a family in Abram's Village took the liberty of making several critical remarks about certain priests. A grandmother listened attentively to the visitor's "shocking" gossip and then proceeded to lecture him: "Did you know, she said sternly, that our Lord said 'He who strikes my priests, strikes me in the eye?'" (TR). Astonished by this sharp and unexpected reply, the stranger asked immediately: "In what book did you read that?" To which the old lady responded: "I read it in better books than you read!" (TR)[17].

It should be said that there were many Acadians of this elderly lady's calibre who respected everything the Church preached. Nevertheless, there were Acadians who did not always follow their priest's instruction to the letter and who even dared disobey him in public. In Mont Carmel around 1880, several parishioners uttered threats against the elderly Father Sylvain-Ephrem Poirier during a quarrel and, what is more, urged their fellow parishioners not to provide firewood for the church or the presbytery since it was not cited as an obligation in either the Bible or the Church precepts[18]. Sometimes these protests were justified because some priests did take advantage of their authority by denouncing and disgracing their parishioners from the pulpit[19]. Generally, however, Acadians held their priests in high esteem. They would often pay their respects to their priest on the anniversary of his ordination and when he moved away from the parish—or even when he left for an important trip abroad—and on New Year's Day. On each occasion they would emphasize his dedication to the parish, enumerate his many qualities and accomplishments and express their obedience as parishioners. In closing, they would present him with a gift which might be a sum of money or a costly item such as a fur coat, a winter carriage, silver plates or other valuable objects.

A COMMITTED CLERGY

It is generally recognized that the clergy's contribution to the development of the Acadians was outstanding. Their influence extended far beyond strictly religious matters. Priests became involved in various areas where they felt they could foster the advancement of the Acadian people. As we shall examine further on, they were involved in education, cultural development, agriculture, colonization, and other areas of social concern.

According to the ultramontane ideology, all these areas were interrelated and should be under the control of the Church, not the State. Was not language the guardian of the faith? Was it not agriculture that would enable Acadians to preserve their language, their faith and their traditions? Did the future of the Catholic Church not depend on the education of young people? Given this perspective, the clergy's involvement in socio-economic spheres constituted a duty of prime importance.

The French-speaking members of the clergy were certainly among the most ardent supporters of the Acadian cause on Prince Edward Island, as was the case elsewhere in Acadia. They became involved in any movement aimed at promoting the social advancement of Acadians and preserving their culture. Since laymen trusted them implicitly, priests often became the principal leaders of these movements. For example, the organizing committee of the first national convention of the Acadians, held in Memramcook in 1881, appointed the priest from each of the Acadian parishes as an *ex officio* member of the convention. The committee explained its decision in the newspaper *Le Moniteur Acadien*:

> The clergy supported our poor people when they were attacked, took care of them in times of adversity, awakened them from their lethargy, and opened up the arsenal of education: the clergy will lay a solid foundation for our future. It is fitting that members of the clergy play a leading role in organizations such as the convention. We are relying, therefore, on their enlightenment to make this national gathering a festivity that will leave a deep and lasting impression on the life of the Acadian people. (TR)[20]

Father Joseph Quévillon
Reg Porter Collection.

Father George-Antoine Belcourt
Public Archives of P.E.I.

The Acadian clergy did in fact participate very actively in this first convention, as it did in the others that were to follow.

THE TEMPERANCE MOVEMENT

The founding of parishes and the presence of resident priests facilitated the development of societies of a religious or socio-religious nature. No other organization was better promoted by the Church and the clergy than the temperance society. In fact, alcoholism was a serious problem which all the Churches considered to be the sin of the century and which they all sought to eliminate. The temperance movement was actually started in Ireland in 1838 and spread quickly to all English-speaking countries. It was firmly established on the Island by 1841, thanks to Bishop MacDonald. Under his leadership, the clergy founded several Total Abstinence Leagues. Father Sylvain-Ephrem Poirier became president of the league he founded in Cascumpec for Prince County. To become a member, one had to promise not to consume alcoholic drinks except in the case of illness. By the end of 1841, there were five thousand members of the temperance movement on the Island[21].

The movement was successful for a long time, although it had its ups and downs. The clergy was obliged to revitalize it from time to time—apparently with the arrival of a new generation. Generally these temperance societies took the form of cultural and educational groups whose members organized variety shows, established bands and libraries, invited guest lecturers and supported both morally and financially any worthy cause.

Father Belcourt, a Québécois priest, organized a temperance society in Rustico in 1860 shortly after his arrival in the parish. Having spent many years as a missionary with the Red River Indians and Métis, he was fifty-six years old when he came to the Island. He named his society the *Institut catholique de Rustico* and chose Saint John the Baptist as patron saint. The purpose of the institute was to educate parishioners and dissuade them from alcohol abuse[22]. The members met regularly to listen to Father Belcourt's talks on topics as varied as education, economics and science. In 1864, he wrote:

> We have lectures regularly every Thursday at our Institute. I attract people with experiments in Chemistry and Physics which interest them enormously. Ferland's *L'Histoire du Canada* also provides a useful collection of facts which interest them just as much and, by varying the topics, help train our schoolmasters. (TR)[23]

Thanks to a very energetic leader, the *Institut* was able to undertake numerous projects. A library was founded and stocked with a wide variety of books and newspapers. There were classical works, scientific books, religious writings, etc., purchased by means of contributions from the members and gifts from Emperor Napoleon III. The latter were obtained with the help of the French historian, Edme Rameau de Saint Père, who was referred to as "The Great Friend of the Acadians" (TR) and who corresponded regularly with Father Belcourt; he had his heart set on the advancement and welfare of the Acadians. These contributions from France enabled the *Institut* to accomplish other projects, as indicated in the following extract from a letter, dated August 3, 1863, which Father Belcourt wrote to Edme de Saint Père:

> I have not given an account of how the money given by His Majesty to the Institute has been spent, because I completely forgot about it. We purchased almost fifty volumes in Quebec for our library, along with a globe of the world, a globe of the heavens, plus an armillary sphere to complete the set. In addition, a musical instrument (harmonium), and part of the salary for a Canadian master hired to play the Church organ which I purchased last autumn, to teach music and to make a model school at the Institute in order to train schoolmasters. All these things were paid for with the money from the Emperor's gift and part of the members' annual contributions. (TR)[24]

The *Institut catholique de Rustico*, which had two hundred and fifty members in 1867[25], contributed substantially to the economic, social and cultural growth of the community. In addition to the activities already mentioned, we should mention that the Farmers' Bank of Rustico was also discussed at the meetings of the Institute[26] and that annual festivities were organized to celebrate its patron saint on Saint John the Baptist Day. The *Institut catholique* operated for a long time as a temperance society and then became a "Good Death Society" (TR) at the beginning of the twentieth century[27], but its most active years coincide with Father Belcourt's stay in Rustico from 1860 to 1869.

The temperance movement was totally reorganized in 1878. The clergy was aware that alcohol abuse still constituted a very destructive factor in society. Consequently, Bishop Peter MacIntyre sent all the parishes a pastoral letter in which he urged his priests to fight harder against this social calamity:

> Redouble your labours in the cause of Temperance, for you well know that drunkenness is one of the besetting sins of our time. Bring the spiritual and temporal evils of this vice before the minds of your people, and exhort them to sobriety in honour of the sacred thirst of our Saviour on the Cross.[28]

The bishop asked priests and laymen to organize societies for total abstinence in their parishes. To facilitate the co-ordination of the movement, he established a central council of which Father Ronald B. MacDonald, the parish priest in Miscouche, became president. An excellent propagandist, Father MacDonald travelled from one parish to another promoting the organization and accepting pledges of total abstinence from new members. According to the *Moniteur Acadien*, the Acadian parishes were among the first to join the movement:

> We note with great pleasure and a true feeling of pride that our compatriots were among the first to respond to the call of their chief Pastor. Moved by the havoc wreaked on populations by drunkenness, that canker of society, Acadian parishes have resolved to stem the curse of our time. (TR)[29]

The propaganda campaign proved to be very effective since most men embraced the cause: 230 in Bloomfield, 330 in Egmont Bay, and 204 in Mont Carmel[30]. To become a member of the Society, you had to take an oath of total abstinence from intoxicating drinks and promise to recite one "Our Father" and two "Hail Marys" to ask for perseverance. Each local society had a vigilance committee that watched over the members and fined them 20 cents whenever they were caught consuming alcohol. Finally, a member would risk being expelled from the organization if he broke his pledge several times[31].

By 1860 most of the parish temperance societies had been transformed in order to join the ranks of the League of the Cross, a new worldwide temperance movement[32]. These organizations were still engaged in essentially cultural and educational activities. As was the case in Rustico, most of them became "Good Death Societies" (TR) at the beginning of the century although they were still called the Temperance. Total abstinence from alcoholic beverages was no longer compulsory and anyone—man, woman or child—who had received communion could become a member on payment of annual dues of about 10 cents. The money collected was used to pay for the religious ceremony at the time of the member's funeral. This type of organization survived in some parishes until the 1970s.

In short, the temperance society played an important role in Acadian parishes since, for many years, it constituted the principal community organization. In addition to fighting the problem of alcoholism, the temperance movement contributed to the social, economic and cultural development of the parishes.

EDUCATION

A QUESTION OF RELIGION

Between 1860 and 1870, Acadian schools were victims of a serious religious and political conflict in the province. By the end of the 1850s, the question of religious instruction in the schools had pitted Catholics and Protestants against each other. The controversy was focussed on the power of the Church and the State in educational matters. A violent debate dragged on in both the newspapers and the Legislature. The School Act of 1877 finally stated that public schools in the province were to be non-confessional, that is, neutral in religious matters.

To appreciate the extent of the debate which divided the province for many years, it should be understood that by the middle of the nineteenth century Prince Edward Island was a pluralistic society from a religious point of view. The members of the various religious denominations wanted their children to be educated according to their beliefs. This demand on the part of parents posed a problem since many communities were comprised of several denominations. The limited population in these communities, not to mention the meagre resources available in the Public Treasury for education, did not justify multiplying schools in order to respect everyone's religious beliefs and practices. The simplest solution was thus to see that public schools

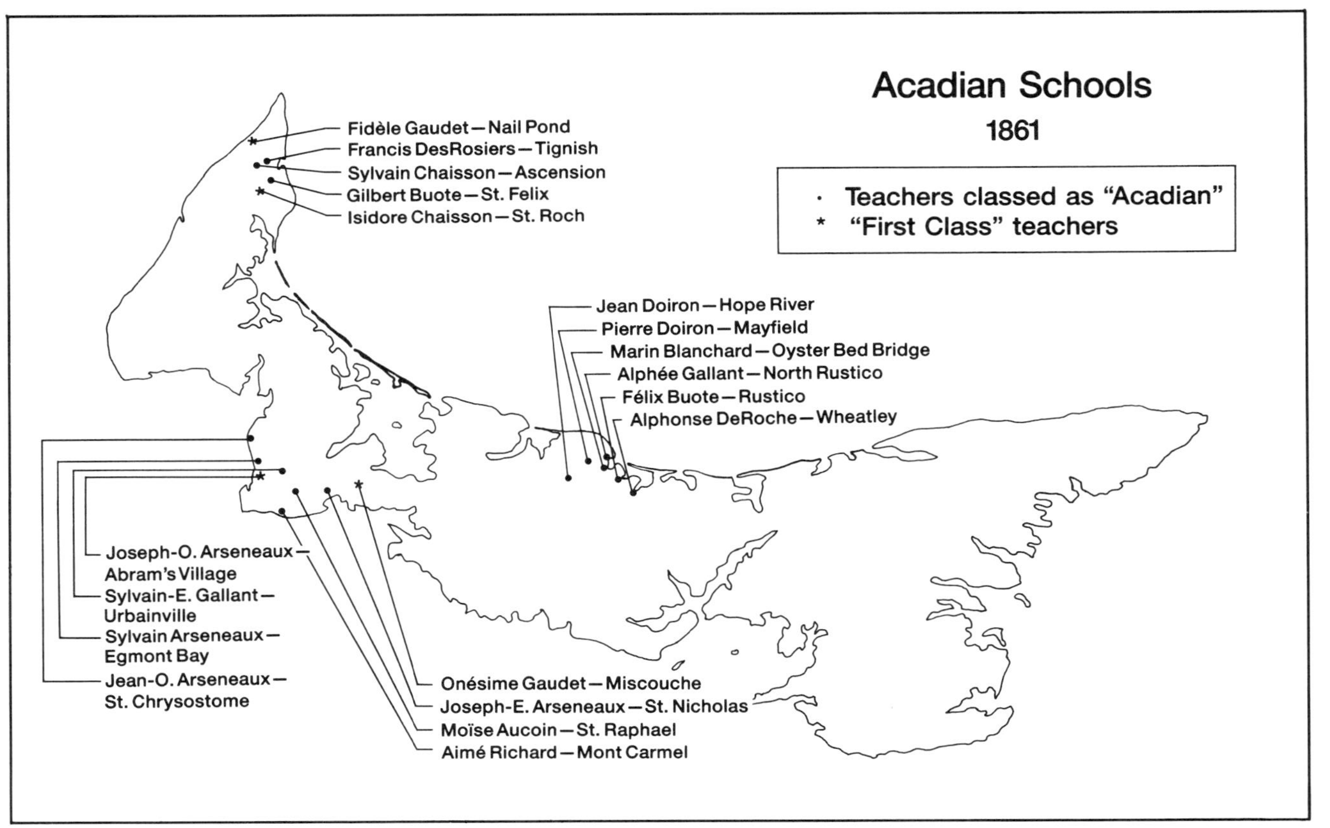
Acadian Schools
1861
· Teachers classed as "Acadian"
* "First Class" teachers
Fidèle Gaudet – Nail Pond
Francis DesRosiers – Tignish
Sylvain Chaisson – Ascension
Gilbert Buote – St. Felix
Isidore Chaisson – St. Roch
Jean Doiron – Hope River
Pierre Doiron – Mayfield
Marin Blanchard – Oyster Bed Bridge
Alphée Gallant – North Rustico
Félix Buote – Rustico
Alphonse DeRoche – Wheatley
Joseph-O. Arseneaux – Abram's Village
Sylvain-E. Gallant – Urbainville
Sylvain Arseneaux – Egmont Bay
Jean-O. Arseneaux – St. Chrysostome
Onésime Gaudet – Miscouche
Joseph-E. Arseneaux – St. Nicholas
Moïse Aucoin – St. Raphael
Aimé Richard – Mont Carmel

remain non-confessional. However, this principle had not yet been laid down by law. Instead, it was left to the Board of Education to make sure that the curriculum and schoolbooks authorized for these schools were devoid of any religious content. When schools did not adhere strictly to the orders of the Board, the authorities turned a blind eye to the irregularities as long as no conflicts arose in the districts concerned.

As we saw earlier, Acadian schools, although receiving grants from the provincial Treasury, enjoyed a special status. Priests were authorized to certify the proficiency of their teachers who were, by necessity, Catholic. Furthermore, the clergy made a point of choosing schoolbooks with a religious content.

But the religious debate that flared up after 1856, following the official opening of the Normal School in Charlottetown, led Protestant journalists and later, Orangemen, to criticize openly the privileges enjoyed by the Acadian schools. They demanded that the government stop giving these confessional schools preferential treatment[33]. They also asked why the government was subsidizing French-language education for Acadians. The newspaper, *The Islander* wrote:

> We reply that the French inhabitants of the Island have no right to expect to be educated in the French language—they have no claims upon the Government—they are the descendants of prisoners of war who secreted themselves in the woods of the Island, and of the neighbouring Provinces. [...] We, on grounds of national policy, object to the encouragement of French schools...[34]

Because of these criticisms, changes were made to the School Act that were to have profound repercussions on Acadian schools. In 1860 an amendment forced Acadian teachers to take the Board of Education examinations in order to obtain a teacher's certificate. If they refused to comply, their salary was reduced from 40 to 35 pounds[35]. Three years later, another amendment abolished the category of Acadian schoolteachers. This meant that Acadian teachers had the same status as other teachers on the Island and that the privileges, which until then had been granted to Acadian schools, were eliminated. Thus, in principle, Acadian schools ceased to exist. A teacher in an Acadian school could in fact be of any denomination, he no longer had to show that he was capable of teaching in French, and he had to attend the Normal School where all teacher training took place in English. The School Act said nothing, however, about the language of instruction in Acadian schools; therefore, one could continue teaching in French. It was a paradoxical state of affairs: before setting out to teach in French, Acadian candidates had to demonstrate their proficiency in English at the Normal School in order to obtain their teacher's licence[36].

According to the school inspector, William Henry Buckerfield, the 1863 amendment to the School Act helped Acadians move ahead by making them learn the language of the country. He wrote:

> The abolition of the Government allowance to Acadian teachers, thus putting the French population on precisely the same footing as their fellow subjects, was, I think, a judicious enactment, and it will tend most strongly to the general introduction of the English language in districts throughout which it has hitherto been of rare occurence. I believe, indeed, that the most intelligent among the French are fully sensible of the disadvantage under which many of them have laboured, from their ignorance of the language in which the business of the country is conducted[37]

The long term effect of this policy was the anglicization of Acadian schools; in the short term several Acadian schools had to close since the School Act did not allow duplication of establishments in the same school district[38]. Consequently, if there was already a recognized English school, the Acadian school would not be recognized as a district school and receive public funds. Even in entirely Acadian districts, there were problems stemming not from the presence of English schools, but from the shortage of licenced francophone teachers qualified to teach unilingual French children. It was a vicious circle, since most Acadian teachers did not know enough English to pass the Board of Education examinations. In some schools in Egmont Bay and Mont Carmel the difficulty was overcome by hiring young women without a licence whose salaries were paid by private donations[39].

Over the years, new amendments to the School Act were to alter this deplorable situation. By 1864, two schools were allowed in districts that were deemed to be densely populated. Acadian Catholic schools were thus tolerated in certain districts[40]. In 1868, urged on by the Honourable Joseph-Octave Arsenault, the Legislative Assembly passed a motion encouraging teachers to become qualified to teach

French. As a result, any teacher who obtained the appropriate qualification was entitled to receive a salary increment of 5 pounds from the government, providing the school district matched the sum[41].

Despite complaints to the Board of Education, textbooks with a religious content were used in the Acadian schools until 1877. The situation was tolerated for a long time merely because appropriate French textbooks without a religious content were not available in Canada[42]. This fact exemplifies, once again, the link between language and faith.

The problems encountered by Acadian schools related, as we have seen, not only to the language of instruction and the training of teachers, but also to religion. As stated earlier, the debate concerning religious instruction in schools divided the province for quite some time. The School Act of 1877 settled the matter to the extent that public schools were to be non-confessional and textbooks standardized. The French books being used in the Acadian schools were thus removed. However, the Act left the whole issue of French-language education unresolved.

The School Act of 1877 could hardly leave Bishop Peter McIntyre indifferent. In fact, he organized an extensive campaign to defend the rights of Acadian schools. According to his interpretation of previous school acts, Acadian schools were legally entitled to teach the Catholic religion and the French language. In other words, Acadian schools were separate schools. Thus, in Monseigneur McIntyre's opinion, the School Act of 1877 contradicted the British North America Act which protected the educational rights which Catholic Islanders acquired before the Island entered Confederation in 1873.

The bishop personally took numerous steps to protest the School Act. He also urged Acadians to petition Ottawa in order to demand justice; in addition he asked them to contest the law by keeping their schools closed. The Acadians followed their bishop's recommendations and began boycotting public schools. But it was a lost cause: the Island government succeeded very quickly in proving that the School Acts, especially after 1863, placed Acadian schools on the same footing as all the other public schools in the province[43]. The only concession the Acadians gained by their action was that they obtained a series of bilingual readers. This success was very relative, however. Inspector William McPhail approved of these readers because they made it easier to translate or, in other words, to learn English [44].

SETTING UP PRIVATE INSTITUTIONS

The Acadian elite, dedicated to defending the special status of Acadian schools, proved powerless in the face of government. It should be emphasized that there was no Acadian member sitting in the Legislative Assembly in 1863 when the amendment to the School Act, eliminating this special status, was adopted. Given this deadlock, the clergy took the initiative and created private Catholic schools in Acadian localities. Fathers Belcourt and Quévillon were the first to promote and set up these schools.

Father George-Antoine Belcourt was an energetic and determined priest. He recognized that the Island needed an institution that could train bilingual teachers. He also wanted to circumvent the amendments to the School Act which, in his view, were designed specifically to anglicize the Acadians[45]. In 1862, therefore, Father Belcourt opened a secondary school in Rustico in order to train Acadian schoolmasters. The teacher he hired was Israël J.-D. Landry, a young man from Montreal who later founded the *Moniteur Acadien* in 1867.

The subjects taught in the model school[46] were French, Latin, Greek, Mathematics, Plain Chant, Music[47] and, in all likelihood, English. Since the school could not qualify for government grants, the teacher's salary came from local contributions and donations which Father Belcourt received from the emperor Napoleon III.

The Rustico school was very successful. In the space of two years there were enough teachers trained in order to fill the requirements of all the Acadian schools on the Island. Proud of the accomplishments of both his school and his schoolmaster, the pastor for Rustico wrote to Rameau:

> ...for two years this master has run a model school here and trained schoolmasters capable of teaching in both languages well above the capabilities of English masters; we have provided all the French populations on the Island with schoolmasters and there are still some available. (TR)[48]

Unfortunately the school only survived a few years, just long enough to train a sufficient number of competent Acadian teachers, one of whom later became a lawyer, another a doctor and a third a senior employee of Canadian National[49].

One of the first convents in an Acadian parish in the Maritime

The Convent in Miscouche
Musée Acadien.

Provinces was opened in Miscouche in September 1864. The building was constructed under the direction of Father Joseph Quévillon who came to the Island from the diocese of Montreal. He wanted the convent to be both a "home of charity" (TR) and a school for Acadian girls. As he explained to his bishop, Monseigneur Bourget, the need was great:

> First of all, our primary aim is to work towards the worldly and religious regeneration of the Acadian people who are living in another century, by giving females a domestic as well as a social education in order to remove them from this sort of subservience in which they find themselves with regard to a foreign people. In the course of time, we must prepare our convent girls to become housekeepers, etc. Secondly, there is not one single Catholic Home, Orphanage or Infirmary on the Island; all these have yet to be established here. To control public disturbances there are but prisons into which poor specimens of both sexes are thrown pellmell. (TR)[50].

Bishop McIntyre did not support the idea of an orphanage because he felt that the convent should become above all an educational institution[51]. Faced with the opposition of his ecclesiastical superior, Father Quévillon handed over the convent, that he had endowed with 700 pounds, to the bishop of Charlottetown who took charge of it henceforth[52]. Bishop McIntyre sent for three sisters from the Congregation of Notre Dame in Montreal who arrived in time to begin classes on September 14, 1864.

Bishop McIntyre took a personal interest in the convent. He requested the help of the people in Miscouche and elsewhere to see that the sisters were comfortable. The following passage, taken from the Convent records, shows how much the sisters appreciated the bishop's dedication and the parishioners' generosity:

> Returning from Tignish, his Lordship was preceded by carriages loaded with eight hundred pounds of flour, two hundred mackerel, two quintals of cod and a tub of butter. This Devoted Prelate spent Sunday with us. It would be impossible to say how thoughful he was. He kindly invited the people to come the next day for the Mass that he would say for them, and to bring several pieces of firewood, and axes and saws to finish the new convent buildings. His Lordship extended this invitation so kindly and so gently that the next day the yard was full of men: some were chopping wood, others were sawing, and others were working on the shed. His Lordship spent the day with them: he was indeed a true Father amidst his children. (TR)[53]

From the time it opened, the convent was not limited to Acadian girls only, although they did form the majority of the pupils. In fact, the convent also accepted girls whose parents were Irish, Scottish or English; several pupils were Protestant. In 1866, there were approximately ninety pupils attending the convent classes which included English, French, Geography, History, Education, Grammar, plus Music and Embroidery[54]. In addition to girls from the parish, the convent also took in resident pupils from elsewhere, even from New Brunswick. There were twenty-five boarders in March of 1871: sixteen Acadians and nine English-speaking girls of whom three were Protestant[55].

The survival of the convent was dependent on continued public support. Consequently, the parishioners often organized large picnics (the ultimate fundraising event) and individuals made donations on a regular basis. For example, Father Sylvain Ephrem Poirier, the parish priest for Mont Carmel, donated a pig to the convent in 1871 and 1872[56]. The school itself relied on tuition fees since it was not entitled to government grants. But according to the *Summerside Progress*, the sisters were having a hard time supporting their convent in 1868 because many of the sixty pupils enrolled could not afford to pay all their school fees. It was thanks to the contributions of benefactors like Fathers Quévillon and Miville that the sisters were able to accept children from poor families at no charge or for reduced fees[57].

In all the institutions of the time, the examination of the pupils in public constituted a great event that everybody would attend, including the clergy and notables from the village. The following passage from the *Moniteur Acadien* gives a very picturesque account of the ceremony and an idea of the subjects studied by pupils in 1869:

> The convent rooms not being large enough to hold the many friends of education at the convent, an outdoor stage was constructed with a bower of fir branches overhead that gave if not a most picturesque setting, at least a most pleasant one. At the outset, the scene was made even more beautiful and more graceful with the pupils dressed in white, the picture of innocence, standing in rows behind the stage. The programme was arranged so as to mix the serious parts of the examination with different pieces of music and singing, along with dialogues and plays, with the result that the audience could spend some very enjoyable moments.
>
> The pupils were questioned seriously by the members of the clergy not only on English and French Reading, Translation, Geography, English and French Grammar, Arithmetic, but also on the higher branches of learning, Rhetoric,

> the Terrestrial Globe, Ecclesiastical History, Modern History, Natural Philosophy and Botany. The pupils answered perfectly all the questions they were asked. (TR)[58]

Tignish and Rustico followed the example of Miscouche by establishing convents under the direction of the sisters of the Congregation of Notre Dame in Montreal: the convent in Tignish opened in 1868, and the one in Rustico in 1882[59]. These convents offered the same bilingual curriculum as the one in Miscouche and were also instrumental in preparing candidates for the Normal School, thus providing Acadian schools with bilingual teachers. The convents were also excellent centres of cultural animation. The sisters gave art and music classes and often put on variety concerts that were greatly appreciated by the public.

Until the beginning of the twentieth century, French appears to have prevailed in these institutions. Since the sisters were from Quebec, the curriculum was exactly the same as the one the Congregation used in their native province. The atmosphere was French even though bilingualism was a must for any public event organized by the sisters involving their pupils.

ACADIAN SCHOOLS

Despite good classes and competent teachers, the convents only reached a small proportion of Acadian school children. The vast majority of pupils went to public schools with all the problems that entailed. In 1885, there were twenty-seven so-called Acadian public schools in Prince County where most of the French population lived[60].

School attendance continued to pose a major problem throughout the province. In fact it was often deplored that classes were so poorly attended. Many young school children would only occupy their school benches during the warm months of the year. In the case of older children, they would often be obliged to stay at home to help work on the farm. Some of them only went to school during the off-season[61].

Even though parents were becoming more and more interested in education and were building and furnishing new schools, often the conditions did not enhance either attendance or the quality of teaching. In some schools there was a shortage of desks and the children were too crowded together, there were no maps, and sometimes there was not even enough firewood. As for the teachers, they were not only obliged to work under disheartening circumstances, but they also had to be content with very meagre wages. In 1875, the average male schoolteacher received 48 cents per day, and his female counterpart 35 cents for the same work. Thus, it is not surprising that so many teachers left the profession which served as a springboard for more lucrative careers[62]. As a result, competent qualified teachers were scarce.

Although this regrettable situation existed throughout Island schools, it was worse for Acadian teachers. In order to receive the same salary as other teachers in the province, Acadian teachers had to write their examinations in English which put them at a definite disadvantage with regard to their Anglophone colleagues. According to the superintendent of education for the province, this fact was likely to discourage Acadians from going into teaching. Relative to this, he wrote the following in 1887:

> The syllabus of Teachers' Examinations is too difficult in my opinion for a French speaking scholar to overcome without devoting more time to its attainment than the after remuneration would warrant. Probably this is one reason why so few of our Acadian brethren adopt the teaching profession.[63]

The duties of Acadian teachers were made even more difficult because they had to teach, with neither method nor appropriate texts, several subjects in English to pupils who generally only spoke French[64].

After about 1880, Acadians started complaining about the deplorable gaps in their teachers' knowledge of the French language. In 1884, a contributor from the Island writing in the *Moniteur Acadien* warned his readers that if the situation did not improve, "every trace of our beautiful French language will be obliterated for future generations. Even nowadays you can hardly get a French word out of either a teacher or a pupil. What will it be like in fifty or a hundred years? (TR)[65]" The anglicizing effect of the educational system supported by the provincial government was becoming increasingly apparent. The quality of French teaching depended almost entirely on initiatives taken by the Acadians themselves outside the system.

Pensionnat de St. Joseph

Sous la Direction des Sœurs de la Congrégation de Notre-Dame, à Miscouche, paroisse de Belle-Alliance, Isle du Prince-Edouard.

Cette nouvelle Institution, qui a été ouverte le décembre 1867, est sous la direction des sœurs de la Congrégation de Notre-Dame, qui s'efforceront de donner aux jeunes personnes, que les parents confieront à leur sollicitude, les vertus et les connaissances convenables à leur sexe. Elles ne négligeront rien de ce qui pourra contribuer à entretenir où à améliorer leur santé, à donner l'habitude de l'ordre, de la propreté et de la bonne tenue. La position heureuse de la paroisse de Miscouche, sa proximité de la mer, l'air pur qu'on y respire, joint à une nourriture saine et abondante et les soins assidus des maitresses offrent aux parents toutes les garanties désirables pour la santé de leurs enfants.

ENSEIGNEMENT.

Le cours d'instruction comprendra la Lecture, l'Ecriture, l'Arithmétique, la Grammaire Française et Anglaise, l'Histoire sainte et l'Histoire profane, l'Histoire ancienne et l'Histoire moderne, la Géographie, la Mythologie, la Littérature, l'usage des Globes, l'Astronomie, la Botanique, la Zoologie, la Philosophie naturelle, la Chimie pratique, la tenue des livres, la Géométrie, l'Algèbre, le Dessein et la Peinture de divers genres, l'Economie Domestique, l'ouvrage à l'aiguille uni et enjolivé, la Broderie, etc.

CONDITION DE LA PENSION.

Pension	$60
Demi pension	30
Quart de pension	15
Musique et Instruments . . .	26
Dessein et Peinture	6
Blanchissage	12

Les parents, avant de faire confectionner le trousseau de chaque élève, sont priés de vouloir bien prendre les informations nécessaires auprès des maitresses.

20 Mai 1868.

Announcement published in the *Moniteur Acadien* in 1868.

What subjects were Acadian children studying at this time? First, the young pupils learned to spell and to read French. In most schools, especially before 1877, English reading was only taught in the second year or, in many cases, even much later. It is interesting to note that boys were taught more English than girls. In 1864, most of the girls at the school in St. Félix, for example, did not learn any English at all.

Prior to 1877, the textbook that was used as a reader was called *Le nouveau traité des devoirs du chrétien*[66]. The more advanced pupils took French Grammar (*Grammaire Bonneau*), Geography (with a French textbook) and Writing. In general it was the older pupils who took English Reading and English Grammar, in addition to Arithmetic taught with the aid of an English book, usually *Gray's and Thompson's Arithmetic*[67]. A bit of music was also taught in a few schools[68] and, in the majority, Catechism was taught outside regular school hours[69].

After the School Act of 1877, pupils learned to spell and started learning to read French and English with the three books in the series of *Royal Readers*. These schoolbooks had English on one page and the French translation on the opposite: the idea being that it would be easier to learn English by translation. A few years after the new School Act was implemented, the Board of Education accepted the *Montpetit* series, French readers being used in Quebec schools[70]. The first four years were thus devoted to Reading and Spelling in English and French. It was only when Acadian school children reached Grade Five that they were able to start English Grammar, Geography and History, all taught with English textbooks[71]. Needless to say, the teaching of French suffered in this system. An Island Acadian, concerned about the situation, wrote in November 1884:

> A great failure I see in Prince Edward Island is the lack of French teaching in our schools. Is it the government's or the teachers' fault? Both, I feel; because if the government gave more attention to the education of our young men, in the French as well as the English language, there would be better citizens living in our towns and cities. [...]
>
> It would be good for our children if French Grammar were introduced into our schools; but in order to do that we need teachers who can teach it, which proves that we absolutely must have a French Department at the Normal School where our young men going into the teaching profession could receive a proper French education. Our public spokesmen should have understood this a long time ago and should have made it their duty to raise this important question. (TR)[72]

It should be noted that this Acadian was writing a few months after the second national Convention which was held in Miscouche. The conventions undoubtedly made the Acadians on the Island more aware of their precarious situation from a cultural point of view. Consequently, they took various steps to counteract the trend towards assimilation. The first priority was to improve French education for young people. At the Convention in Miscouche a motion had already been passed requesting that the provincial government: raise the standard of teaching French in the Acadian districts to the same level as the teaching of English; pay Acadian teachers the same salary for teaching French as other teachers; and have the inspection of Acadian schools take place in French[73]. It was not until the 1890s that the government agreed to some of these demands.

ADULT EDUCATION

Around this time people started becoming interested in education for adults, especially for men. As we have already seen, the temperance societies established in all the parishes stimulated interest in a variety of topics. Another educational forum for adults developed in the form of debating and discussion clubs. Men would meet in order to debate topical issues and to practice the art of public speaking. A debating club was set up in 1874 in Abram's Village[74], 1876 in Miscouche[75] and in Rustico in 1878[76]. The *Moniteur Acadien* announced the founding of a club in Abram's Village where practical and amusing topics would be discussed every week and lectures given by the members during the winter. The editor of the newspaper said he was so pleased about this initiative that he hoped that Acadians in the other Maritime Provinces would follow this wonderful example[77]. It was Father Ronald B. MacDonald who organized the club in Miscouche. Like the *Institut catholique de Rustico*, this debating club had a library and a reading room. The *Moniteur Acadien* explained how it operated in its issue of June 1, 1876:

> This group, whose meeting place is located across from the Church, has a spacious meeting room, a library, a reading room where members can go every day to read the Island newspapers, the best newspapers from Canada and the United States, etc. From time to time there are sessions during which highly topical issues are discussed, lectures given by the founder, Rev. R. MacDonald, or by one of the members or an outsider invited for this purpose. (TR)[78]

The members of the club in Miscouche, like those elsewhere, were most interested in agricultural improvements. Like the temperance societies, these clubs went through periods of activity and inertia.

The Political Arena

We have already seen that the restrictions preventing Catholics from voting and sitting in the Prince Edward Island Legislature were finally abolished in 1830. As a result, politicians naturally began canvassing for the Acadian vote. However, it was not until 1854 that an Acadian, Stanislas F. Perry, was elected to the Legislative Assembly. For the first few years after the Acadians obtained the right to vote their leaders do not appear to have encouraged them to take part in the electoral process. An Acadian, lamenting his elders' attitude, wrote in 1880:

> . . .it was hardly thirty years ago that some of our more influential men were saying to us: "Friends, don't pay any attention to the government of the province; don't get involved in politics; don't go to the polls. It's all well and good for the English, but it's not good for you." And we listened so well to that advice that we allowed ourselves to be fleeced by the English, the Scottish, and even the Irish, just like so many sheep. Truly, we must have been sheep indeed to have let them pull the wool over our eyes like this. (TR)[79]

To a certain degree, one can understand the Acadians' reticence with regard to politics. One must remember that, for the most part, they were tenant farmers. At election time their landlord or his agent would often stand as candidate, and for fear of reprisals, the Acadians always voted for him[80]. Consequently they did not really have a free vote.

Acadians did, however, find several Anglophone members who were sympathetic to their problems. One should name, among others, Nicholas Conroy, Benjamin Davies and William Cooper who made the government and the public aware of the injustices that landlords and their agents were inflicting on the Acadians[81]. These men belonged to a political movement fighting for major reforms in the colonial government and the land tenure system. In fact, they were demanding that the government and the Legislature represent the interests of the majority of Island residents rather than a clique of rich citizens. Indeed, the clique in power represented mainly the proprietors and their agents.

The Liberal Party, comprised of reformists, gained power in 1850. They achieved almost immediately their coveted aim of responsible government. In other words, an executive council (cabinet) was made up of elected representatives chosen from the Legislature. Prior to that, the powerful executive council was comprised of members appointed by the Lieutenant-Governor and was, therefore, not responsible to the electorate.

Within a few years, the new Liberal government reformed the public educational system to make it more accessible and brought in a program enabling the government to purchase the lands of the proprietors and sell them to the tenants.

It is not surprising that the first Acadian candidates to run for public office were members of the Reform Party. Stanislas F. Perry (Poirier), a native of Tignish, was elected in 1854 under the Liberal banner. He did not seek election in his own riding but in the one that included the parishes of Egmont Bay, Mont Carmel and Miscouche. However, he was elected in his home riding of First Prince in 1870.

Fidèle Gaudet, also from Tignish, was the second Acadian to win a seat in the Legislative Assembly. It would appear that Fidèle Gaudet was successful in the general elections of 1858 thanks to a political manoeuvre conceived by his Liberal colleagues which enabled him to secure the Acadian vote[82]. However, his stay in the Legislature was very short. Since no party held a majority, the Assembly was dissolved after sitting for two days and elections called[83]. On this occasion, the Liberals in Tignish abandoned their Acadian candidate in favour of influential Irishmen[84].

In 1867, Joseph-Octave Arsenault, a merchant and former teacher from Abram's Village, was elected in the riding of Third Prince. (We might point out that both Perry and Gaudet had also been teachers before becoming involved in politics). Arsenault was elected as a Liberal and sat in the House until 1895 although he joined the Conservatives in 1870.

Only the Acadian communities in Prince County were able to elect Acadians to the Legislative Assembly. In constituencies elsewhere

Stanislas F. Perry, politician.
Reg Porter Collection.

they were too small a minority (ethnic or religious) to be elected.

Thus, Stanislas F. Perry and Joseph-Octave Arsenault dominated the Acadian political arena on Prince Edward Island for the entire 1860 to 1890 period[85]. In 1870, nearly all the Catholic Members of the Assembly belonging to the Liberal Party, including the two Acadians, left the government and joined the Conservative Opposition with the aim of forming a coalition government. They did this because their Protestant confreres were against giving grants to sectarian educational establishments like Saint Dunstan's College and the convents. Consequently, the Catholic Members turned to the Conservatives who were in favour of grants for denominational schools.

Under the coalition government, Stanislas F. Perry became Speaker of the Legislative Assembly, a prestigious position which he

Joseph-Octave Arsenault, politician.
Musée Acadien.

held until 1874 when he was elected to the House of Commons in Ottawa. He was the first Acadian Member of Parliament in the country. He joined the Liberal Party which was in power at the federal level. He lost his seat in the elections of 1878 when the Liberal government was defeated. As a result, he returned to provincial politics and was re-elected in 1879, still as a Liberal. At this time the religious distinction between Conservatives and Liberals was no longer as blatant. In 1887, the politician from Tignish resigned from the provincial Legislature and was re-elected to the House of Commons.

Stanislas F. Perry's political career had its difficult moments. Early on he was poorly treated by the leaders in the party, who prevented him from running for election in 1863 so that an Anglophone could be elected. However, in the next elections (1867) he did stand as a candidate for the Liberal party. He complained about his party's intrigues in his nomination speech, but at the same time he announced his allegiance clearly and defended the right of Acadians to be represented politically. This part of his speech was reported in the following manner by *The Summerside Journal*:

> Hon. S. Perry did not come to defend the Government, was a Liberal and would support the Liberal Party. Had sacrificed as much for the Liberal Party as any man in it. Gave up his claims in the Third District for Mr. Warburton. Considered that the Liberal Party had used him badly, but is nevertheless no Tory. The French people are the pioneers of the country. They have broken the road for those who came after them. The French population of the Colony are as loyal as any of Her Majesty's subjects. Is not ashamed of being a Frenchman.[86]

The Acadian member of the Legislature did not always enjoy his compatriots' support and admiration. Towards the end of his career he was even accused of not having fought very hard for the national and religious rights of the Acadians during his long stay in parliamentary circles. He was also accused of having played on patriotism merely to get the Acadian vote at election time[87]. The newspaper, *The Examiner*, accused him of changing his position too often with regard to important political issues[88]. In an homage to Perry at the time of his death, one of his fellow members of Parliament emphasized that in fact what characterized Perry's career was his great loyalty to the Liberal party[89].

Unlike Perry, Joseph-Octave Arsenault remained highly respected by his compatriots throughout his long political career and did not occasion such severe criticism. His continued support for the Conservative party and his great commitment to the Acadian cause won him the admiration of his contemporaries. As a reward for his long political career, he was appointed senator in 1895. At the time of his death in 1897, *The Patriot* of Charlottetown paid him a moving tribute which sums up well the high regard held for this Acadian pioneer in politics:

> In the councils of his country and on the floor of the House he was characterized for his unassuming disposition, sound judgement and moderation in debate.
>
> In business life he was noted for his strict integrity, keen business insight and indefatigable industry, while socially Mr. Arsenault was a whole souled gentleman, possessing many of those qualities which distinguish Acadians.[90]

During this period the Catholic clergy were often accused of becoming involved in politics and trying to influence the way the faithful voted. This applied especially to Bishop Peter McIntyre who used his ecclesiastical power to make sure that Catholic voters and politicians defended the cause of the Catholic Church in the province[91]. Known for their submission to the clergy, Acadians were particularly affected by this. In 1863, an Irishman from Tignish complained, in the Catholic newspaper *The Vindicator*, about the undue influence of the bishop on the French voters during the recent elections in his area[92].

During his stay in Rustico, Father Belcourt took an interest in politics. He urged Acadians to take an active part in fighting against the unfair treatment they were receiving in the area of religion, education and land tenure. Convinced that it would help small tenant farmers, he supported, for example, the Island entry into Confederation. He explained his position in a lecture which he gave in Rustico in 1865[93].

Like most Islanders, the Acadians appeared at first to be against union. In 1867, their two representatives in the Assembly spoke out against Confederation. Joseph-Octave Arsenault, suspected of being a unionist, stated that people on the Island did not need the Canadians in order to govern themselves[94], and Stanislas-F. Perry even went so far as to say that he would leave the Island if it were annexed to Canada[95]. Several years later, the project of union seems to have been more attractive to Acadians, at least in Egmont Bay. As a matter of fact in 1870 these Acadians said they supported entry into the Canadian Confederation provided the federal government granted a loan to purchase the lands of the absentee landlords and subsidized the construction of the railway[96]. One month later the Honourable Arsenault declared that he was not anti-union. He explained that he regarded the project as "an alliance with a people like ourselves, and not with a foreign country or despotic government"[97].

Some Acadians felt that the entry of the Island into Confederation would make it easier to enforce their linguistic and religious rights. A young leader from Egmont Bay, Jean J. Arsenault, expressed himself clearly on the matter in the *Moniteur Acadien* in 1870. He stressed the fact that a large percentage of the population of the new nation was made up of French-Canadians who were thus in a position to command respect. According to the young writer, it was in the interest of the Acadians on the Island to rally behind the French-Canadians under a central government that would be more understanding with regard to Francophones. "Why, he wrote, would we not go where our old grievances will be redressed and where we would find justice and equality?" (TR)[98]

We have quoted many times articles that appeared in the *Moniteur Acadien*. It would be impossible to overemphasize the importance of this newspaper, founded in 1867, as a voice for Acadians. Indeed, most of the Acadian elite on the Island subscribed to this first newspaper. Members of the elite regularly contributed articles and letters related to the important political debates of the moment and to specific Acadian issues. They discussed in particular the lack of Acadian representatives in government, the importance of political unity, and the scarcity of Acadians in the public service.

POLITICAL PATRONAGE

One very political question that the Acadians were brandishing at this time, in the English as well as the French press, was their representation in the civil service. Already for many years these positions, paid out of the public Treasury, were distributed after elections to the supporters of the party in power. For a long time, lack of education had prevented Acadians from occupying their share of these positions. After 1860, however, this was no longer a problem since the number of Acadians with the necessary education was constantly increasing. In 1870, an Acadian from Tignish complained openly that public offices were granted almost exclusively to Englishmen in the Acadian parishes[99].

The subject of public offices came up again after the coalition government was formed in 1870. The Acadians expected to be rewarded by the new government that their two members had helped form. As usual, the appointments took a long time. One Acadian did not hesitate in exposing in the press the grievances that were annoying Acadians of all political persuasions:

> Now sir, when the present Government was formed, I was under the impression that from the support it got from our Acadian Representatives that we would

> be recognized by appointing some of us to the Offices which became vacant, but we have been sadly disappointed. The fact is, when the Acadians are wanted at an Election they are brought on a par with their neighbours, but as soon as they voted manfully and help to a large extent to put a party in power, there is no more talk of them.[100]

The editor of the newspaper *The Examiner* proved to be sensitive to the Acadians' complaints. He asked the government to correct this situation which he deemed unacceptable, expressing the hope that the discrimination against the French in the province would soon be a practice of the past:

> We hope the day is not far distant when the fact of an Islander being of French descent will not disqualify him from holding some of the positions of honour and emolument in this Island. There are twelve thousand Acadians in the Island, and though they have elected two representatives to the House of Assembly, there is no Acadian in any office of importance.[101]

The government appointed several Acadians to public office in order to placate the critics. But, in the long run, the situation did not improve very much. Acadians often felt cheated by politicians because they did not receive their share of appointments. On the eve of the provincial elections in 1893, Gilbert Buote, the editor of the newspaper *L'Impartial* published in Tignish, recalled for his readers the experience of previous elections. He reminded the Acadians in his riding of their weight in the electorate and urged them to elect to the Legislature a fellow Acadian who could do them justice:

> Let us beware of false promises. Let us not forget that we have been shamefully betrayed in this very manner. We have already been insulted by the fact that a Frenchman was appointed Road Master and then replaced by someone else who had no right to the position; certainly, not one of us has forgotten that insult. The time has come for revenge. It is up to us to help ourselves and to prove, once and for all, to these people who have no sympathy for us that we are tired of their duplicity and clever tricks. Let us show that we are equal to the occasion by rejecting these shameful intrigues unworthy of any honest man and designed to corrupt us and to spread hatred and discord amongst us. (TR)[102]

Gilbert Buote was unquestionably one of the fiercest defenders of the Acadians at the time. As we shall see further on, he demanded unceasingly, by means of his newspaper, that Acadians be treated fairly in every area.

Agricultural Economy

COLONIZATION

Land rental continued to be a problem on the Island until the end of the 1870s. Many Acadians remained tenants of absentee landlords until the collapse of the land tenure system which began after some of the proprietors agreed to sell their lands. Subsequently the provincial government passed the Land Purchase Act in 1875 after the entry of the Island into Confederation. This law forced the last of the proprietors to sell their land to the Island government. The purchase was financed by a loan from the federal government obtained by virtue of a promise made to the people of the Island during negotiations prior to the creation of the province in 1873.

Before the land tenure system was ultimately abolished, however, the Island Acadians found themselves more and more crowded together in overpopulated parishes and on farms that were too small. Some landlords or their agents were not anxious to rent out new land to them[103]. Consequently, the younger generation did not know where to settle.

We have already examined Father George-Antoine Belcourt's role in Rustico concerning education. His influence in the area of agriculture was equally important. When he arrived in 1859, he saw the extent of the problem of his 2,245 parishioners, almost all of whom were farmers and fishermen and who were confined to a territory that was far too small. "The entire community has developed so that half the population is on twenty-five acres of land, three-quarters of the other half live on fifty acres, and the remainder occupy one hundred acres" (TR), he wrote[104]. He immediately drew up plans to solve this enormous problem.

First of all, Father Belcourt advocated creating a people's bank, a type of credit union. This financial institution would enable Acadians who stayed in the area to keep up the properties they were living on and to buy new land. Next, he started an important wave of emigration

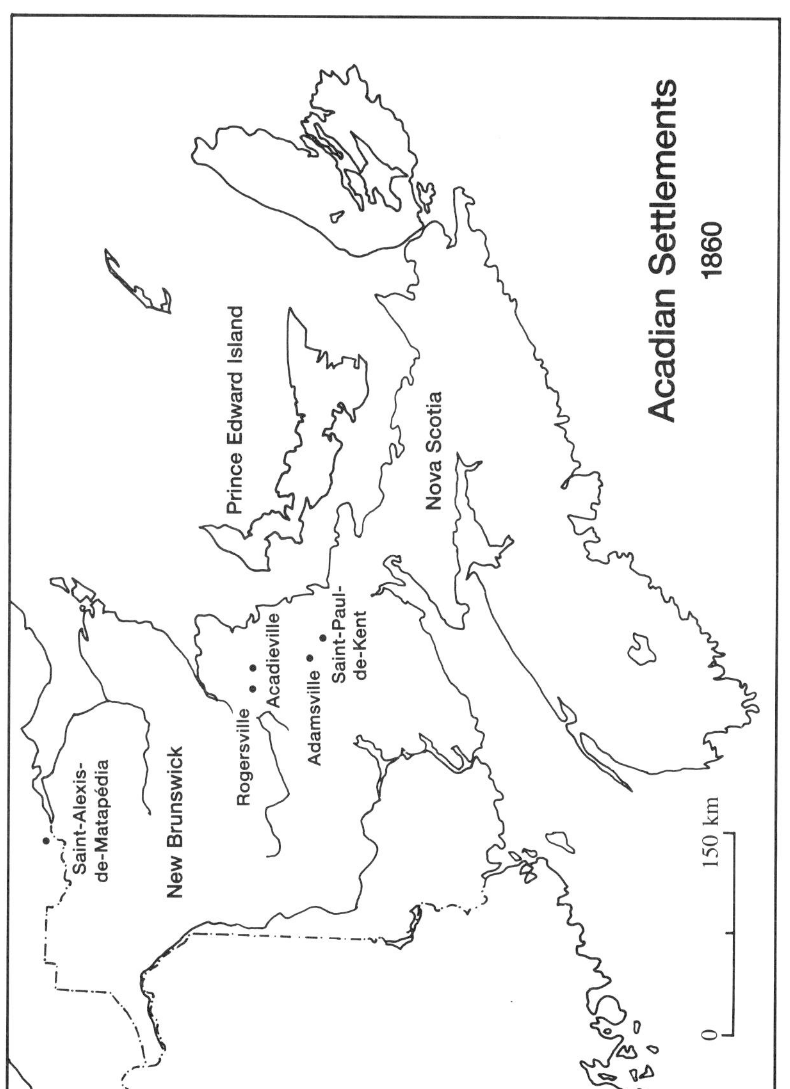

Communities where Island Acadians settled from 1860 onwards.

of young Acadian families who left Rustico to found new settlements on Crown Land in the Matapedia Valley in Quebec and, later, in Saint-Paul-de-Kent in southeast New Brunswick. His aim was to get half of his parishioners to emigrate[105]. He also recruited young colonists and supporters in the other overpopulated Acadian communities on the Island and in New Brunswick[106].

The emigration to New Brunswick continued after Father Belcourt's departure, with a marked increase around the time of the Acadian national conventions in the early 1880s. As we shall see, the emigrants headed mainly for Rogersville and Adamsville. After the last of the absentee landowners were forced to sell their properties, Acadians were able to acquire land more easily on the Island. As a result, several families left Rustico around 1880 to found a small settlement, which they called *Nouvelle Acadie*(New Acadia), in Lot 43 in Kings County. Between 1860 and 1890, other families also moved away from Rustico to resettle in the area of Bloomfield, Prince County[107].

THE FARMERS' BANK OF RUSTICO

The founding of the *Banque de Rustico* was without question the most interesting economic initiative of the period. Conceived by Father Belcourt, it was created in 1861 but only became chartered in 1864 under the official name of the Farmers' Bank of Rustico[108]. With an initial capital of only 1200 pounds, it was the smallest chartered bank in Canada and perhaps even in the whole of the British Empire[109]. It was also the first people's bank in Canada and operated successfully until the expiry of its charter thirty years later.

When the parish priest in Rustico created this banking institution his desire was to develop a spirit of thrift and entrepreneurship amongst his parishioners. He encouraged people to invest in the bank by purchasing shares and opening a savings account. At the same time, he gave instructions on how to run the institution so that the farmers of Rustico were soon managing the bank on their own. The bank offered Acadians distinct advantages, including the possibility of borrowing at better rates than from lenders or commercial banks. Consequently, the people in Rustico were able to gain greater control over their economy and even save their farms from the grasp of greedy creditors. The Farmers' Bank also served anglophone customers and Acadians living elsewhere on the Island.

With the entry of the Island into Confederation in 1873 the eventual disappearance of this public bank was predictable. The Canadian constitution gave the federal government sole jurisdiction over banking institutions. In 1871, an act in the House of Parliament which set $500,000 as a minimum capital resulted in the dissolution of small banks. After several extensions the charter of the Farmers' Bank of Rustico finally expired in 1894[110].

Nevertheless, the spirit of the first public bank in Canada lived on. The founder of the *Caisses populaires* (credit unions), Alphonse Desjardins, studied the *Banque de Rustico* which served as an inspiration for his now international movement[111].

Parish Hall in Rustico which housed the Farmers' Bank.
Public Archives of P.E.I.

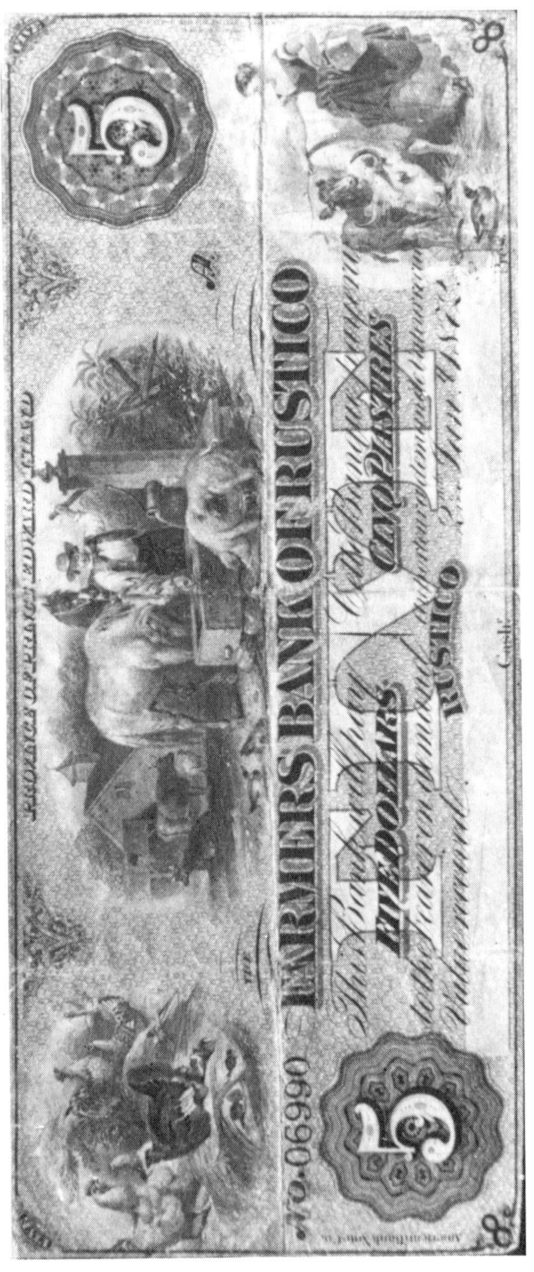

A five-dollar note from the Farmers' Bank of Rustico.
Francis Blanchard Collection.

GRANARIES

At the beginning of the 1860s another type of co-operative institution was set up by Acadian farmers on the Island. It was a sort of agricultural bank commonly known as a "granary" (TR). This time, it was the farmers in the parish of Egmont Bay who started the project, motivated perhaps by Father Belcourt[112]. A granary was, in fact, a bank for seed grain that operated along the same lines as a regular bank except that all the transactions took place in kind. Interest, shares and dividends were counted in bushels of grain. The *Moniteur Acadien* explains how granaries worked:

> About one or two hundred farmers join together, each contributing the equivalent of ten bushels of oats, creating a stable capital. This does not represent a big amount for each farmer. In the spring, the members who need seed grain get it from the bank, undertaking to reimburse in the fall five bushels for every four borrowed. This constitutes a fairly low interest which does not hurt the borrower at all.
>
> The interest more than pays for administrative fees; thus the capital increases each year to the advantage of the shareholders in the association. (TR)[113]

This co-operative formula proved very useful for Acadian farmers who often had to go into debt to pay for very highly priced seed grain in the spring, thus perpetuating the cycle of chronic indebtedness. In 1868, Acadian farmers had their institution incorporated by the Island Legislature. The bill was entitled: "An Act for the incorporation of Societies for the sale and distribution of Seed Grain on credit"[114]. This Acadian initiative attracted the praise of the anglophone press who urged other farmers in the province to copy the example of their French-language compatriots. *The Examiner* wrote:

> The French Acadian inhabitants of Egmont Bay gave our small farmers an example of self-help and co-operative effort which they would be well to follow. [. . .] This industry [the grain bank] does infinite credit to the intelligence and the independence of the Acadians of Egmont Bay. If such societies were established all over the Island, there would be no necessity for the Government to come to the assistance of the farming population of the Island even in the scarcest years.[115]

Granaries spread quickly. By 1880, there were at least twenty-four of these grain banks—with one exception, all were in Acadian localities. In fact, every parish of French origin had several. Tignish had the most: eight were incorporated between 1870 and 1878[116].

For various reasons most of these granaries had ceased their operations by 1920. On the one hand, the quality of the grain used for reimbursement was no longer reliable because of weed infestation. On the other hand, the granaries were made somewhat obsolete because bartering was no longer used and the quality of seed grain on the market had improved[117]. The Urbainville granary was the last to close its doors after having served the community well from 1869 to 1946[118].

THE PATH OF PROGRESS

Agriculture formed the economic basis of the Acadian communities as it did for the Island as a whole. The Acadian nationalist ideology, as we have already stated, was modelled on the ultramontane doctrine according to which a life devoted to farming was synonymous with a religious and moral life. In both Quebec and Acadia it was felt that without farming the French-Canadian nation could not flourish. The following are the words of Father Marcel-François Richard, one of the greatest Acadian nationalists:

> Acadia has no future except in agriculture. Her stability depends on this key industry. Let us devote ourselves to our national soil, let us love and cherish our dear Acadia. [...] To be truly Acadian, we must walk in the footsteps of the pioneers who first cleared and farmed this land. The life or death of the Acadian homeland will depend on this. (TR)[119]

The years between 1860 and 1880 represent a period of both nationalism and openness to progress. According to an Acadian writing in *The Summerside Progress* in 1868 the younger generation was open to changes in agriculture whereas the older farmers were still clinging to outmoded ideas and practices[120]. Thus, for the first time Acadian farmers were beginning to attend lectures and meetings to discuss their problems and look for solutions. These meetings usually took place within the framework of the debating clubs and temperance societies like the *Institut catholique de Rustico* under the direction of Father Belcourt.

Since, in general, the directors and the vast majority of the members of these societies were farmers, agricultural issues dominated the agendas. Such was the case for the discussion circle founded in Miscouche in 1876. The *Moniteur Acadien* wrote that being "composed almost exclusively of farmers, the society does not neglect agriculture. On the contrary, it appears to be the main goal promoted and most of the meetings are devoted to discussing the best ways to raise the standard of this noble profession" (TR)[121]. In Abram's Village the debating club was also dominated by farmers. In November 1874, shortly after it was founded, the club organized a ploughing competition[122].

Within the context of the Maritime Provinces, Acadian farmers on the Island appear to have been ahead of their compatriots in both New Brunswick and Nova Scotia. Shediac native, Pascal Poirier, pointed this out in a speech he gave in Quebec City in 1880. After a trip to the Island in 1890 a mainlander described the situation of the Acadian farmers in an article published in *L'Évangéline*:

> Several Island parishes are remarkably prosperous due to the industry of people living on farms. Let us hope that this noble activity of our Island neighbours will be passed on to their children: this activity in farming indicates a great wealth of patriotism, a rightful love for well-being granted to the most sanctifying of labours for which man was created. (TR)[123]

On the whole, the Acadians benefited from the overall improvement that took place in agriculture on the Island. In their own milieu, however, they were greatly stimulated and supported by the Farmers' Bank of Rustico, the granaries and educational meetings organized by various groups.

LAND USE

Spurred on by increasingly widespread education, Island farmers began seeking better ways of exploiting the land. All the newspapers of the time showed a keen interest in farming. They reminded their readers frequently that cultivating the soil was a science and that to succeed in agriculture one had to keep abreast of new techniques and put them into practice.

The major problem in agriculture around the middle of the nineteenth century was the impoverished soil and lack of fertilizer.

As of 1860 the problem was solved in part when the virtues of mussel mud were discovered and it began to be applied as a general practice. This mud, taken from river beds, is made up of decomposing shells and is an excellent source of calcium and other necessary soil nutrients. The geologist and naturalist, Francis Bain, wrote in 1886:

> "Mussel mud" has been a fortune to Prince Edward Island. A real treasure of the deep lavished on the wealth of her agriculture. Every acre of arable land dressed with this rich fertilizer has with fair treatment, its productiveness doubled for fifty years to come...
>
> Mudding increases the oat crop—the staple export of the Island—and improves the quality of the grain. It makes wheat more certain. Potatoes are increased in bulk though not in quality. Turnips have their burden of fodder doubled and greatly enriched, while the pastures are thicker, sweeter and vastly more nutritous.[124]

Since the production of oats was the main source of income for Island farmers the application of mussel mud thus constituted a remarkable asset.

In addition to this soil dressing composed of shells, farmers also fertilized their land with lobster shells from the packing plants, or even with herring or mackerel which, most of the time, was very cheap. Sometimes the farmer caught the fish himself.

In general, the crops were rotated on a seven year cycle with fertilization taking place in the first year only[125]. Since there were few farm animals the limited amount of manure made this type of rotation necessary.

CROPS

During the 1860 to 1890 period, oats and potatoes were the main crops on the Island. Acadians appear to have followed quite closely the production trends of the province. Although oats constituted the leading commercial crop their production posed serious problems because the fertility of the soil was exhausted very rapidly. Consequently, the quality of the oats tended to deteriorate over the years from lack of proper fertilizing.

Potatoes regained importance after a series of blights during the 1850s and 1860s. Thus, production went from three to seven million bushels between 1860 and 1890[126].

Hay also became a very important crop. Production increased considerably with the use of mussel mud. The editor of *The Summerside Progress* stated in 1867 that the average yield had quadrupled in the space of fifteen years [127]. Other important crops of the period included turnips and barley.

Wheat, on the other hand, did not contribute substantially to the Island economy. Crops were destroyed too often by disease to make production worthwhile. It will be remembered that before 1840 wheat production was quite widespread in the province, but since that time the crop had diminished considerably since many farmers had stopped growing wheat altogether. As a result, the province had to import flour and wheat[128]. Only towards the 1870s with the construction of the railway linking the Maritimes to Ontario was a better variety of wheat introduced to the Island and production encouraged[129].

In 1868, a bad agricultural year throughout the Island, farmers in the Abram's Village area met to discuss the situation and to decide which crops it would be best to grow at this difficult moment. A report of the discussion appeared in *The Summerside Progress*, providing an interesting glimpse of the quandary a group of Acadian farmers were facing at the time:

> Several gentlemen addressed the meeting and nearly all of them concurred in the idea that the poor farmer, who can barely raise enough on his farm to support his family, should sow no oats or very little, and advising him to cultivate corn, buckwheat, barley, beans and peas, which would yield more than oats if the soil were properly tilled. They contended that although the poor farmer should raise a large quantity of oats, the best part of it would go to market, and he would find himself without bread and without means to buy it. To cultivate a large garden was, also in their opinion, a good means of living at a small expense.
>
> Other parties argued that if oats were not sowed by a large number, the farmers would be left without fodder to feed to their cattle. They held that what was taken out of the farm should return to it in the shape of manure, if no other means of making manure were at hand.[130]

The produce that farmers used as payment to rent their church pew gives an indication of the importance of the various crops over the years. In Cascumpec in 1863 almost all the Acadian farmers paid for their pews in bushels of oats. From 1875 onwards potatoes formed part of the payments, and in 1889 they also included wheat and sometimes barley. In that year the average contribution, Dominique Gallant's for instance, included twelve bushels of potatoes, five bushels of oats, two bushels of wheat and one bushel of barley[131].

In Abram's Village in 1880, the Honourable Joseph-Octave Arsenault, merchant and politician, paid farmers 38 cents a bushel for a large quantity of oats, and likewise for potatoes[132]. In 1887, the *Évangéline* reported that the yield of oats was quite high and of good quality in Abram's Village but that the price was only around 25 to 27 cents a bushel, while potatoes were fetching between 25 and 30 cents a bushel[133].

One distinctive crop grown by Acadian farmers was flax. In fact, this plant was grown very little on the Island outside the Acadian communities. Flax filled various household needs: it was used to make sheets, towels, curtains and clothing[134]. There was no mill on the Island for the treatment of flax, so all the procedures for making linen were carried out on the farm[135].

The census of 1881 shows clearly that the Acadians took a special interest in growing corn. However, production was small-scale and probably only for home consumption[136].

LIVESTOCK

A common complaint in the newspapers of the time was that farmers kept too many animals for the amount of feed available. As in the past, most farmers continued to winter their cattle on straw, for lack of anything better. Nevertheless, there was a marked increase in livestock numbers during this period.

There is little information on the Island Acadian farmers' livestock for this period. According to the historian Andrew Hill Clark, compared to other Island farmers at the beginning of the 1860s, the Acadians raised fewer cattle[137]. One might assume that they were more interested in growing cereals as evidenced by their desire to establish granaries. Livestock would thus be kept mainly for domestic needs.

For the Island as a whole cattle numbers almost doubled in the space of ten years, i.e. between 1871 and 1881[138]. The more prosperous farmers made an effort to improve their breeding stock. Their slogan was: "The Scrub must go!" In fact, the more perspicacious recommended raising quality animals for market to solve the problem of soil exhaustion resulting from cereal production[139]. It should also be noted that home-made butter and cheese provided a good source of income for the farmer of the time[140].

With regard to other livestock, sheep appear to have been highly prized since, in 1880, there were four times as many sheep as pigs on the Island[141]. The farmer sold wool for cash while pork was raised mainly for home consumption[142].

The sale of eggs constituted another source of cash income for farmers. Poultry-raising developed particularly during the 1880s on the Island. The egg market was located in the United States. We know the main exporters: the Honourable Joseph-Octave Arsenault from Abram's Village; Honoré V. DesRoches, Gilbert DesRoches and Jean S. Gaudet from Miscouche[143]; and Joseph D. Buote from Rustico[144].

The horse was probably the most prized animal and, in fact, greatly sought after as a draft animal. It replaced the ox formerly used in the province. The Island gradually acquired an excellent reputation in the Canadian and American marketplace for the quality of its thoroughbreds[145]. The race horse also gained in popularity and races became extremely popular amongst Islanders.

The Sea

The Reciprocity Treaty signed in 1854 between Britain and the United States was largely responsible for the expansion of the Prince Edward Island fishery. Tignish was one of the areas in the province that benefited the most: numerous fishing companies were established in the region, including Hall and Myrick which set up in both Tignish and Sea Cow Pond[146]. By 1867 the company owned seventy-five boats of varying tonnages with a crew of three to five men, exporting about 4,000 quintals of dried cod mainly to the West Indies, and about 2,500 barrels of salt mackerel to the United States[147].

Despite the growing number of Islanders involved in fishing, they were still outnumbered by American fishermen in Island waters. In 1868 the editor of *The Summerside Journal* felt that it was unfair that Americans were coming to fish here every year, while young Islanders were having to emigrate to find work:

> The waters around the Island swarm with fish, which while they afford a lucrative employment to thousands of people from other countries, are comparatively useless to us. It is certainly an uncomfortable and humiliating spectacle, to see our neighbours sending their immense fleets of fishing vessels year after year to our shores, while our youth, for want of employment, are leaving the land of their birth to seek their fortunes elsewhere. We want men of capital to take hold of the fishing business, in order to make it pay. . .[148]

The lieutenant-governor also deplored this state of affairs. He wrote in 1872 that ties with farming were so profound that people were not giving the fishing industry the attention it deserved. He pointed out that it was American investors who were supporting the P.E.I. fishery[149].

Nevertheless, the fishing industry was becoming increasingly important throughout the Island, particularly in Acadian villages. Eighty-seven boats and 535 fishermen in Rustico caught $59,993 worth of mackerel, herring and cod in 1876. The industry was not yet very sizeable in Egmont Bay where only mackerel and herring were fished: in that year, there were only ten boats and thirty men who brought in $6,350 worth of fish[150]. Because of the abundance of mackerel in the area, Miminegash developed very rapidly into an important fishing village. There were ten "stages" in 1877 and about thirty the following year[151]. Most of the fishermen were either Acadian or Irish. According to the fisheries inspector's 1878 report for Miminegash, there were 530 fishermen on 135 boats with exports amounting to 4,000 barrels of mackerel, 400 barrels of herring, 200 quintals of cod and 500 of hake, 150 gallons of fish oil and 57,600 tins of lobster[152].

LOBSTER FISHING BECOMES SIGNIFICANT

The lobster fishery did not exist on Prince Edward Island before the 1870s. Although this shellfish abounded in Island waters, since there was virtually no market it was not caught on a commercial scale. Farmers only used lobster as fertilizer.

It was during the 1870s that lobster fishing really developed on the Island. In 1871, 6,711 pounds of lobster were canned. But by 1882 the figure had increased to five million pounds[153]. As a result, lobster canneries sprang up almost overnight all along the coast. By 1884, there were ninety-five factories operating in the province[154].

Many of these packing plants were built in the Acadian parishes, in particular along the coast between Mont Carmel and Egmont Bay where previously fishing had not constituted an important part of the economy. In 1884 there were ten factories in operation[155]. As the fisheries inspector, J. Hunter Duvar, noted, this proliferation gave rise to disputes between the factory owners:

> Factories, especially along Egmont Bay have been erected in clusters at intervals of a mile, or even much less, so that it would be impossible now to lease effective areas, seeing that it takes a shore frontage of about three miles to work a lobster factory satisfactorily. From this cause continual disputes arise among the factories as to the overlooking of traps.[156]

Given these circumstances, some of the lobster canneries did not survive for long.

There were several Acadians who were owners or joint owners of canneries, including Captain Francis Gallant in Nail Pond, Moïse Chiasson in Tignish, the Honourable Joseph-Octave Arsenault in Egmont Bay[157], and Jean-J. Gallant in Mont Carmel[158]. Several Acadian businessmen from south-eastern New Brunswick were among the first to build factories in Mont Carmel and Egmont Bay[159] since they already had a certain amount of experience in this industry which had started up earlier in their province than on the Island.

The increase in the number of lobster canneries inevitably resulted in over-fishing. After a few years of intensive fishing, the quantity and the size of lobsters decreased to such an extent that it was even thought that the lobster season would have to remain closed for several years in order to allow the stocks to replenish[160].

During this period, each lobster cannery would hire about twenty men and ten women for two or three months. Most of the men worked as fishermen on the company boats while the remainder, along with all the women, worked in the factory. The employees would usually be housed on the premises in quarters provided by the factory owner.

The impact of these numerous canneries on the economy of the region was considerable; with the creation of seasonal jobs young people were able to stay on the Island rather than having to look for work in the United States[161]. These jobs also gave women the rare opportunity of working for a salary close to home. They were mainly young unmarried women or widows who were anxious to earn a living in order to bring up their children.

In 1891, a journalist with the *Moniteur Acadien*, visiting the Acadian communities on the Island, was struck by the effect that the fishing industry had on the local economy. With regard to Egmont Bay, he wrote:

> Lobster-fishing is the main industry along the coast, here and elsewhere on the Island.
>
> I dare say that several members of almost one third of the families are either fishing mackerel or lobster, or else are employed in the canning factories. It is a most interesting process to observe. (TR)[162]

As a result of the fishing industry, jobs were created in other sectors even during the winter; wood had to be cut, boats built, traps and crates made for the fishermen and the packers. Already in 1880 J. Hunter Duvar, fisheries inspector, had remarked on the positive impact of this new growth in the fisheries:

> A large amount of ready money is circulated by this industry. Besides the erection and repair of buildings, tin and iron work, boat-building, fuel-cutting, truckage, and much other outlay, fair wages are paid, directly or indirectly to perhaps two thousand hands, male and female. Hence the industry is of considerable importance in the political economy of the Province.[163]

OTHER FISHERIES

After 1880 lobster was almost always the leading fisheries product on the Island. Other important catches such as mackerel, herring, oysters and cod continued to be profitable. Statistics for 1889 provide information on the relative commercial value of each type of fish: lobster—$247,313; mackerel—$198,662; herring—$135,760; oysters—$123,771; cod and hake—$117,829[164].

Mackerel fishing appears to have been very good in 1880 around Rustico and on the Island generally, as was pointed out in the *Moniteur Acadien*:

> Mackerel fishing is infinitely better than last year. The fish is a better size, it fetches a better price and is more abundant. In various fishing communities on the Island, boats are bringing in between three and four thousand a day.

> The average daily catch per boat is between twelve hundred and eighteen hundred mackerel. This is a godsend for everyone, including the fishermen and the fish merchants. (TR)[165]

The following year, however, mackerel was much scarcer. The fishermen in Rustico said the decrease was caused by a proliferation of lobster traps in the fishing grounds[166]. The prime market for mackerel was in the United States. It was usually sold salted, but by 1886 it was already being shipped on ice as far away as Boston[167].

Herring was caught mainly in the spring and was used as bait for mackerel, cod and lobster fishing, and also for home consumption. It was normally salted.

During this period the oyster trade, stimulated by the construction of the railway, constituted quite a sizeable portion of Island exports. Miscouche was one of the main export centres for oysters. According to a contributor to the *Moniteur Acadien* in 1884, three local businessmen were exporting large quantities of oysters to Montreal and Quebec City. He was referring to Gilbert DesRoches (nicknamed the "Oyster King" (TR)), Honoré V. DesRoches, and Jean S. Gaudet[168].

Cod and hake also constituted significant species for both fishermen and exporters. The fish was salted and dried for both export and local consumption. There was also a market for cod liver oil and cod sounds and cheeks.

In addition to the fish already mentioned, a wide variety of other species were also fished in smaller quantities, including salmon, gaspereaux, haddock, halibut, trout, smelts, bass and eels. Most of these fish were consumed locally as fresh products[169].

FISHERMEN AND FISH PLANT WORKERS

It is true that the expansion of the fisheries, especially lobster, did result in the creation of many jobs on the fishing boats and in the fish-processing plants. While attracting large numbers of Acadian men and women, these jobs were nevertheless seasonal and poorly paid. But at a time when there was little money and when jobs on the Island were scarce, even meager salaries were not to be scorned. In 1881 the fisheries inspector wrote the following on this matter:

"The wages they earn during the summer help them get through the long hard winters during which they have no remunerated work." (TR)[170]

These jobs only lasted for two or three months. On an average, in 1887 men employed in lobster factories received 30 dollars a month, and women 12 dollars a month[171]. As we have said, the majority of men worked as fishermen and the women were employed in the plants. However, any fisherman who did not own his own boat did not really receive a salary. In fact he was paid according to his catch—in other words about 55 cents for one hundred lobsters[172]. Obviously the men who could afford their own boat had a higher income depending on the size of the catch, which varied from one year to the next. Needless to say, a bad season played havoc with the welfare of the fishermen. Such was the case in 1882. That year the *Moniteur Acadien* predicted hard times for fishermen: "This misfortune is going to weigh heavily on the fishermen who, for the most part, have no other means of subsistence." (TR)[173]

Many fishermen depended entirely on fishing and, in general, could barely subsist. Their small income did not enable them to provide a decent living for their large families. They were forever indebted to their employers who gave them loans to outfit their vessels and to buy molasses, flour and other staples. In many cases these same employers also owned the stores.

The fishermen and fish plant workers were often either farmers' sons or farmers themselves. Fishing enabled them to supplement the meager income from the farm. Their situation was less precarious than men who depended entirely on fishing since at least they could feed their families with the produce from their farming operation.

The shortage of available farmland for the younger generation and the dividing up of existing properties forced young men who wanted to stay on the Island to turn to the sea. Indeed, these circumstances prevailed in most of the Acadian parishes. The large parish of Tignish was no exception, as Pascal Poirier pointed out in 1875:

> The parish of Tignish is comprised of eight hundred families, almost all of whom are Acadian. The vast majority of the inhabitants are involved in fishing and farming. [...] The soil is very fertile and it would appear that the farmers in Tignish know how to exploit this fertility. But the head of the household cannot expand or increase his holding for the simple reason that there is no

> more vacant land available. This means that he is often forced to share his property with his children so that the resulting parcels of land are too small to provide for the needs of everybody. Consequently, fishing has become more or less a necessity. And this state of affairs will become worse as time goes on[174]

Pascal Poirier recommended emigration and resettlement as solutions to the problem. He was careful not to promote fishing, because, like most Acadian leaders of the time, he maintained that the well-being of the Acadians depended on farming. As an occupation, fishing was considered to be considerably inferior to agriculture and even disastrous for the Acadian economy. However, the Honourable Stanislas F. Perry did not share this view. During a meeting with the inhabitants of Nail Pond, near Tignish, he assured his audience, comprised mainly of fishermen, that their work was useful and worth encouraging. He told them that "fishing was not a contemptible activity as some people believed and should not be trod upon; fishermen had the right to receive help and encouragement because there is no other occupation more lucrative than fishing" (TR)[175]. However, speeches of this kind were not heard at the National Conventions of the Acadians. If the fisheries issue was raised, it was generally in negative terms.

The National Conventions Of The Acadians

The Acadians on Prince Edward Island were not the only ones overwhelmed by social, economic, cultural and political problems. In fact, francophones throughout the Maritimes found themselves in a more or less similar situation. It was logical that Acadians from the Island join forces with their compatriots to examine their status and the direction their development should take. Between 1881 and 1890 they met for three large congresses or conventions, as they were called at the time, which were held in Memramcook (New Brunswick), Miscouche (Prince Edward Island) and Church Point (Nova Scotia). A fairly large number of Islanders were in attendance.

Actually, the first important meeting of Acadian leaders took place in Quebec city in 1880 for Saint-Jean-Baptiste Day, the national holiday of French Canadians. That year, the *Société Saint-Jean-Baptiste* in Quebec city invited North American francophones to gather for a

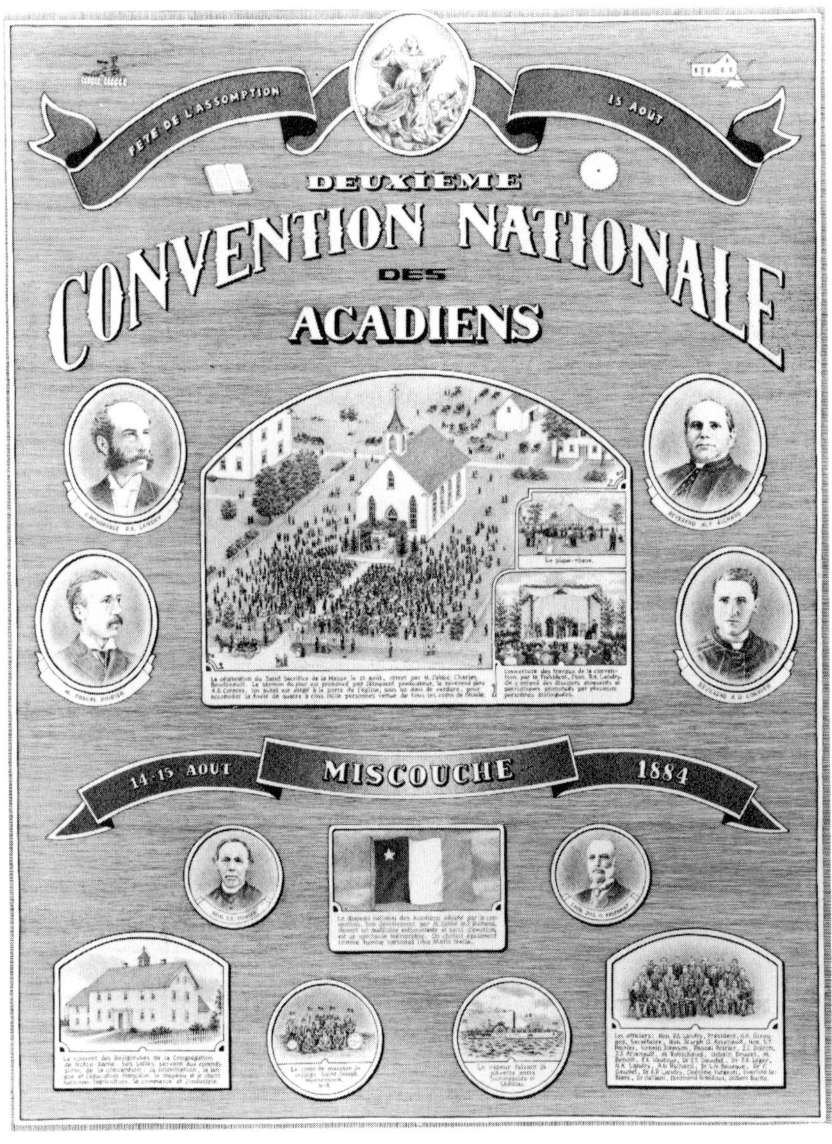

Environment Canada, Parks; Bernard LeBlanc.

convention to analyze their situation. The organizers created a special committee for the Acadian delegates.

Led by the Honourable Joseph-Octave Arsenault, the Island delegation was comprised of nine men chosen during public meetings which had been organized in the parishes[176]. At the first of these parish assemblies, held in Egmont Bay, the Honourable Arsenault explained why an Island delegation should attend the Saint-Jean-Baptiste convention. He felt that a great deal would be gained. Solutions might even be found for pressing problems like the lack of land for the younger generation. The *Moniteur Acadien* summarized his remarks:

> It is there, under national banners, that we the Acadian people, will find the strength and resources to gain respect for our rights which have been ignored for too long, and to preserve the integrity of our national character and the language we love and that our mothers taught us; in short, everything that is of concern to our nation: religion, education, science, industry, and colonization. He made us realize that we could benefit from joining our Canadian brothers to form one national family. Above all, the Honourable Arsenault emphasized the question of colonization. Since this issue is on the programme of the convention, it would be very much in our interest to be well represented, if only to discuss a subject that concerns us so much; our properties are already too small and we shall soon be forced to seek settlements elsewhere for our children, and that will certainly be in Canada. (TR)[177]

At the close of the meetings the Acadian delegates at the convention in Quebec decided to hold their own convention the following year in Memramcook "to address the general concerns of the Acadians" (TR)[178]. An organizing committee was appointed immediately. It was comprised of leading Acadian politicians including Joseph-Octave Arsenault and Stanislas F. Perry from Prince Edward Island.

The purpose of this historical gathering was voiced with clarity in the committee's manifesto announcing the first national convention for Acadians:

> [It is] to cement the unity that is absolutely essential in order for French Acadians to assert themselves as a strong and dynamic people, a friend of progress and seriously concerned about its future. For too long we appear to have been ignored. Force has taken precedence over privilege. The time has come to assert our rights to a just equality that the straightforward and practical side of our conquerors will not be able to refuse much longer. (TR)[179]

The convention in Memramcook and subsequent conventions were important events that attracted crowds of more than five thousand people. About two hundred Acadians from Prince Edward Island attended the gathering in Memramcook. Not everyone took part in the discussions. The study sessions were reserved for the delegates representing each parish, members of the clergy ministering to Acadians, Acadian members of Parliament and other public figures appointed by the organizing committee. The public only attended the religious ceremonies and the plenary sessions where they listened to reports on the discussions and stirring patriotic speeches. The convention provided the occasion for a welcome picnic where everyone enjoyed various forms of entertainment.

In the study sessions the delegates discussed virtually every aspect of Acadian life: the French language, education, agriculture, emigration, colonization, trade, industry, the French language press, and above all national symbols. The delegates at the 1881 convention chose a national holiday, the Feast of the Assumption, celebrated on the 15th of August. Other symbols that would help unite Acadians and distinguish them from other peoples in the country were chosen during the second convention, held in Miscouche in 1884. The French tricolour with a gold star in the blue stripe was adopted as the Acadian flag, and the tune of the Latin hymn in honour of the Virgin, *Ave Maris Stella*, was chosen as the national anthem. The motto, *L'union fait la force* (Strength through Union), was selected along with a badge which portrayed a star, a sail boat and the Acadian motto[180].

The national conventions aroused a spirit of nationalism and patriotism in the Acadians on the Island that impelled them to fight harder against creeping anglicization. Participants from the mainland attending the 1884 congress in Miscouche were astonished to discover the extent to which the Acadian community on the Island had been anglicized. Very disturbed by this fact, an Acadian from the Island wrote the following in the *Moniteur Acadien* several months after the great gathering:

> During the convention in 1884, I must admit that I was ashamed to hear the way my fellow Islanders spoke to each other. It seems to me that it must have been annoying for outsiders to see their brothers from the Island forever talking in English in an Acadian assembly, or to be more exact, an Acadian convention. Everything was in English: dinner tickets, programme, mottos, etc. (TR)[181]

The Acadian flag, chosen at the 1884 Acadian National Convention held in Miscouche.
Georges Arsenault.

By participating in the conventions and meeting Acadian leaders from the other provinces, Island Acadians became more aware of the overwhelming dangers of assimilation. Motivated by the atmosphere of solidarity between the provinces that prevailed during the convention, the more militant patriots began fighting for their rights and looking for solutions to their social and economic problems. They profited from the active support of influential and prestigious Acadians like Pascal Poirier and Valentin Landry who came over to the Island from New Brunswick to give advice on how to recover the ground that had been lost in the schools in the area of French instruction[182].

Henceforth, the Acadians in the Maritimes helped each other promote and defend the Acadian culture and identity. The *Société nationale l'Assomption*, now called the *Société nationale des Acadiens*, was founded during the first national conventions. Comprised of representatives from the three provinces, it organized several other conventions and dealt with numerous major issues.

CHAPTER IV

SUCCESSFUL INITIATIVES

1890–1945

A New Beginning

The evolution of the Acadian community between 1890 and 1945 is marked by a series of important and diverse projects undertaken by members of the elite to preserve and promote French life on the Island. Spurred on by the nationalist fervour resulting from the first national conventions, Acadian leaders devoted themselves to finding appropriate ways to stem the growing tide of anglicization. Given this spirit, the last decade of the nineteenth century constituted a crucial period in the history of the Acadians on Prince Edward Island.

The most outstanding event of the decade, if not of the entire period, was unquestionably the creation of the French-language newspaper, *L'Impartial*. Founded in Tignish in 1893 by the school teacher Gilbert Buote and his son, François-Joseph, the paper set out to defend the cause of the Acadians, as the editor stated in the first issue:

> To advance the Acadian cause in social, intellectual and moral domains, such is the goal of *L'Impartial*. The interests of our people will form the object of our most active vigilance whenever there is a question of gaining recognition of our rights. (TR)[1]

The first French-language newspaper on Prince Edward Island contributed a great deal to promoting Acadian identity by making Acadians aware of the richness of their language and culture. Realizing that French on the Island was in peril, Buote sought every possible way of preserving the ancestral language. For almost twenty years *L'Impartial* served as the mouthpiece for Acadian nationalism and published innumerable articles on the French language, on Acadian history, education, religion, agriculture and colonization[2]. Gilbert and François-Joseph Buote and the contributors to the newspaper strongly encouraged Acadians to set up institutions that would foster their development and to participate in their nationalist and patriotic associations.

L'Impartial also served as a forum where its more educated readers could exchange ideas and criticize each other publicly. One of the longest debates revolved around the possibility of establishing an Acadian college on the Island. The idea was kept alive in the columns of the newspaper from 1903 to 1907 and stimulated so much interest that many people undertook to subscribe financially to the project.

Unfortunately, there was no one to take over and organize the project so it did not get beyond this forum[3].

The Buotes' newspaper did, however, successfully give rise to other projects, in particular the *Association des instituteurs acadiens de l'Île-du-Prince-Édouard* (Acadian Teachers' Association) which was to play a major role in French education and the survival of the Acadian culture. We will examine the activities of this organization further on.

Published for almost twenty years, *L'Impartial* disappeared from the scene in 1915 because of financial difficulties resulting mainly from the economic climate brought on by World War I[4].

The establishment of the *Société Mutuelle l'Assomption* (Mutual Assumption Society) on the Island in 1905, proved to be an important stage in the evolution of Acadian nationalism. Founded in 1903 by Acadians in Massachusetts, the society spread almost everywhere there was a sizeable Acadian community. Its aims were to promote the social, intellectual and moral well-being of Acadians, to administer an insurance fund to protect Acadian families, and to set up a scholarship fund to help train an elite[5]. The Mutual Society paralleled and complemented the activities of the National Assumption Society which was founded during the first national conventions and later renamed the National Acadian Society.

L'Impartial.

--Proprietaire. "L'Union fait la Force."

Tignish, Ile du Prince Edouard, Jeudi le 28 Septembre, 1893.

Un Monstre Humain.

Middletown, N. Y., 18—La femme Halliday, qui est retenue prisonnière par la police pour le meurtre des deux femmes McQuillan et de son mari, a tenté de s'étrangler hier soir avec ses jarretières: Le constable Scatt s'en aperçut heureusement à temps pour l'empêcher de mettre fin à ses jours; elle était déjà presque étouffée. On la surveille avec soin depuis ce moment-là.

Depuis la découverte du cadavre de son mari qui avait été déposé sous

Un Bon Conseil.

Dit La Patrie, de Troy:

Pères et mères chrétiens qui vivez au Canada, né laissez, pour aucune considération, vos filles seules venir aux Etats-Unis. C'est une grande imprudence, c'est un crime et vous êtes grandement coupables en agissant ainsi. Si l'amour du lucre vous pousse à sacrifier l'honneur et la vertu de vos filles, vous devenez criminels. Au contraire, si votre bonne foi est surprise par ses embaucheurs, nous vous mettons en garde contre eux et vous

Une lettre etrange du roi Leopold

Bruxelles, 23.—Le roi des Belges, Léopold, a remis entre les mains des ministres, de la nouvelle constitution, une lettre cachetée; cette lettre ne devra être ouverte qu'après la mort du roi.

Elle est l'objet de beaucoup de commentaires; certains prétendent que le roi désapprouve la nouvelle constitution et en décline la responsabilité; d'autres disent qu'il donne des avis pour les changements à venir ou bien qu'il exprime ses regrets de que le

Gilbert Buote
Reg Porter Collection.

By 1920 there were seven branches of the Mutual Society on the Island, located in Palmer Road, Bloomfield, Egmont Bay, Mont Carmel, Rustico, Summerside and Charlottetown. The members met regularly at the branch level to talk about the Acadian cause. In 1933, for example, a motion was adopted in the Rustico branch asking every school district in the region to demand that teachers in French schools make the children speak French during recess[6]. Indeed, the Mutual Assumption Society was interested in any measure that helped foster French education and the French fact. The scholarship fund enabled the Society to sponsor the education of a good number of young people, including many from the Island. On several occasions the Mutual Society helped the Acadian Teachers' Association by covering the travel expenses of members attending their congress.

The members of the Mutual Society on the Island held their first provincial assembly in 1932. Presiding at the meeting, Charles M.

Arsenault explained that his reason for bringing the branches together was to nominate a permanent committee responsible for finding ways to keep the nationalist spirit alive. He spoke as follows:

> We have several local organizations on the Island, but not one of them has official status and thus cannot exercise any authority or undertake anything that might be of benefit to all Acadians. (TR)[7]

Therefore, a committee was formed to organize an annual congress for the provincial branches of the Mutual Assumption Society which became the voice of the Acadians on the Island. It was to share the role with the *Société Saint-Thomas d'Aquin* (Saint Thomas Aquinas Society) from the 1940s to the 1960s at which time the branches of the Mutual Society were dissolved.

In addition to the annual assembly, the Mutual Assumption Society organized so-called "national" conferences to study the Acadian situation on Prince Edward Island: the first one took place in Egmont Bay in 1932 and the second in Mont Carmel in 1938. Not only were delegates from the branches of the Mutual Assumption Society invited to attend, but also representatives from all the Acadian groups in the province. Patriotic speeches flowed at these large gatherings. Stock was taken of the problems and accomplishments of the Acadian community. The main topics of discussion were the French language, education, agriculture, the Catholic press and participation in patriotic societies. These conferences were aimed chiefly at making Acadian Islanders more aware of their distinctiveness and vulnerability as a cultural minority and stirring them to work harder to ensure the advancement and survival of French culture in the province.

Simultaneous to the establishment of the Mutual Assumption Society on the Island, a similar organization was founded in Tignish: the Acadian Mutual Benefit Association (otherwise known as the Mutual). It set up branches in the parishes of Miscouche, Wellington, Palmer Road and Hope River[8]. The members met regularly and discussed questions concerning the preservation of French culture on the Island.

Other important events took place at the beginning of the twentieth century that helped keep the Acadian national spirit alive on Prince Edward Island. In 1913 Tignish was given the opportunity of welcoming delegates from all three Maritime Provinces for the seventh national convention of the Acadians. A delegation from Quebec, organized by *Le Devoir*, visited the main Acadian areas in the Maritimes in 1927. The group, led by the great nationalist, Henri Bourassa, visited Egmont Bay where Acadians from all over the Island had gathered to listen to stirring patriotic speeches. The speakers proclaimed their keen interest in all matters relating to the survival of the French minorities in Canada. It was on the occasion of this visit that Professor J.-Henri Blanchard launched his book, *Histoire des Acadiens de l'Île du Prince Édouard*, in order to introduce the Québécois to the history and current status of the Acadians in his province[9]. The work also enabled his Island compatriots to learn more about their past.

The Key Issue: Education

During the period 1890 to 1945, the Acadian ruling class devoted considerable energy to promoting education and particularly French education. They wanted to make sure that French was taught properly in Acadian schools and undertook to find ways of increasing substantially the number of Acadians in the professions.

The provisions of the School Act of 1877 pertaining to French education had not been modified. Authorities in government did, however, show benevolence with regard to the steps being taken by the Acadians, and, as we shall see, granted certain privileges.

A wave of optimism prevailed among the Acadians during the 1890s. Several events contributed to this positive atmosphere. In 1890 the Model School at Prince of Wales College hired an Acadian as principal, namely, Joseph-Octave Arsenault (not to be confused with his uncle, the Honourable Joseph-Octave Arsenault). In 1892, still keeping his position at the Model School, he became the first francophone inspector of Acadian schools. He also taught French at the college[10]. These appointments were the results of a memorandum presented to the Board of Education by the Scottish priests, Dugald MacDonald and Ronald MacDonald, in Tignish and Rustico. In their memorandum they requested a better system of French education for Acadians[11].

The Acadians were very pleased with these appointments. Up to that point the position of inspector had been given to anglophones

The seventh Acadian National Convention, held in Tignish in 1913. François-Joseph Buote (left) and Pascal Poirier (right) are standing on the platform. The Wellington Brass Band can be seen in the foreground. *Henri Gaudet Collection.*

with little knowledge of French. Now the inspector of Acadian schools could have a better relationship with the Acadian teaching staff, the pupils and the parents. It would now also be possible to supervise the quality of French teaching and promote education in the Acadian communities more easily. Although Joseph-Octave Arsenault only held the postion for nine years, it existed until 1972 and was always filled by an Acadian[12].

These encouraging steps were followed by the founding of *L'Impartial* by the teacher, Gilbert Buote, and the creation of the Acadian Teachers' Association.

THE ACADIAN TEACHERS' ASSOCIATION

When Gilbert Buote started publishing his newspaper he did not give up his position as director of the Grammar School in Tignish. The whole question of education for the Acadians was of great concern to him, particularly the teaching of French. After discovering that the Acadian teachers had not been invited to the educational conference in Kensington, he suggested to Inspector Arsenault, in his editorial of August 3, 1893, that Acadian teachers be convened to a special convention to discuss "the main points that need to be examined concerning the best way to promote French education in our schools (TR)[13]".

The idea was received very favourably by the inspector who immediately invited interested parties to meet in Charlottetown on September 27, 1893. The Acadian Teachers' Association was founded during this meeting with the aim of "fostering the teaching of French in public schools on the Island (TR)[14]". It was agreed that the Association hold an annual meeting in a different Acadian parish each year.

The first convention after the founding meeting was held in 1894 in Egmont Bay. The success of the event was enhanced by the presence of the Bishop of Charlottetown, Monseigneur James MacDonald, and the Quebec historian, Abbé Henri-Raymond Casgrain. Presentations were given on reading, writing, and the necessity and methods of teaching French[15]. The president of the Association, Inspector Arsenault, expressed his optimism with regard to the organization and how it would benefit the Acadians in his annual report to the Chief Superintendent of Education:

> I might say that the [convention] opened a new era in Acadian educational matters in the Province. As this coming together of the Acadian teachers is to be henceforth an annual occurence, I look forward with pleasure to the great good these meetings are capable of accomplishing [. . .] Conventions of this nature are necessary, as the teachers have not only to ground their pupils in the English language but also in the French. The Acadian teachers are peculiarly situated in this respect.[16]

The Acadian Teachers' Association met every year, usually for two days during the month of August, until 1971. The convention was attended by most Acadian teachers, along with priests from Acadian parishes, Acadian public figures, and a large number of parents mainly from the parish where it was held.

Every year several teachers or other concerned individuals were invited to talk about teaching and the French language. The audience was encouraged to comment on the content of these presentations which formed the basis of the meetings. For example, at the eighteenth convention held in Tignish in 1910 seven people gave presentations on the following topics:

—The Role of Religion in Public Education, J.-H. Blanchard
—Corporal Punishment, Denis D. Arsenault
—The Noël Method, Jean O. Arsenault
—Our Duties as Teachers, Théodore Gallant
—The Language Spoken in the Home, Arsène Arsenault
—Our Language, Adrien Arsenault
—Advice to Young Teachers, Marin Gallant (TR)[17]

For several years, a session was reserved for answering questions submitted by the participants on various subjects ranging from grammatical difficulties to proper ways of "stimulating the pupils' ambition and curiosity" (TR). The agenda also included religious services, a variety concert and guest speakers. The conventions would close with the adoption of a series of motions proposing ways to increase teachers' salaries or obtain more French schoolbooks or make Acadian history better known, and expressing thanks to all the people who had supported the Association in one way or another. The following example gives the text of a resolution adopted in 1930:

Delegates at the 1898 Conference of the Acadian Teachers' Association of P.E.I. held in Miscouche.
Musée Acadien.

> Be it resolved that the Convention agree that members make an effort to increase their knowledge of Acadian history in order to correct pupils and the numerous historical errors in schoolbooks, thus stimulating patriotism in every Acadian and imparting a greater love for the French language at home and in the community. (TR)[18]

The clergy was well represented at these conventions and occupied a place of honour. Members of the clergy took part in all the discussions and, more often than not, presided over the committees that were set up either to examine important issues or to petition the provincial Department of Education on behalf of the Association.

On the whole, Island teachers had every reason to be proud of their Association, the first of its kind organized by Acadians in the Maritime Provinces. It contributed greatly to the advancement of the French cause on the Island.

Father Désiré F. Léger from Saint-Paul-de-Kent (New Brunswick), attended the 1910 convention in order to see how the Association operated. The following year, he organized, in Saint-Louis-de-Kent, the first Acadian educational convention in New Brunswick[19]. Numbered amongst the important accomplishments of the Acadian Teachers' Association are the creation of regional assemblies (1894), the founding of the Saint Thomas Aquinas Society (1919) and the organizing of French competitions (1930).

REGIONAL ASSEMBLIES

At the 1894 convention the participants felt it would be desirable for teachers to meet periodically to discuss matters relating to their profession. It was agreed, therefore, that meetings be organized for the teaching personnel at a regional level. With that end in view, the Acadian school districts were divided into four sections with one person in each section responsible for organizing the meetings and reporting to the annual convention. The number of organizers was later increased so that meetings could take place in all the Acadian parishes.

These meetings were called "regional assemblies" (TR). From the outset, parents were encouraged to attend the assemblies which thus took the form of parent-teacher meetings, the first of their kind in Prince Edward Island and perhaps in all of Canada.

The assemblies followed more or less the same format as the conventions of the Association. Several teachers gave presentations which the audience was invited to comment upon. There were also discussions on practical matters such as: "What is the best way to make children attend school?" (TR), "Summer holidays" (TR), "Should one give more attention to the pupil who is less intelligent than to one who is more intelligent?" (TR).

Report of a regional assembly held in Mont Carmel in 1900.

On the invitation of Mr. Emmanuel Arsenault, president of the Mont Carmel section, the teachers met at the Mont Carmel School on Saturday, the 17th of this month. The following were present:

Father Arsenault, Messrs. André Doiron, Nazaire Poirier, Emmanuel Arsenault, Bruno Martin, Mathurin Gallant, teachers, and a host of ratepayers who, by their very presence, showed they are interested in education.

Mr. Jean J. Gallant presided.

The following subjects were examined:

1. Studying lessons under parents' guidance
2. The advantages of regular attendance and the disastrous consequences of irregular attendance
3. The respect that parents and children owe the teacher
4. Hygiene
5. Cleanliness
6. The monthly visit by the trustees
7. Care of books, etc.

Father Arsenault, Messrs. André Doiron, Bruno Martin and Em. Arsenault spoke to the assembly. Their speeches were greatly appreciated by all and certainly did not fail to produce the desired effect.

After the subjects had been examined sufficently, a vote of thanks was given to Mr. André Doiron for his active part in the meeting.

After singing the National Anthem the participants dispersed, satisfied with the excellent lessons they had been given.

(*L'Impartial* December 6, 1900) (TR)

Thanks to the regional assemblies and the annual conventions which were open to the public, taxpayers took a greater interest in education. They informed themselves about their responsibilities for the maintenance of the schools, and above all, the proper education for their children. Extremely impressed by this progress, the Chief Superintendent of Education, Alexander Anderson, remarked in his annual report of 1907:

> No section of our people puts forth more effort to secure Education for their children, and none are more self-denying and none more enthusiastic than the Acadians. There is no Acadian District but votes a good supplement to its teacher. They have generally good schoolhouses and school grounds planted with shade trees and are well supplied with the necessary apparatus. In all these respects they are far in advance of districts older and much wealthier.[20]

Regional assemblies continued to be held in some parishes, albeit irregularly, right up until 1953 when the Home and School Association, as it exists today, was created on the Island. It is interesting to note, however, that even in its final years the Acadian Teachers' Association always included in the agenda of its convention a report from the regional parent-teacher assemblies.

THE SAINT THOMAS AQUINAS SOCIETY

To a certain extent, it was the conventions of the Acadian Teachers' Association that gave rise to the Saint Thomas Aquinas Society, an organization that was to become the principal voice of the Acadian community on the Island. It was founded at a public meeting on August 18 during the 1919 convention, held in the parish of Bloomfield. The meeting had been called to discuss the formation of a society that would be responsible for "raising funds for the education of young Acadians" (TR)[21]. The need for this type of organization was obvious to the members of the convention who knew full well that the majority of Acadians were small farmers and fishermen by trade and thus could not afford to have their numerous children educated in colleges and convents. Yet the Acadians desperately needed educated people capable of contributing to the growth and preservation of their culture.

Professor J.-Henri Blanchard was one of the founders and one of the most ardent supporters of the Saint Thomas Aquinas Society. In a speech to his colleagues attending the 1920 convention, he spoke very optimistically about the benefits the Society could bring:

> With the moral support and the pecuniary help of all our friends, we soon expect to see numerous priests, doctors, lawyers and other Acadian professionals graduate from colleges and universities and champion our religion, our race and our rights. The Society will therefore have to be largely instrumental in bringing closer the day of complete rehabilitation of the little Acadian group on the Island. (TR)[22]

Although the immediate objective was to collect money for the education of young Acadians, the overall goal of the Society was to see French and Acadian life flourish on Prince Edward Island[23].

Thanks to the work of its leaders, recruited amongst the clergy and the more educated Acadian laymen, the Saint Thomas Aquinas Society succeeded in collecting enough money to be able to award several scholarships each year. Funds were obtained from private individuals, collections and evening recreational activities organized by the directors of the Society[24]. In Charlottetown, for example, an evening of card games was organized to help pay for the studies of a young man from Rustico who planned to enter the priesthood[25].

An important event took place in 1937 that was to have a profound effect on the Society and its activities. It was in that year that the second Convention for the French Language in Canada was held in Quebec City. Professor Blanchard was invited to speak about the status of French in his native province. In a well prepared lecture, he described the precarious state of French life and education on the Island, emphasizing the scarcity of professionals amongst Acadians, be they doctors, lawyers, priests, teachers or civil servants. He also stressed that the Island community lacked the means for financing post-secondary studies for its young people:

> We do, of course, have the Saint Thomas Aquinas Society which collects some monies to pay for the higher education of two students. But this is so little, given the dangers that threaten us from all sides. If we wish to train the required leaders without whom we, as a French-language group, shall surely disappear, then we must act as speedily as possible; otherwise it will be too late. (TR)[26]

J.-Henri Blanchard

The speaker from the Island found a sympathetic and receptive audience. Following his talk, members of the audience suggested that he canvass colleges in Quebec to procure scholarships for Island Acadians; he visited the institutions in 1937 and 1939. He was given a warm welcome and, in 1937, seven Acadian boys began their classical studies in Quebec. By 1939 there were twenty-two enrolled[27]. The few existing Acadian colleges also took in their share of students from the Island. The Saint Thomas Aquinas Society co-ordinated the distribution of all the scholarships.

This generous outside support gave the Society new momentum; efforts were made to build a more solid foundation and even to increase the sphere of activities. About thirty branches, mainly involved in recruiting new members and fundraising, were created in the Acadian school districts[28]. In addition to awarding scholarships and bursaries, the Saint Thomas Aquinas Society gave grants to Acadian schools to purchase French books for their libraries, distributed hundreds of books donated by French-Canadian patriotic societies, and subscribed schools to the newspaper *L'Évangéline*[29]. All these endeavours were designed to foster reading in French. As the years went by, the Society extended its work and activities with the result that it became, as we shall see, the principle voice for the Acadian community.

ACADIAN SCHOOLS

Thanks to the progress made in the educational field, the growing interest of Island Acadians in their children's education was shown plainly by an increase in the number of schools and schoolchildren. Some one-room schools were enlarged and "graded", in other words divided into two sections separating the primary grades from the more advanced grades. On the whole attendance was deemed to be quite good by the inspectors of Acadian schools.

In 1899, there were forty-three Acadian schools comprising fifty classrooms used by 2,226 pupils of which approximately three hundred were non-francophone. It should be noted that not all Acadian children had access to Acadian schools. According to the calculations of Inspector Joseph-Octave Arsenault, about two hundred Acadian children were attending schools where French was not taught at all[30]. About thirty years later, Professor J.-Henri Blanchard stated that nearly half the Acadian school children, approximately eleven hundred, had to attend entirely English-language schools[31].

With regard to private schooling, the convents in Tignish, Miscouche and Rustico continued to provide a good education for young girls. However, faced with overwhelming financial difficulties, these convents schools were forced to abandon their status as private institutions between 1902 and 1922 so that they could become integrated into the public school system and thus benefit from government grants. The convents were then obliged to follow the official public school curriculum which meant less French. Little by little, the French atmosphere in the convent schools diminished so that by 1942, only eight out of seventeen teaching sisters were French-speaking[32].

Professor J.-Henri Blanchard paints a fairly accurate picture of the amount of time allotted to the instruction of French in the Acadian schools. His observations of 1937 are valid for almost the entire 1890 to 1945 period:

> The French curriculum in the sixty-two schools in Acadian localities is limited to instruction in reading, grammar, dictation and a bit of composition. A few rare schools teach the history of Canada in French. In some schools French is used for arithmetic and geography, but as a general rule these subjects are taught in English. In most schools even beginners are introduced to the different subjects by means of the English language.
>
> In several schools where French is encouraged more, the pupils learn to read French. They start learning English at the end of their first year, after which the languages are taught concurrently. Ordinarily in these schools the morning lessons are devoted to French reading and the afternoon ones to English reading. (TR)[33]

Due to numerous obstacles even this curriculum was not always respected. First of all, a shortage of francophone teachers meant that some districts were obliged to hire teachers with little or no knowledge of French. Inspector Joseph Blanchard pointed out in 1902 that schools in that predicament did not obtain very satisfactory results: "Imagine a teacher with no French and children with little or no English, and you can form an idea of the thoroughness of the work done[34]". In 1926, for example, seventeen of the sixty-three teachers responsible for Acadian classes were English-speaking[35]. Another obstacle resulted from the fact that many Acadian teachers were poorly qualified to teach French since almost all their training had been in English. It was not surprising, therefore, that the teaching of the Acadians' mother tongue left much to be desired. Inspector J.-Wilfred Arsenault sounded the alarm in his report of 1936: "I have concluded that, unless our present system of teaching French and preparing teachers for our Acadian Schools is immediately revolutionized, the French Acadian Schools of our Island will soon be French in name only[36]".

Acadian communities began to take more and more interest in the upkeep of their schools. Matters concerning the cleanliness, appearance and furnishing of schools would often be discussed at the Acadian Teachers' Association conventions and at regional assemblies. During the 1890s Acadian schools started celebrating Arbor Day, a school holiday instituted in the province in 1885[37]. On that day pupils would

Hélène Doiron-Gallant with her pupils at the Duvar School in 1938.
Oscar and Hélène Gallant Collection.

clean up the school and decorate the schoolyard by planting flowers and trees.

After the Women's Institutes were organized in 1913, taxpayers took an even greater interest in their schools. One of the main concerns of these women's circles, founded under the auspices of the Department of Agriculture, was to improve the school districts. The women organized benefits to pay for school equipment and maintenance. They also supervised the sanitary conditions in schools. In 1916, for example, the Women's Institute in Miscouche bought a new blackboard, a teacher's desk, a fountain and cups for all the students in the public school[38]. Over the years, the Institutes became popular in many of the Acadian school districts. The school inspector often encouraged women to form them.

There were several important events during the school year that broke the daily routine. One such event was public examinations, the most important of which took place at the end of the year. Pupils were questioned in front of their parents, the priest and other interested people on the subjects studied during the year. On this occasion the pupils also sang and recited and prizes were given out.

The school fair constituted another popular event that took place for many years. All the pupils from a parish would gather together for a day in the fall at one of the schools in the district. It was a small agricultural fair to which the pupils would bring animals, vegetables, handcrafts, cakes, etc. The best exhibits would receive a prize. The aim of these fairs was to stimulate interest and enable young people to improve their knowledge in farming and domestic arts.

From 1930 onward, another event attracted the attention of Acadian students: the French competition, organized by the Acadian Teachers' Association under the direction of Professor J.-Henri Blanchard. It was designed to encourage school children to take a greater interest in learning French reading, grammar and composition. The competition usually took place on a Saturday in the spring. Pupils from several neighbouring districts would meet in the same school to take written examinations that were later corrected by a provincial jury. The prize-winners were given readers. The competition stimulated a great deal of interest and lasted, almost without any changes, until the end of the 1960s.

THE TEACHING STAFF

As we have seen, Acadian teachers were very active during this period; they met regularly to share their knowledge and discuss their problems. Taxpayers usually attended these meetings, although teachers would also have their own meetings from time to time in order to improve their teaching skills and their French.

The shortage of Acadian teachers still constituted a major problem. It was caused by various factors including poor salaries which prompted many individuals, after several years of teaching, to turn to more lucrative careers. This was particularly true for men who, up until the beginning of the twentieth century, formed the majority in the profession. More and more men were leaving the classroom to the care of young female teachers who would also abandon teaching after a few years in order to raise a family. Some teachers left for western Canada to try their luck where teaching positions were better paid. Consequently, between 1906 and 1920, the inspector for Acadian schools complained on numerous occasions that his best teachers, both men and women, were leaving for the Prairie provinces. There was a strong demand in the west around that time for bilingual teachers to work in the newly founded French-Canadian parishes. The two world wars also caused a drain on the teaching personnel on the Island. During World War II, especially, many men and women left the teaching profession to join the army or work in factories in large industrial centres where salaries were more attractive.

The entrance exams and the language of instruction at the provincial Normal School further hindered the recruitment of young teachers originating from Acadian communities. Since English only was spoken at the School, the French-speaking students had to work much harder to succeed than their classmates[39]. This state of affairs was not conducive to attracting very many Acadians into teaching.

At the beginning of the century all female teachers received less pay than their male counterparts. The matter was the subject of discussion on numerous occasions during the Acadian teachers' conventions. The minutes for the 1907 convention indicate the general drift of the discussion:

> Mr. F. J. Buote pointed out the injustice done to female teachers, seeing that they do not receive as much pay as male teachers although they do just as much work. Rev. P.C. Gauthier is also in favour of equal pay for male and female teachers and proposed the following motion which was adopted unanimously. Given that a distinction is made in the salary between male and female teachers in this province, be it resolved that the salary paid to female teachers be just as high as that paid to male teachers. (TR)[40]

This discrimination lasted for a very long time since it was not until 1947 that female teachers finally received equal pay.

One encouragement for Acadian teachers was that, as a token of the taxpayers' esteem, they were awarded a supplement in addition to their salary from the government. This did not happen in all provincial school districts. Alexander Anderson, Superintendent of Public Education, expressed his delight concerning the matter in his report of 1908. He wrote: "It is very satisfactory, again, to feel bound

Students, teachers and visitors at the 1938 summer school held at the Convent in Miscouche.

to commend the spirit and generosity of the rate-payers in the French-Acadian districts in which there is no teacher but receives a supplement[41]."

The French training of teachers assigned to Acadian schools still left much to be desired. The Board of Education was not the least bit interested in the matter. Most of the time the quality of teaching depended entirely on the personal drive and initiative of teachers who had their heart set on improving the way their mother tongue was taught[42]. In 1937, Professor Blanchard explained the situation in the following manner in his speech in Quebec city:

> All our schools, with the exception of the three convents in Tignish, Miscouche and Rustico (all under the direction of the sisters of the Congregation of Notre Dame in Montreal), are directed by lay men and women with teacher's certificates from the Normal School in Charlottetown. Their training in teaching as well as their language training leave much to be desired. Acadian men and women have to take exactly the same course as English-language candidates. It is true that all our teachers, without exception, have to take French classes for at least two years. But these classes are limited to studying grammar, a bit of translation and, to make matters more preposterous, the grammar textbook is written in English, as are all the explanations. Therefore, it is scarcely of any use to French-speaking students. That is the weakest point in the organization of teaching French in our tiny province. (TR)[43]

As we have seen, the speech by the Island delegate had happy consequences. Several French-Canadian organizations, sympathetic to the Islanders' predicament helped the Acadian Teachers' Association organize summer courses for its members. In 1938, the nationalist newspaper, *Le Devoir*, even launched a subscription campaign to collect the funds required for financing the courses. As a result, for ten years, very competent French-Canadian professors came to the Island to teach the two-week-long summer courses. They were sent by the following groups: the *Comité permanent de la survivance française*, the *Société Saint-Jean Baptiste* in Montreal, the *Alliance des professeurs catholiques de Montréal* and the Quebec Department of Education. The P.E.I. Department of Education also helped finance the courses[44].

These summer courses took place in Miscouche in 1940 and the majority of the Acadian teachers enrolled. Four professors from Quebec and Ontario gave courses on French parsing, composition and grammar. Another course focussed on how to teach beginners to read. The summer sessions proved to be very useful: back in their classrooms, teachers tried to put into practice their newly acquired skills[45]. For the first time, Acadian teachers on the Island had the opportunity to perfect their French education and pedagogical training in their mother tongue.

ADULT EDUCATION

Throughout this period attention was given to adult education. The temperance societies which had played such an important role in this area lost their momentum at the turn of century. But after

1894, debating clubs became very popular in Acadian circles. The members would meet regularly throughout the fall and winter. A topic for discussion would be chosen ahead of time and all the members invited to state their point of view during the debate. A vote would be taken afterwards to determine which side of the question had won the most supporters.

The editor of *L'Impartial* was delighted to see these clubs being formed. According to him they could contribute greatly to the training of young men:

> We cannot do too much to promote these societies that have been taking shape lately in the form of debating clubs in several of our French centres. It is certainly one of the best ways for our young men to become accustomed to speaking in public, as well as acquiring a great deal of useful information that can be applied to ordinary everyday tasks. (TR)[46]

The subjects debated were varied and often quite educational:

—Which has the greater influence: wealth or education?
—Which is the better form of vote: the ballot or open declaration?
—Which country offers the greatest chances of success for a young man: Canada or the United States?
—Who causes the greatest harm to the public or to society: the vendor of liquor or the drunkard?
—Which is the better form of government: the monarchy or the republic? (TR)[47]

Some of these clubs did not last long, but after a brief lapse they reappeared at the beginning of the twentieth century and operated again for a few years.

New clubs for farmers organized in Acadian localities at the end of the nineteenth century constituted an excellent source of information for the agricultural community. People met on a regular basis mainly to improve their knowledge in the field of agriculture. These clubs will be examined in detail in the section on farming.

On several occasions at the turn of the century, genuine evening courses were organized for young men in some Acadian school districts. In his annual reports of 1898 and 1928, the inspector for the Acadian schools mentions that these courses existed[48].

The most important development with regard to adult education on the Island was the formation of a movement of study groups. Founded in 1936 during the Depression, this movement was based on the Antigonish Movement, a program of social and economic development at St. Francis Xavier University. Dr. John T. Croteau, professor of Economics and Sociology at St. Dunstan's and Prince of Wales Colleges, directed the movement on the Island under the aegis of the Adult Education League[49]. Within a few years, virtually every Acadian community had a study club designed to promote and teach appropriate ways for ensuring community development from an economic, social, religious or educational point of view. Thus at regular meetings during the off-season, small groups of men would practice leading assemblies, learn how co-operatives worked, study the needs of their communities and organize projects in aid of their locality. These study clubs, in which the local teacher played an essential role, made an invaluable contribution to the growth of Acadian communities. Credit unions, co-operative stores, fishermen's unions and other such organizations were formed. Thanks to these study groups, people also became more interested in schools and new ones were built in several districts[50].

Religion And The Church

At the turn of the century, the Acadians on the Island appear to have escaped the bitter struggle that took place in New Brunswick within the Church between the Acadians and the Irish. Although the Acadians formed the majority of the Catholic population in New Brunswick, all the important ecclesiastical positions were held by Irish clergymen quite unsympathetic to the Acadian culture and the aspirations of the Acadians. In 1890, when the Acadians began exerting pressure to obtain a bishop of their own nationality, they were strongly opposed by the Irish and all the bishops in the Maritime Provinces[51]. This long and difficult battle consumed virtually all the energy of the Acadian leadership. Victory finally came in 1912 when the Acadians were able to greet with joy their first bishop, Monseigneur Edouard LeBlanc, appointed to the episcopal seat in Saint John.

The battle between the French and the Irish within the Catholic

Church in Canada was not restricted to New Brunswick. Similar battles took place both in Ontario and in the west where the ecclesiastical hierarchy had been, up until then, French-Canadian. Language was the main bone of contention. On the one hand the French Canadians maintained that language was the guardian of the faith: anyone who became anglicized risked losing the Catholic faith. On the other hand, the anglophone clergy, particularly of Irish descent, was convinced that English would sooner or later become the dominant language of the country: consequently it should be favoured to ensure the expansion and the unity of the Catholic Church. Besides, how could one attract Anglo-Protestants to Catholicism if, influenced by their anti-French heritage, they identified the Catholic Church with French Canada[52]?

Even in the absence of overt struggles, the will to anglicize on the part of the English-speaking clergy became evident on Prince Edward Island, especially during and after the 1920s. The Acadians began to lose ground with regard to the use of French in their religious life. Parishes where a high percentage of the faithful were French-Acadian thus fell into the hands of almost exclusively English-speaking priests who were unable to respect either the language or the culture of a large proportion of their congregation. Some members of the clergy actually opposed the Acadian cause. This was serious to the extent that it hampered the efforts to promote and preserve the French language and Acadian identity. We have already seen the influential role played by Acadian priests in that area. A visitor from New Brunswick wrote in 1924: "Wherever French is still intact, there is a zealous Acadian priest who, with the support of his obedient parishioners, is upholding the respect for the ancestral language (TR)[53]".

The Acadians were not particularly receptive to this form of anglicization which the clergy was fostering. Having been told for so many years that they must preserve French, the guardian of their faith, they now found the clergy depriving them of their right to listen to a sermon in their mother tongue and even to learn their catechism in French.

The scarcity of Acadian or bilingual priests rarely justified this situation. The clergy in the Diocese of Charlottetown was, in 1937, comprised of seventy priests, eight of whom were Acadian. Only four of them served on the Island: the others were assigned to the Magdalen

Father François-Xavier Gallant and his parishioners in Bloomfield, 1910.
Alban and Jeanne Arsenault Collection.

Islands[54]. Sometimes Acadian priests ministered to parishes that were totally English-speaking. Other Acadian priests born on the Island were given parishes in western Canada or the United States.

Despite this rather discouraging state of affairs, the Island Acadians were able to rely on the support of several energetic native priests who left their mark on their community—the most notable of these being Fathers Jean Chiasson, Célestin Gauthier, Pierre-Paul Arsenault and François-Xavier Gallant. They took on the leadership of various social, economic and religious movements with the goal of ensuring the growth of the Acadian community. They promoted and defended education and the French language, encouraged farming and colonization, and propagated temperance and mutual insurance.

MASTER BUILDERS

Many priests became involved in organizing the construction of the magnificent churches and stately presbyteries that characterize the Acadian landscape. They were thus continuing the work their predecessors had begun mainly in the 1860s with imposing structures like the beautiful brick church in Tignish and the famous red sandstone parish hall in Rustico that originally housed the Farmers' Bank of Rustico. While glorifying God with these grandiose buildings, the priests also wanted to provide their parishioners with monuments they could be proud of and which would prove that the Acadians, without being the wealthiest class on the Island, were capable of great and beautiful accomplishments. No doubt the personal glory of the priests responsible for these remarkable structures was also enhanced.

At a time when money was scarce, the organizational skills of the priests and their talents as fundraisers largely determined the financing of these famous buildings. A popular and effective way of raising money was the parish picnic which used to be called a "tea party". This important event was organized by the priest and took place during the summer, often on the feast of the Assumption (August 15). The festivities lasted all day long. They would begin with a solemn Mass that was often followed by a procession and speeches by guest speakers. An effort was usually made to procure a band to liven up the celebrations and enhance the religious ceremonies. Included in the money-making events were meals, merry-go-rounds, games of chance, games of skill, raffles and a dance. Lotteries and variety concerts also constituted efficient ways of raising money. In Mont Carmel, Father Pierre-Paul Arsenault, a very resourceful priest, started a popular way of paying for the construction of a brick church. His gimmick consisted of "selling" bricks to donors whose names were inscribed in the register for special Masses. His call for funds was explained in a leaflet stating the conditions of the donations:

> **A Generous Appeal to the Devout Servants of Notre-Dame de Mont Carmel**
>
> For every five cents donated to the construction of the Church of Notre-Dame de Mont Carmel, P.E.I., you will have the honour of owning a brick in this house of God.
>
> Your names will be kept in a register and you will also have a share in the offering of two Masses celebrated each year in this Church. (TR)[55]

Father Arsenault indicated the dates for these annual Masses in the parish register: one would be said on July 16 for the living benefactors, the other would be celebrated for the deceased subscribers on the first available day after All Saints' Day.

The success of these projects depended essentially on the generosity of the parishioners who offered their assistance in time, in kind and in money. The priest would usually prepare a plan according to which the men in the parish would contribute a certain number of days of labour towards cutting and transporting lumber, making bricks, digging the basement for the building and other such work. Often the parishioners would donate farm produce which the priest could sell in aid of the building fund.

Benefiting from their very enviable prestige and a remarkable sense of administration, the clergy generally succeeded in completing, with the help of the parishioners, magnificent projects to the honour of the Acadian parishes.

SISTERS

We have already seen that from the middle of the nineteenth century onwards, teaching sisters contributed a great deal to the educational and cultural development on the Island. It will be remembered that it was the sisters of the Congregation of Notre Dame in Montreal

Émilienne Arsenault (Sister Saint Fulbert), the first native Island Acadian to become a nun.
Musée Acadien.

who founded the convents in Miscouche, Tignish and Rustico that were among the first on the Island. This religious order took in many Acadian women including Emilienne Arsenault (Sister Saint Fulbert) from Egmont Bay who was the first native Island Acadian to become a nun. She became a novice in 1874.

Many young Acadian women took the veil in various religious orders throughout North America[56], and particularly in the Sisters of the Holy Family in Sherbrooke, Quebec. Mother Évangéline Gallant, an Island Acadian born in Egmont Bay, became highly distinguished in her congregation. She entered the Sisters of Charity (Grey Nuns)

Mother Évangéline Gallant, Superior General of the Grey Nuns in Montreal, with her Inuit godchild, Clara Jacobson, the first baptized Catholic in Maitland Point on the Arctic coast, 1942. *Musée Acadien.*

in Montreal in 1901. A nurse by profession, she first worked in various missions located in the United States and western Canada. Her administrative talents enabled her to hold high offices in her Order. She became Superior General of the Order and filled the position from 1935 to 1946[57].

A religious vocation was a very honourable estate for all good Catholics. Any family who gave a nun, a priest or a brother to the Church and the community was highly respected. Families who had aroused several religious callings amongst their children were held up as an example.

RELIGION-BASED SOCIETIES

Over the years the number of societies of a religious or socio-religious nature gradually increased in the parishes. Temperance societies still existed although they lost their momentum at the beginning of the century when they became Good Death Societies and their educational and cultural role was taken over by other organizations.

With the founding of convents, societies for young girls were established: the Infant Jesus Society, the Guardian Angels Society, and the Children of Mary. Other religious groups for adults sprung up during the 1890s. The Holy Family Society and the League of the Sacred Heart were established around 1893[58]; the Holy Rosary Brotherhood and the Holy Name Society (for men only) appeared later in the diocese. Generally these organizations were concerned with moral instruction and promoting worship. The number of societies in a parish depended on the zeal of the pastor and the presence of a convent.

Other Catholic organizations were formed after 1920, such as the Catholic Women's League whose first chapter on the Island was founded in Charlottetown in 1921. The Catholic Women's League was interested in Catholic education, the family and ecumenism[59]; as a movement it spread quickly into several parishes in the province including ones with a strong Acadian element. This organization operated in English only.

Around 1936, the Egmont Bay priest, Father F.-X. Gallant, asked parishioners enrolled in the Women's Institute (sponsored by the Department of Agriculture) to form a French-Catholic society under the name of the Altar Women's Society[60]. Acadian women responded to their priest's request and set up a parish-wide organization with a branch in nearly every school district thus replacing, in most cases, the Women's Institute. Several years later the women in Mont Carmel joined the society. This new organization filled the same role as the Catholic Women's League and the Women's Institute, except that it functioned in French. Mrs. Madeleine Gallant, one of the founding members, described the activities of the Altar Women's Society:

> You might well ask yourselves why the Altar Women's Society was organized. Obviously in the parishes where there are no convents there are no sisters

> available to take care of the sanctuary and the altar. Our society has thus been called upon to fill this void. We attend to the upkeep of altar hangings, we purchase ornaments and flowers and we see to the cleaning of the church. Like the Women's Institutes, we also assist with the maintenance and the furnishing of our schools.
>
> At Christmas time we send clothing and toys to the orphans in the diocesan orphanage [. . .] We support any campaign aimed at helping worthy causes. (TR)[61]

It should be added that the monthly meetings included in their agenda an educational session on religious subjects.

It was during the 1930s that Acadian women in the parish of Bloomfield formed the Saint Anne Club whose activities resembled those of the Altar Women's Society. Along with other things, they promoted the worship of Saint Anne[62]. There was also a branch in Rustico.

A certain number of mutual societies were created during the period 1890 to 1945. Although not exactly religious organizations, they were nevertheless only open to Catholics and always under the spiritual direction of a priest. The first of the mutual societies that spread into the Acadian parishes was called the Catholic Mutual Benefit Association, a national co-operative organization aimed at providing life insurance benefits. After the establishment of the first branch on the Island in 1893, the movement spread quickly into almost all the Acadian parishes. Soon, however, new mutual societies grew up in the Acadian parishes that were more directly concerned with French-Acadian interests. The *Société des Artisans canadiens-français* (French-Canadian Tradesmen Society) was thus established in Tignish in 1902 and in Rustico in 1903, and, as we have seen, several branches of the Mutual Assumption Society were founded in the province from 1905 onwards. The Acadian Mutual Benefit Association, founded in Tignish in 1905, also succeeded in setting up several branches on the Island.

LIVING ONE'S FAITH

Acadians expressed their faith in ways that went far beyond the important place given to the priest in their religious life and the beautiful churches manifesting their ties to the Catholic religion. Indeed, religion for the Acadians was a way of life imbued with traditional beliefs and practices, established ceremonies, and precise regulations laid down by the Church. It was within this framework that Acadians lived their faith and communicated with God and the saints.

For centuries Acadians were profoundly marked by their religious heritage, brought mainly from France by their ancestors. Passed down for generations, it was comprised of partly religious and partly superstitious beliefs and practices, undoubtedly dating back to pre-Christian times; and of a rigour typical of the Catholic religion practised by the early settlers. A negative approach was characteristic of this Catholicism with a stern, omnipresent God always ready to punish the slightest error. This perspective of the Catholic religion was perpetuated in the new world by a clergy trained for a long time according to the Jansenist doctrine.

No doubt the prolonged absence of priests amidst the Acadians, throughout the eighteenth and nineteenth centuries, contributed to keeping alive beliefs and practices that often related more to superstition than to religion. Traces of this traditional mentality can still be found today. Let us look at some of the manifestations of popular beliefs which, it should be pointed out, are not always specifically Acadian and are often shared by other Catholic peoples.

To ensure that this omnipresent God protected them, the Acadians surrounded themselves with numerous holy objects. The crucifix and holy pictures would always be given a place of honour in most rooms in their dwellings. Consecrated branches were also placed throughout the house and outbuildings, usually near a window as protection against thunder. Holy water was also used during storms and sprinkled on the stove, windows and mirrors to protect against lightning. According to some beliefs, holy water also had medicinal qualities: it was rubbed on different parts of the body to cure all sorts of ills. Consecrated medals were so popular that it would be unheard of not to wear one since they ensured divine protection. When Acadian women were still wearing the traditional dress, their costume would not have been complete without a little cross around the neck, or failing a cross, a medal[63].

The worship of saints was also a well established practice. Their intercession could be of assistance in obtaining favours from Heaven. The Blessed Virgin, among the most popular of saints, was chosen as the patron saint of the Acadians in 1881 and referred to as Our Lady of the Assumption. She was often implored in times of misfortune to soothe the afflicted.

Known for her miracles, Saint Anne, mother of the Virgin Mary, also earned the affection of the Acadians. By 1887, a group of Islanders had already made a pilgrimage to Sainte Anne de Beaupré in Quebec[64]—a tradition which continues today. Other saints were invoked, including Saint Antoine of Padua to help find lost objects, Saint Gerard to help give birth without difficulty, and Saint Benoît and Saint Barbe to protect against thunder. Saint Benoît medals placed on window sills were trusted to guard against lightning. They were often accompanied by with the following prayer addressed to Saint Barbe:

> Saint Barbe, you who hold the key to thunder Protect us from all danger. (TR)[65]

FROM MORNING 'TIL NIGHT

Worship and prayer punctuated the Acadians' day from the moment they arose until the moment they went to bed. The number and frequency of religious exercices varied according to the time of year. Advent and Lent constituted the high points of the liturgical calendar. But throughout the year, both the individual and the family observed a daily "program" of prayers.

The first devotion was the morning prayer which was silently recited by each person while kneeling. Only the children, still at the learning stage, would recite aloud in front of their mother. This devotion was quite long and included a series of prayers transmitted orally from one generation to the next. Before the meals, everyone would say the *Benedicite* to ask the Lord to bless the food, and afterwards, Grace to thank Him for the daily bread. At noon the *Benedicite* was preceded by the recitation of the Angelus, a prayer commemorating the Incarnation.

The rosary, the main family prayer, was always recited after supper. This long repetitive prayer was usually followed by litanies to the saints, prayers for the souls in Purgatory, the Holy Father, temperance and other intentions. This lasted at least fifteen minutes.

Finally, before bedtime, each person said the evening prayer which was a repetition, almost word for word, of the morning prayer.

Before getting into bed one crossed oneself with holy water and said a short invocation such as:

> Holy water I taketh you
> On my body, on my blood.
> Holy Guardian Angel
> Please remain with me
> The whole night through. (TR)[66]

And thus ended in prayer a typical day for an Acadian.

In addition to these prayers encouraged but not imposed by the Church, there were certain religious obligations that had to be observed at the risk of mortal sin. On Fridays, Catholics abstained from eating meat. The interdiction was not lifted until 1965. The Church required that every person in good health attend Sunday Mass; it was in Latin until 1965. Often Sunday Mass was followed by another religious service, the blessing of the Holy Sacrament, which took place during the summer months on Sunday afternoon after Vespers and was attended by many parishioners. Sunday was, of course, a day of compulsory rest; ordinary tasks were set aside completely and only with the priest's permission could one, in case of necessity, work in the fields, for example. Even small tasks like knitting were forbidden on the Lord's Day.

FROM BIRTH TO DEATH

The important stages of the life of the individual were marked by a series of rituals, both profane and religious. As soon after birth as possible the baby was baptized by the parish priest. The godfather and godmother were usually chosen from within the family circle. Generally the child was given a name with a religious significance. Biblical names such as Judith, Moïse, Elie and Sara were just as popular as saints' names like Bruno, Anne, François and Madeleine. Almost every family had at least one Joseph and one Marie. Tradition also dictated that parents name children after the saint whose feast day coincided with their birthday.

The most important religious ritual during childhood was certainly First Communion which, at the beginning of this century, took place at the age of twelve. This important stage in the Catholic religion

Funeral in Miscouche, circa 1900.
Georges Arsenault.

was preceded by lessons on the catechism given in the church by the priest during the summer holidays. Children would walk to church every day for several weeks to learn about the mysteries of their religion and the precepts of the Church. If finally, after these classes, the children's religious instruction was deemed sufficient, they would be allowed to take communion. The long-awaited day was the scene of an imposing religious ceremony for which the young girls were clad in white from head to toe, while the young boys, also in their Sunday best, wore a white ribbon on their left arm.

Confirmation was another even more imposing ceremony with a similar setting. It was particularly noteworthy, however, since it only took place every three or four years and it was the bishop himself who administered the sacrament. As they had done before their First Communion, the children went to church for several weeks to attend catechism lessons given by the priest.

The very simple marriage ceremony took place in front of several witnesses early in the day at morning Mass. Normally several couples exchanged vows at the same time. The wedding festivities, on the other hand, were on a much larger scale and might even last more than one day since nothing was spared for what was considered to be a memorable event. In some families the wedding would be ended by saying the rosary and the evening prayer.

Normally it was not long after marriage before children were born; the children were many in Acadian homes. Large families were, in fact, blessed by the Church, whereas couples were disapproved of if they tried to limit the number of births. Therefore any couple who, for any reason except illness, decided not to have any more children was committing a grave sin in the eyes of the Church. The clergy used diverse ways of getting the message across. An example is the missionary who told women that all the children they prevented from being born would tug on their skirts and make it harder to fly to heaven[67]!

When they were elderly, parents still remained in their own home with the family of the son who was to inherit the family estate. It was there that they would die, surrounded by their loved ones. The priest was called to the deathbed to administer the Last Rites at the appropriate time. In those days the wake would be held at home in a death chamber improvised for the occasion. The devotional objects in the house, such as crucifixes and holy statues and pictures, were placed in the room. Friends and relatives kept vigil over the body for two days and, at various moments, recited prayers for the dead, the rosary and litanies. They also sang hymns, a tradition which was lost at the end of the nineteenth century[68].

The body was then carried to the church, draped for the funeral service, and finally taken to the cemetery to be buried in the presence of the priest, the family and friends. The priest recited the last prayers asking the Lord to have mercy on the soul of the deceased. Finally, the priest threw a shovelful of earth on the coffin which had been lowered into the grave, and declaim: "Remember that thou art dust and unto dust thou shalt return."

Acadians had a great deal of respect for the dead and did not forget them in their prayers. An effort was made to have a Mass sung regularly for the repose of their souls. It was believed that deceased persons who benefited from fifteen masses said for their intention would go to heaven[69]. Acadians who had the means almost always left a certain sum in their will so that masses would be celebrated for the repose of their soul.

FROM ADVENT TO ALL SOULS' DAY

In addition to the daily and weekly exercises that punctuated the spiritual life of the Acadians, the Church had a calendar year filled with religious activities that all Catholics made it their duty to observe. The calendar included periods of penitence and prayer along with numerous feasts of obligation such as Epiphany (January 6), All Saints' Day (November 1) and the Immaculate Conception (December 8) which were to be observed to the same degree as Sundays. We will examine briefly some of these religious traditions.

Advent opened the liturgical year of the Catholic Church. It is a four week period of spiritual preparation for Christmas. In the past, there were no dances or marriages during this period and people carried out various penitences such as giving up candies and sweets. Christmas was essentially a religious festivity that began with midnight Mass. As is the case today, the priest and the choir took great pains to prepare for this celebration, one of the happiest and most beautiful of the year. On Christmas afternoon families would go to the church where children could see the crèche. On New Year's Day, a holy day of obligation, people of all ages would visit their fathers to receive the paternal blessing[70].

Among the religious ceremonies celebrated in the church during the winter, there was Candelmas Day (February 2) when candles were blessed. People would take home several candles that would be lit on special occasions during the year: for storms, for novenas, and during the final hours of the dying. The feast day of Saint Blaise was celebrated the next day. People went to church to have the priest bless their throats with prayers and consecrated candles. They had great faith in this ceremony as a way of preventing sore throats.

Lent was undoubtedly the most demanding period of the liturgical calendar. For the forty-six days that preceded Easter, the Catholic Church prescribed a very strict regime of penitence. It was above all a period of fasting and abstinence which varied in stringency depending on the era. Here are the rules for Lent in the Charlottetown diocese in 1894:

1. Meat is permitted for all three meals on Sundays.
2. Meat is permitted once a day, i.e. for the main meal on Mondays, Tuesdays, Thursdays and Saturdays except for Ember Days and Good Saturday.
3. According to a decree granted to this ecclesiastical province on May 10, 1889, the use of lard and other fat is permitted for the preparation of food for all meals on days of abstinence as well as for meat days. However, two days are set aside: Ash Wednesday and Good Friday. (TR)[71]

People gave up sweets or candies during Lent and many men would abstain from smoking and drinking alcoholic beverages. Amusements were few and far between, whereas events of a strictly religious nature increased in both length and number. People who lived close to the church attended Mass regularly during the week and everyone would do the Stations of the Cross at home and in the church.

Lent came to an end with Holy Week and the lengthy ceremonies called *Tenebrae* during which cantors interpreted the Lamentations, long plaintive songs. Good Friday was a day of great mortification. Some people fasted all day while others observed strict silence. Everyone attended the afternoon service. Lent ended with another series of religious ceremonies held in the church on Saturday; this marked the end of fasting and the beginning of the celebration.

Easter was a day for feasting on all the things that one had gone without for over forty days. People ate a lot of eggs. It was believed that when the sun rose Easter morning it danced, and that spring water collected before sunrise had medicinal qualities.

The month of May is a very important month for Catholics since it is dedicated to the Virgin Mary. This was particularly true for the Acadians who attended church every evening and said prayers for the month of Mary. People who were unable to get to church easily set up a small altar at home in honour of the Virgin. A statue of the Madonna or else a large portrait surrounded by greenery, flowers and candles was placed in a prominent position on the altar where the family would gather in the evening for the rosary and perhaps to sing hymns such as "Tis Mary's month, the finest month" (TR) ("C'est le mois de Marie, c'est le moi le plus beau").

Corpus Christi, a solemn ceremony in honour of the Holy Sacrament, took place towards the end of May or in June. It marked the occasion of the most impressive religious event of the year and one of the most spectacular pageants. A large procession was formed outside the church after High Mass. Children, members of the choir, altar boys and members of various parish societies, each following behind its respective banner, all took part in the procession. The priest, walking under a dais, carried the monstrance containing the Holy Sacrament. He was preceded by a group of young girls, dressed entirely in white, who scattered the route with flower petals or confetti. The route was marked with flags and the procession stopped to pray at several wayside altars. To mark the occasion, people often sported new clothes for the first time. In short, it was *the* outing of the year.

The blessing of the fleet was a very popular and picturesque ceremony which was normally held on the Sunday before the opening of the lobster season. Fishermen and their families went by boat to where the blessing was to take place and where they would be met by the priest, accompanied by several altar boys and a number of cantors. The people who were not able to be on the boats gathered on the shore to watch the ceremony.

The Assumption of the Blessed Virgin, the Acadians' feast day on August 15, often gave rise to spectacular celebrations attended by thousands of people who came from all over the province and from elsewhere. The festivities began with religious ceremonies and ended, as we have seen, with a picnic in aid of a parish project.

Blessing of the fleet in Mont Carmel, circa 1900.
Georges Arsenault.

According to the Catholic liturgical calendar the month of November is dedicated to the memory of the dead. The first of the month is All Saints' Day. It used to be a holy day of obligation. It is followed by All Souls' Day which was also celebrated in church by most parishioners. The collection for the day paid the honorarium for the Masses for the souls in Purgatory. Sometimes the priest and the faithful went in procession to the cemetery to pray for deceased parishioners. In some parishes farm produce, handcrafts and various items donated by parishioners were sold at an auction following Mass. The proceeds were turned over to the priest's fund again to pay for the Masses for the souls in Purgatory. According to popular belief amongst the Acadians of the time, the souls of the dead returned to earth on All Souls' Day. As a result you were not supposed to plough on that day for fear of hurting them.

The Feast of the Assumption

The main national event in 1893 took place in the parish of Bloomfield, an event which was a great success according to the newspaper *Le Moniteur Acadien*:

...The music was under the direction of R.M. Gallant and Professor F. Pitre, both skillful and distinguished musicians. One would have to go to the large cities of our country in order to hear a stronger and a better trained choir than the one we heard during Mass. A powerful orchestra, conducted by R.P. Arsenault, gave added splendor to the circumstance. A twenty piece band rang out joyful tunes before and after holy Mass...

After Mass, a procession took place, composed of the band, the societies of the League of the Cross and of the Holy Family from Tignish and Bloomfield along with the Assumption Society from Tignish.

At noon there were at least three thousand people on the grounds, and the tables and different amusements were very well patronized. During the afternoon there were speeches given by Mssrs. Perry, Howland and Arsenault. At six o'clock, the gathering dispersed to the majestic sounds of *Ave Maris Stella*... (TR)

Le Moniteur Acadien, August 22, 1893

The religious customs, beliefs and practices that we have described give a general idea of the religious life of the Acadians until the middle of the twentieth century. Religion played a very important role both in everyday life and throughout the main stages of life, thus providing a constant focus for all Acadians. It permeated their character and directed their daily existence.

Seeing the innumerable rituals and duties interspersed throughout the Acadians' life, one might have the impression that there was very little room left for joy and pleasure. In fact, while their religious ties were strong and they were generally faithful to the precepts of the Church, the Acadians also liked to enjoy themselves very much. Their folklore provides eloquent proof of this: a rich and extensive repertoire of music, songs, dances, tales and legends has survived to this day. One should not be surprised to discover in this legacy of oral traditions an abundance of songs and stories that are somewhat risqué! What is more, when the priest prohibited dancing some parents even dared challenge his authority by holding dances in their own homes. In their opinion there was nothing sinful in supervised entertainment of this kind. They preferred to be able to see their children having fun rather than have them out of sight and perhaps misbehaving.

Political Issues

The publication of *L'Impartial* by the Buote family added a new dimension to Acadian political life. Contrary to the newspapers of the time that declared their party affiliation, the new Acadian paper announced from the beginning that it would be "impartial". Defending the rights of the Acadians was considered more important than political allegiance and partisanship. The Buotes described their position in the following terms:

> With regard to politics, *L'Impartial* is strictly independent. We respect equally the two major parties which divide public opinion concerning the affairs of our country; consequently, our columns are open to both of them without any differentiation. However, should one of our own canvass for votes with the view of serving the State, then *L'Impartial*, will, in accordance with its motto, side with the nationality and will leave no stone unturned to promote our rights.(TR)[72]

However, *L'Impartial* had a hard time maintaining this neutrality. Various political, religious and economic circumstances forced the editors to take sides. They first turned to the Conservative Party, especially from 1896 and onward. It was during that year that *L'Impartial* directed a bitter campaign against the Acadian Liberal Member of the House of Commons, Stanislas F. Perry, accusing him of treachery for having voted against the Catholic cause in a Bill pertaining to French Catholic Schools in Manitoba. *L'Impartial* was thus partially responsible for Perry's defeat in the federal elections of 1896. After that, the paper continued to flog the federal Liberal Party and its leader, Wilfred Laurier, whom it accused of neglecting Acadian supporters in public offices. But around 1904, disillusioned by the Conservative Party, the Buotes stopped supporting it and sided with the Liberal Party then in power[73]. The latter had just appointed the first Acadian judge on the Island, Stanislas Blanchard[74]. The paper remained faithful to the Liberal Party until its own demise in 1915. In its final years, this Acadian publication even claimed to be "the French-language organ of the Liberal Party in the Maritime Provinces" (TR).

Despite its shifting loyalties, *L'Impartial* played an important role in Acadian political life. First of all, it often tried to make Acadians realize that they were sufficiently numerous in certain electoral ridings to be able to elect one of their own—if they united rather than dividing their strength between different parties. *L'Impartial* also constantly demanded that Acadians be treated fairly by being given their share of public positions, even in the highest echelons. It made one of these pleas on the eve of the 1904 elections:

> The only way to claim our right is to unite. Let us put politics aside in order to consider our situation. If the law of the land guarantees us equal rights, we are certainly far from enjoying this equality. Why not make demands, and if they are refused, we make them again. The time has come, the time is right.
>
> Let us urge our candidates on both sides to defend our cause, after all we only want fairness, nothing more.
>
> There is undoubtedly enough intellectual ability amongst our Acadians to be able to fulfil the requirements of these positions just as advantageously as English, Irish and Scottish gentlemen. (TR)[75]

One question which *L'Impartial* was the first to raise, and which still preoccupies Acadians today, is that of an Acadian senator for Prince Edward Island. Shortly after the appearance of the newspaper in 1893, one of the Senate seats for the Island became vacant. *L'Impartial* immediately asked that it be filled by a francophone:

> We still only have one Acadian in the Senate for all the Maritime Provinces, and it would seem reasonable that, given our numbers in Prince Edward Island, New Brunswick and Nova Scotia, the government acknowledge that we merit a second senator. We have amongst us the Honourable J.O. Arsenault and the Honourable S.F. Perry, both eminently qualified for the position from every aspect. (TR)[76]

The Acadians missed out on the vacant seat this time. But when Senator George W. Howlan was named Lieutenant-Governor of Prince Edward Island the following year (1894), *L'Impartial* took up the cause once again. The paper asked Acadians to unite in order to demand a seat in the Senate. The campaign was successful. In February 1895, Joseph-Octave Arsenault, after twenty-eight years in the provincial Legislative Assembly, was appointed to the Upper Chamber of the country. English as well as French newspapers were pleased with the choice. According to *The Charlottetown Herald*, no other appointment in the province to such an honourable post had ever been more deserved[77]. Not to be outdone, *The Summerside Journal* stated that this felicitous nomination crowned an irreproachable and honourable political career[78].

J.-O. Arsenault's career as a senator was of short duration. He died in 1897 at the age of sixty-nine. Thus ended the very brief Acadian participation in the Canadian Senate. Since then, despite numerous requests, the Acadians have never succeeded in obtaining one of the four senatorial seats reserved for the Island. In 1925, they mounted an impressive campaign to get an Acadian appointed to one of the two vacant seats representing the Island. Requests, resolutions and personal letters were sent to the Prime Minister by the Acadians of Prince Edward Island with the support of French-Canadian societies, newspapers and Members of Parliament. Finally, a small delegation of Acadians went to Ottawa to present a request directly to the Prime Minister. Once again they were disappointed, even frustrated; neither of the two seats was given to an Acadian[79].

Since Stanislas F. Perry's death in 1898 there has never been an Acadian from the Island elected to the House of Commons. The proportionately small number of Acadians in the federal ridings does

Aubin-Edmond Arsenault, politician and judge.
Public Archives of P.E.I.

not weigh in their favour, hence the zealous efforts to capture a seat in the Senate. In 1927, Professor Blanchard wrote:

> The Acadians constitute [. . .] about one seventh of the population. The Island sends eight representatives to Ottawa, four senators and four members of Parliament. Therefore in all fairness there should be a representative of the Acadian race. Besides, the Senate was created to facilitate the representation of minorities, all the more reason to let an Acadian in, given the fact that they are scattered in the various ridings and cannot elect a member to the Commons. (TR)[80]

At the provincial level from 1894 onwards the Acadians in Prince County succeeded in electing two of their candidates to the Legislative Assembly. Their members are from the constituencies of First and

Third Prince. Normally, when an elected Acadian is a member of the party in power, he is appointed to the cabinet as a minister without portfolio.

In 1917, the Acadians were delighted to see one of their compatriots become Premier of the province. The lawyer, Aubin-Edmond Arsenault (son of Senator Arsenault), became leader of the government after Premier Mathieson resigned. He was the first Acadian to become a provincial premier in Canada. However, his government was defeated in the elections of 1919. He was appointed Judge of the Supreme Court of Prince Edward Island, a position he occupied until 1946. The other Acadian Members of the Legislative Assembly who became ministers without portfolio during this period were: Benjamin Gallant, Jérémie Blanchard, Marin Gallant and Adrien Arsenault.

Despite the demands of *L'Impartial* and the Acadians, few Acadians were able to find positions in either the provincial or federal civil service. The rare posts they did occupy were of minor importance. The shortage of educated candidates and the lack of political influence contributed to this state of affairs.

If Acadians were conspicuous by their absence in the civil service, they were proportionately over-represented in the armed forces during the two world wars. The campaign against conscription led by the Québécois did not appear to have affected the francophone community on the Island. The large Acadian families there provided numerous young men to defend the country, many of whom died in action.

Agricultural Changes

GOVERNMENT ASSISTANCE

World War I, the Depression during the 1930s and World War II had a devastating effect on the international economy, affecting even the smallest Island farmer. But before the turn of the century, federal and provincial government intervention caused a total restructuring of farming on the Island. As we have seen, the cultivation of oats and potatoes for export had depleted the soil; even spreading mussel mud was not enough to restore all the nutrients to the land. It was thus necessary to find a way of using the land that would be less destructive.

The federal Department of Agriculture made the first move. The government representative for the dairy industry, Dr. James W. Robertson, came to the Island in 1890 to preach the virtues of dairy farming. He explained to the farmers the advantages of producing butter and cheese on a commercial scale. Rather than selling grain, it should be kept as feed to produce profitable quantities of milk. The manure could be used as fertilizer[81]. The basic concept was to complete the natural cycle by putting back the nutrients that cultivation had removed from the soil.

The federal government made a concrete commitment to launch the new industry. Under the direction of Dr. Robertson, the government helped farmers get together to organize and build cheese and butter factories. It became directly involved in these processing plants by providing construction grants, making sure the personnel was properly trained and finding markets for the products. The direction and assistance provided by the federal government proved to be highly beneficial. The first cheese factory was constructed in 1892. Ten years later there were forty-four throughout the province[82].

As a result of the growing interest in farming, the provincial government founded its own Department of Agriculture in 1901[83] which intervened at once by providing the farmers with numerous assistance programs designed to make their operations profitable. The federal government again made a substantial contribution to the improvement of agriculture by establishing an experimental farm in Charlottetown in 1909[84]. All these measures were greatly appreciated by farmers. A correspondent from Egmont Bay wrote in *L'Impartial* in 1905:

> If agriculture as a science remained for such a long time in obscurity, it was because our people were not supported by government as they are today. (TR)[85]

Acadians actually profited from the help provided by the Departments of Agriculture. In Rustico they joined together with the farmers in the surrounding English villages to found, in 1894, the New Glasgow cheese factory[86]. Similarly, the farmers in Egmont Bay and Mont Carmel turned to dairy farming and co-operated in the construction of a cheese factory in Abram's Village in 1896[87]. The Acadian farmers and their English-speaking neighbours did likewise in Tignish and Palmer

Cheese factory in Abram's Village, circa 1900.
Musée Acadien.

Road in 1898[88]. Butter factories were constructed in St. Louis and Wellington at the very beginning of the century, but only operated for a short time[89]. As we shall see, Acadian farmers also benefited from the creation of agricultural institutes and all the advantages they entailed.

EMIGRATION

In spite of all these transformations, the majority of Acadian farmers had no capital and were farming small acreages usually consisting of impoverished and badly drained soil. They were rarely able to provide a decent living for their large families. Looking for additional income, they began to turn increasingly to fishing or other sources of remuneration. Some farmers merely left the province. As in the past, emigration appeared to be the only solution for some Acadians on the Island. Good acreage was no longer available and, tempted by the abundance of jobs in the industrial heartlands of the United States, the new generation preferred self-exile to the difficult and uneconomic life of the small farmer. The poor economy of the Island, and the Maritime Provinces generally, resulted in a steady emigration that caused a significant drop in the Island population. It fell from 109,000 to 88,000 between 1891 and 1931[90].

This flow south of the border distressed Acadian leaders throughout the Maritimes. They feared that living in American cities, Acadians would lose their language, their culture and their religion. In the hope of stopping this movement, they recommended colonization even more vigorously so that new Acadian parishes could be created on crown land in New Brunswick. This argument was heard especially after the first National Convention of the Acadians (1881) during which a colonization society had been established. Several leaders on the Island supported this trend by encouraging their compatriots to become pioneers in the new settlements. Consequently, many families left the Island at the end of the nineteenth century and settled in Rogersville and Adamsville in New Brunswick, while other households joined the Acadian settlement of Matapedia in Quebec[91]. An Acadian from Tignish, living in Rogersville, wrote to *L'Impartial* in 1895 urging his compatriots to move to Rogersville instead of crossing the American border:

> I invite our young men who are not afraid of using their arms to come here and get good land which can be had at very advantageous terms, rather than ruining their health and becoming slaves on the other side of the border.
>
> Since we are condemned to earning our living by the sweat of our brow, it is not harder to work in Rogersville than elsewhere... (TR)[92]

The idea of leaving the Island to resettle elsewhere disturbed many people at the time. The issue was discussed at debating clubs. The question was asked in Duvar in 1896: "Is it wise to advise our young people to emigrate to Matapedia?" (TR)[93] The following year people in St. Louis also broached the topic and asked: "Under the present circumstances, is it more advantageous for our Acadians from the Island to emigrate to neighbouring provinces rather than staying at home?" (TR)[94]

Whereas many families went to settle in the new parishes, young men preferred the industrial cities of New England to the virgin forests of New Brunswick and Quebec. They emigrated to the United States in great numbers up until the Depression in the 1930s which slowed down the migration considerably.

The arguments in favour of colonization and of farming went hand in hand. The leaders of the time sought to keep Acadians in farming which they felt offered greater economic stability and a more promising future than fishing. The editorial staff of *L'Impartial* frequently repeated remarks such as:

> If one were to compare those who entrust their future to cultivating the land with those who stick to income from fishing, one would quickly reach the conclusion that the sooner they leave the coastline and follow the plough, the better off they will be. Let us work the land, it is our future. (TR)[95]

As we have already seen, ultramontanism, still the dominant ideology of the Church, made a connection between farming and the preservation of both the French-Canadian culture and the Catholic religion. Jean-François Arsenault, praising agriculture during a speech in 1932 at the first National Convention for Island Acadians, reiterated familiar phrases: "Farming is the basis and mainstay of our religious and educational institutions. It is farming that supports the country and that will preserve our language, our religion and our traditions[96]". During the same gathering, Judge Aubin-Edmond Arsenault declared that agriculture was the key to the national revival of the Acadians. Moreover he deplored the fact that educational establishments did not give agriculture the place it deserved in the school curriculum[97].

Acadian leaders often complained that farmers lacked scientific information. Most people believed that anybody could become a good farmer. Speaking to Island Acadians during the 1932 Convention, Father L. Guertin from Saint Joseph College in Memramcook, said: "The education in our schools does not encourage agriculture at all. To be a good farmer, you need an education. To carry out intelligent cultivation, the farmer has to work with his head more than his arms. A good farmer can never be too knowledgeable (TR)[98]". The possibility of establishing an Acadian school of agriculture on the Island was even considered in 1907 in order to provide young people with "the training required to make good and useful farmers (TR)[99]". Although this school was never created, a large number of agricultural organizations were founded over the years. As we shall see, these organizations provided valuable support to farmers from an economic as well as an educational point of view.

AGRICULTURAL ORGANIZATIONS

Interest in agricultural societies had manifested itself by 1898 in the Acadian communities. It was during that year that an agricultural club was formed by the farmers in Abram's Village[100]; their example was soon followed in Urbainville (1899), Tignish (1899) and St. Louis (1901)[101]. *L'Impartial* announced the formation of the Urbainville club in the following way:

> The people in Urbainville have just founded an agricultural club whose president is Mr. Laurent A. Arsenault. There are now seventy members of the association including several of the most prominent farmers in the beautiful parish of Egmont Bay. Regular meetings are held every fifteen days at which the main issues concerning ways to improve cultivation are examined. (TR)[102]

These clubs played both an educational and an economic role. The members co-operated in buying seed and selling their produce[103]. According to *L'Impartial*, "by joining this club, farmers took away from foreign merchants and buyers the right to monopolize prices and only pay what they want when buying from farmers. It is farmers, not others, who have the right to fix the prices of their products (TR)[104]".

As soon as the provincial Department of Agriculture took over these clubs in 1901 they multiplied and were henceforth called Farmers' Institutes. As a matter of fact, one of the first projects which the new Department of Agriculture on the Island undertook was to organize a network of Farmers' Institutes similar to the one that had already existed in Ontario for about fifteen years[105]. Department representatives visited farmers with the aim of encouraging them to form thirty-three institutes, each one overlapping two Lots. Each institute duly formed received a grant of fifty dollars[106].

Acadian farmers, who had already organized clubs in several places, welcomed this governmental support. For many years, the institutes located in their townships had the largest membership and were among the most active in the province[107].

The activities of Farmers' Institutes were varied. First, the regular meetings gave the farmers a chance to share their knowledge and experience. Often they had experts, provided by the Departments of Agriculture, give lectures on practical matters like the care and feeding of dairy cattle, soil cultivation and moisture content, and weed identification[108]. In addition, the Institutes purchased for their members purebred animals, farm equipment, seeds and chemical products. The farmers, for their part, co-operated in the marketing of their products. The Union Institute, which included farmers mainly from the parishes of Egmont Bay and Mont Carmel, was quite successful—as confirmed by the president's report given at the 1908 annual meeting:

> Several lecturers visited us during the course of the year to keep us up-to-date with the most recent farming methods; we have greatly improved our livestock, especially pigs and cows, by purchasing purebred stock. Several of our most dedicated members have won numerous prizes for their exhibits in Charlottetown and Summerside, and Mr. Elie E. Arsenault has just recently honoured the "Union" club by winning six prizes at the Exhibition in Amherst that brought him the tidy sum of twenty-five dollars.
>
> This shows the strength of the union and the spirit of emulation which the club has created amongst our farmers and encourages us to progress with zeal along the path we have laid out for the advancement of our profession. (TR)[109]

The institutes also stimulated the organization of co-operative groups like clubs for shipping animals to market, stallion clubs, and

Members of the Farmers' Institute in Urbainville, circa 1915.

Making hay in Wellington, circa 1910.
Fédora Arsenault Collection.

circles for egg production. The latter were established on the Island in 1913 and regrouped the following year to form the Egg and Poultry Co-operative Association of Prince Edward Island[110]. This movement proved to be important for farmers since the sale of eggs brought in an appreciable income. We should also add that the institutes took a keen interest in the younger generation, and organized school fairs and clubs for young livestock producers.

One of the main accomplishments of the institutes in the parishes of Egmont Bay and Mont Carmel was the organization of an agricultural fair. In 1903, the Urbainville branch of the Union Institute decided to organize an exhibition for its members. The event was so successful that it was repeated the following year but with the participation of the other Egmont Bay branches. The ones in the parish of Mont Carmel joined in 1905; thus was formed the Egmont Bay and Mont Carmel Exhibition Association which is still operating today[111].

Acadian priests played an important role in the organization and promotion of these societies. Some of them were influential farmers who practised the best methods of cultivation and livestock production. Disposing of greater financial means than most Acadians, they were able to procure purebred stock, the best seeds and the most modern farm machinery. Father Pierre-Célestin Gauthier was first president, then secretary of the institute in Palmer Road. Father Pierre-Paul Arsenault's influence was felt in Mont Carmel for a long time. When he died in 1927, someone wrote: "He merits the title of the apostle of agriculture and co-operation for his work towards the improvement of agriculture, and for his help in the founding of the Farmers' Clubs, Agricultural Fairs, and the Prince Edward Island Co-operative Egg and Poultry Association and many other such ventures (TR)[112]". Monseigneur Jean Chiasson from Rustico and Father F.-X. Gallant, a priest in Bloomfield and Egmont Bay, also distinguished themselves as leaders through their support of Acadian farmers.

LAND USE

Based on the dairy industry, mixed farming gradually replaced extensive farming which, as we have seen, produced mainly oats and potatoes for export. The new system helped to maintain the fertility of the soil.

Mussel mud was used in place of limestone for soil improvement until the 1930s. With the production and marketing of potatoes at that time, farmers stopped using mussel mud because they discovered that it increased the likelihood of a scab developing on the tuber. In addition, commercial products such as lime and chemical fertilizer proved to be more efficient and easier to obtain[113].

Drainage posed a considerable problem on Acadian farms, particularly in Prince County. Many of these farms were located on poorly drained, thus unproductive, lowland[114]. After 1915 the provincial Department of Agriculture helped farmers install drainage systems. Two methods were used: either a trench or an underground system of clay tiles. The first experiments on the Island were carried out in Mont Carmel and neighbouring districts[115]. This work improved the situation somewhat.

After the 1920s, the arrival of the tractor and farm machinery transformed farming methods on the Island and elsewhere. However, purchasing this equipment required both a large amount of money and a fairly large acreage. Most Acadian farmers were not in a position to fully benefit from these technological advancements. On the one hand, they did not have the necessary financial resources, and on the other hand their farms were too small to justify an investment of that order. Moreover, tractors were not very suitable for their lowland farms.

CROPS

The development of dairy farming resulted in certain changes in the acreage used for various crops. Hay production increased especially between 1890 and 1920[116], while oats as a monoculture declined. Farmers switched to what was considered better feed for cattle: mixed grains with oats as the major constituent. Wheat production dropped to the point of becoming almost insignificant for farmers on the Island. This was due to the abundance of cheap wheat originating from western Canada[117].

As we have seen, potato-growing increased considerably between 1860 and 1890, although there was a decline between 1890 and 1920 mainly because of the development of dairy farming. It was only after the 1920s that potato-growing increased and that P.E.I. became internationally renowned for the quality of its seed potatoes. Potato farming was to become a major industry. We should also mention the importance of the root crops like turnips and mangels (beets) that were grown mainly as fodder.

Around 1940 the average Acadian farmer owned about sixty acres of which approximately forty-five were cultivated: twenty acres in clover and timothy, four in cultivated crops (turnips, mangels, corn), sixteen in oats or mixed grains, and five in potatoes. The remaining fifteen acres were left for pasture[118].

LIVESTOCK

Since the tractor constituted a luxury unsuitable for some types of terrain, the horse still remained an important animal on Island farms throughout this period.

The number of cattle increased between 1891 and 1901 when dairy farming was subsidized by both governments. As in the past, livestock improvement was recommended and the Farmers' Institutes attempted to comply. The number of sheep decreased considerably compared to the previous period. The decline was attributed to the advent of dairy farming. Efforts were made, however, to revive and protect sheep raising. This resulted in the formation of the P.E.I. Sheep Breeders Association in 1913[119]. Sheep were raised just as much for their wool as for their meat. With regard to pigs, there was little change in the numbers in relation to the previous period. Poultry, on the other hand, increased steadily and surpassed the value of swine and sheep. Thus, in 1931, the proportional value of each category of livestock was reported as follows: horses 44.6%, cattle 38.1%, poultry 7.6%, sheep 5.2%, swine 4.5%[120].

According to the farm economist, J.-Edmond Arsenault, around 1941 the average Acadian farmer owned 3 horses, 6 cows, 15 sheep, 6 pigs and 100 hens[121]. The more prosperous farmers had larger herds.

Fishermen Organize

The end of the nineteenth century and the beginning of twentieth century marks a difficult period for the fishing industry in the Maritime Provinces. This was due to a decline in the demand for salt and dried fish in favour of fresh fish. It was hard to find the capital in the Maritimes to modernize the industry so that fresh fish could be transported to the major markets located primarily in the United States[122]. As a result, fishermen hardly received anything for their catches, if they were able to sell them at all.

Lobster fishing on Prince Edward Island, still the leading fishery, encountered serious problems: overfishing due to competition between too many lobster processors resulted in bankruptcies. In 1896 the editor of *L'Impartial* wrote about the lack of security in the industry:

> I do not question the value of the fishery off our shores, but you must admit that for the past five or six years the number of factories has increased so rapidly that a good many small businessmen have gone bankrupt, and today find themselves with neither factories nor land, victims of their own recklessness. (TR)[123]

In addition to these problems, it should be mentioned that the poor quality of canned lobster that some packers shipped to market spoiled the reputation of the product. Consequently, there was a drop in demand[124].

The innumerable canneries did create many seasonal jobs for fishermen but the ridiculous price they received for lobster and other fish was not enough to provide a decent living for a family. If there was a profit it was pocketed by the factory owners. Even then there were many bankruptcies. Fishing proved to be an unstable and rarely profitable way of earning a living. In 1897, at the end of a poor season, *L'Impartial* undertook once again to remind Acadians of this fact:

> The fishing season is drawing to a close. The relative lack of results will inevitably leave a good number of families in a miserable situation as winter approaches. For several years fishing has not been a very encouraging occupation for those involved. Generally, it is a waste of time and people become poorer and poorer. We absolutely must conclude from this experience that it is essential for us to find other more lucrative ways of obtaining the necessities of life. (TR)[125]

It goes without saying that the "other ways" meant farming; in closing, the author writes: "Let us conquer the soil, there lies our salvation" (TR).

Over the years definite attempts were made to modernize the fishing industry. The advent of facilities like refrigerated boxcars enabled fresh fish and lobster to be transported. But these innovations demanded large capital investments that the majority of the small canneries typical of the Island could not afford.

With the arrival of motor boats, the fishermen's work was made a little less difficult and less dangerous. By 1920 almost all the sailing boats had been replaced. With a motor boat fishermen could move around faster and fish farther out, even when there was no wind. If a storm came up they could take shelter in much less time than with sails.

The advent of motor boats did not change the fisherman's life from an economic point of view, however. Markets were still mediocre and prices relatively low. During the 1920s and 1930s, herring was relatively worthless so that fishermen were forced to sell their catches at an absurd price to farmers for use as fertilizer. Félix Gallant, a fisherman from Abram's Village, recalls these hard times:

> The only price paid for herring was fifty cents a barrel, at the beginning of the season, that is, when the herring was scarce. But, later, it went down to thirty cents a barrel. These were sold to trucks for the North Side fishermen. When these fishermen were well supplied, some would sell their herring to farmers at thirty cents a barrel, and others would exchange the herring with farmers for potatoes. The farmers used the herring as fertilizer for their land. The deal being one barrel of herring for one bushel of potatoes, which then was as low as eighteen cents a bushel. Herring had to be fished with the use of gasoline boats, so after gas, oil, and nets were paid, no profit was accomplished.[126]

Fishermen depended above all on lobster fishing in order to derive some sort of income from their work, but even then the net profit was negligible. A fisherman from Mont Carmel, for example, remembers one year when he only had $6.50 left after he had paid his expenses at the end of the season[127]. The meagre income from fishing forced many young men to work for several months at harvest time on the local farms, or leave for the mainland to work in lumber camps, or else as longshoremen in ports like Saint John[128]. It should be emphasized that unemployment insurance did not exist at the time.

CO-OPERATION

In comparison to farmers, fishermen enjoyed neither the same benefits nor the same favours. We saw how, after the middle of the nineteenth century, farmers began uniting to help each other and educate themselves. Acadian farmers established the Farmers' Bank of Rustico, granaries, and later on, agricultural clubs. Agricultural issues were promoted in temperance societies and debating clubs. Therefore it was the farmers, not the fishermen, who enjoyed the support of the Acadian leaders who were often themselves model farmers. Nevertheless, some members of the elite did take an interest in the fishing industry, but being fish-plant owners they were not inclined to support the organization of fishermen.

There were other factors to be taken into account. For quite some time the majority of fishermen had no control whatsoever over the means of production. While farmers owned both their land and their farm implements, most fishermen owned neither boats nor even fishing gear; they were merely employees, often indebted to their employer. This situation did not facilitate the formation of fishermen's groups, particularly since they had no educated leaders who shared their position. Moreover, government support similar to that given to farmers was a long time in coming.

In 1909, thirty-nine fishermen in North Rustico were the first in the province to join forces in order to run their own cannery because they were dissatisfied with the price paid by the local buyers. This regrouping turned out to be possible because, unlike Acadian fishermen elsewhere, the majority of the fishermen in North Rustico owned their boats[129]. The experiment brought about definite advantages, even though the group still had to negotiate with the local dealer who continued to fix prices. He was the one who bought the canned lobster, sold the fishing gear, and who sold supplies on credit during the off-season[130].

It was in Tignish in 1923 that the first real fishermen's union was born. Under the leadership of a local lawyer, Chester P. McCarthy, a group of Acadian and anglophone fishermen founded their own company in the form of a co-operative. By 1925 they were packing their own lobster and marketing the product themselves, bringing in much more than the prices private companies were paying[131].

Tignish Wharf

Five generations of the Poirier family in Tignish. From right to left: Colas (98 yrs.), Gilbert (69 yrs.), Jean (47 yrs.), François (27 yrs.) and Joseph (5 yrs.). Photograph taken in 1903.

There was nothing unusual about the problems encountered by Acadian fishermen on the Island; they were shared by fishermen throughout the Maritimes. Because of this general malaise, in 1927 the federal government set up a Royal Commission to examine the problems of the fishing industry in the Maritime Provinces and the Magdalen Islands[132]. The Commission recommended that fishermen form co-operatives in order to have a greater influence on the industry. To facilitate the process the Commission suggested that the government help organize a campaign to educate fishermen. The government reacted favourably to this proposal and in 1929 entrusted Father Moses Coady with setting up the program. Based in Antigonish at St. Francis Xavier University, he was to be the principal originator of the Antigonish Movement, a program of economic and social development which, as we have already seen, served as a model for the development of study groups and the co-operative movement on Prince Edward Island during the 1930s[133].

Father Coady and McCarthy, the lawyer from Tignish, exerted strong pressure on Island fishermen and before long they had the support of Dr. Croteau and his collaborators in the Adult Education League. Following the Tignish experiment several fishermen's unions were founded. Acadian fishermen belonged to the unions that were formed in Mont Carmel (1931), Miminegash (1935), North Rustico (1936), Egmont Bay (1938) and Skinners Pond (1939). These unions or "co-operatives" played an important part in the life of both the fisherman and his community. He quickly discovered that it was possible to improve his lot by putting into practice the well-known slogan "unity is strength". As soon as the fishermen had formed their associations and were operating their own factories, they received a better price for their catch. But the advantages went far beyond money matters. Thanks to unions, fishermen were able to meet to learn about economics, discuss their problems and try to solve them. This co-operation amongst fishermen contributed greatly to enhancing their trade which had been scorned for so many years.

The Prince Edward Island fishing industry was stimulated by World War II. Lobster and fish prices skyrocketed. There was a strong demand for mackerel and hake. These species were packed in the canning factories and sold to an international agency that supplied European clients and war victims. This upswing in the market improved business considerably for the fishermen's unions. The fortunate turn in the economy strengthened the fishermen's confidence in the merits of co-operation.

French Culture: A Difficult Struggle

Over the years it became increasingly difficult for French culture to survive and flourish on Prince Edward Island. It is true that between 1890 and 1910, the Acadian community seemed to be under full sail as it tried to regain the ground that had been lost in the past. During that time various institutions appeared, such as *L'Impartial*, the Acadian Teachers' Association and branches of the Mutual Assumption Society. In addition, the government agreed to appoint a francophone inspector for Acadian schools. None of these measures succeeded in stopping the anglicization already under way. Nevertheless, the tide was stemmed somewhat. When Senator Pascal Poirier spoke to the annual convention of Acadian teachers on the Island in 1909, he recalled for his audience the pessimistic outlook he had had around 1880 with regard to the survival of French on the Island. However, he stated that he was "happy to observe that it did not prove to be valid and that today French is loved and spoken more than ever (TR)[134]". Just the same, as Senator Poirier knew well, anglicization had not disappeared. On another occasion (1907), he declared: "In no other place in Acadia is the French feeling more alive than on Prince Edward Island; but, at the same time, in no other place is English more universally spoken in the home, and there lies a great national danger (TR)[135]".

It was not long before statistics proved Pascal Poirier's concern to be well-founded. According to the 1921 census, French was no longer the mother tongue of about seventeen percent of the approximately twelve thousand Islanders of Acadian origin[136]. Twenty years later, the figure had risen to twenty-eight percent[137].

There were numerous causes for this situation. One of the most important that should be mentioned is the matter of French education. While it is true that the Department of Education granted the Acadians definite privileges allowing them to include a little more French in the curriculum, in the final analysis the concessions made by the

Department did not amount to very much. French as a first language was only taught as a supplementary subject and was not compulsory. The curriculum in Acadian schools was thus heavier than in English schools. Moreover, the Department of Education did not take any steps to provide teachers in Acadian schools with appropriate training. It left the entire matter in the hands of the Acadians, without giving them the necessary tools and resources to carry out the task.

Other serious problems adversely affected the Acadian schools. Some schools, faced with a shortage of francophone teachers, were obliged to call upon the services of English-speaking teachers with little or no knowledge of the French language. In other situations, several school districts were mixed which meant that Acadian pupils were plunged into a school environment where English was the dominant language and French often not taught at all. It should be added that in Charlottetown and Summerside, where the Acadian population was growing continually due to increasing urbanization, there was no French education whatsoever available for Acadian schoolchildren.

Living in a milieu where the French language and culture were not highly regarded outside the home, many Acadians lost interest in a French education. In spite of their efforts, the leaders did not always receive the support required to correct this state of affairs.

World War II marked an important stage in the economic, social and political evolution of Canada in general and Prince Edward Island in particular. With peace restored, Canadian society progressed at a rapid pace. The development of technology and communications contributed to the total transformation of traditional life in Canada. Swept up by these extremely profound changes, the Acadian community found it harder and harder to protect itself against cultural assimilation.

CHAPTER V

THE POST-WAR PERIOD

1945–1980

A Rural Society In A State Of Flux

The Second World War was a major factor in the changes that took place in Canadian society. Even a small agricultural and rural province like Prince Edward Island did not remain untouched by these changes. However, the transformation was not as rapid as elsewhere in the country, particularly in central Canada.

Industrialization brought on a wave of urbanization which affected young Islanders and youth throughout Canada. Like their ancestors who had emigrated to the United States in the nineteenth century and early twentieth century, the sons and daughters of small farmers and poor fishermen moved away from the Island where only a few badly paid jobs were available and made their way to the industrial centres of Canada.

The Island could not keep pace with the economic and social development taking place in the rest of the country mainly due to a lack of financial resources. The majority of Island farmers had no capital and were thus unable to expand and modernize their operations in order to compete in the national and international marketplace. Reduced to living below the poverty line on their own land, thousands of small farmers were often forced to become mere wage-earners[1].

The educational system also reflected the poverty of the Island. Of all Canadians, Islanders invested the least in their education[2]. As a result, the level of education and literacy was considerably below the national average.

During the 1940s and 1950s steps were taken to modernize the province: the means of production began to be centralized and the economy became more diversified. Electricity was extended to all the smaller communities, roads were gradually paved, and radio, telephone and eventually television made their way into most homes. The consolidation of rural schools began in the early 1960s. All these changes contributed to the greater well-being of Islanders and raised their standard of living. Small communities which formed the basis of traditional Island life began to lose their economic and cultural independence, however, as a result of this modernization.

The Development Plan for Prince Edward Island, a joint federal-provincial program, was set up in 1969. This was an agreement which was to bring to the Island hundreds of millions of dollars designed to support a variety of development programs which would supposedly enable the creation of economically viable companies. This government intervention radically transformed the socio-economic fabric of the province and, in fact struck a blow to traditional rural and village life.

The Development Plan

This Plan is based on a development strategy that would bring about full economic exploitation of the Island's large and potentially profitable resources for agriculture. Other main features of the stategy are: a considerable development of tourist facilities; better utilization of forest assets; rationalization of fisheries; extension of education programs and training for the full development of the labour force potential; increased efficiency and some expansion in processing and manufacturing industry; investment in housing, health and welfare services and other infrastructures required for effective development.

Development Plan for Prince Edward Island. Ottawa, Department of Regional Economic Expansion, 1969, pp.23–24.

During the first ten years of the implementation of the Plan, the Island underwent profound changes: modernization of the educational system, diversification of the economy and increased governmental services. All this brought about a temporary resurgence in the economy. For the first time in a century there were more people immigrating to the Island than there were emigrating[3].

Nevertheless the Development Plan was not considered to be totally successful since several important objectives were not met[4]. Moreover, the authors and those who implemented the Plan were often accused of being insensitive to the preservation of local culture. The Acadians were particularly concerned about this matter since the Plan took no account whatsoever of the francophone communities in the province. There was never any focus on the development of a policy that would enhance the cultural and linguistic vitality of the Acadians. At most, the publications designed to describe the Plan to the general public were translated into French. Even this was merely to fulfil the new requirements of the federal government pertaining to the official languages[5].

Economic Transformation

FARMING

Contemporary times have been marked by the disappearance of thousands of small family farms and the growth of large commercial operations. The trend began after the First World War and increased considerably after 1945. There were over fourteen thousand farms on the Island in 1911 but by 1941, thirty years later, there were only ten thousand[6]. This number decreased with the passing decades so that by 1980 there were only three thousand farms left on the Island[7]. Those that did survive became proportionately larger.

Since the Second World War, agricultural products have remained more or less the same, the most notable change being in the area of production which became more and more specialized. Mixed farming had been the dominant trend on the Island up until the end of the 1960s. The following list[8] shows the commercial value of various agricultural products in 1979:

potatoes	25%
beef	21%
pork	16%
dairy products	14%
other crops	12%
other	9%
eggs and poultry	3%
	100%

Agriculture is still the main industry on the Island. Even though the number of farmers has considerably diminished since the turn of the century, production has actually increased due to the modernization and commercialization of the industry. The average farm today is a relatively complex operation involving large capital investments, professional management and, of course, a well-trained farmer. In addition, there are now innumerable rules and regulations controlling the quality and even the quantity of agricultural products.

Sylvère and Léo Arsenault's dairy farm in Abram's Village.

THE ACADIAN FARMER IN A CHANGING WORLD

Most Acadian farmers were not able to keep up with these transformations. Their farms were small and poorly drained and they themselves lacked both the money and the education which facilitated modernization. In addition, the Acadian youth appeared to be less and less interested in this rather unprofitable traditional activity. Apparently due to an absence of competent leaders, even agricultural organizations, so dynamic at the beginning of the century, lost their impetus.

Faced with this alarming situation, the Saint Thomas Aquinas Society set up an Agriculture Committee in 1944 under the direction of the agronomist J. Edmond Arsenault. Because of a lack of funds, the Committee did not last long but it does have several accomplishments to its credit, the most notable of which was the creation of scholarships to send students to the Agricultural School in Sainte-Anne-de-la-Pocatière (Quebec). Thanks to the financial support of the P.E.I. and Quebec governments, these scholarships enabled about twenty farmers' sons to take an intermediate course in agriculture between 1945 and 1961[9]. One of the goals of the Committee was to stimulate the interest of young people in agriculture. The provincial and federal Departments of Agriculture were already attempting this by helping with the formation of clubs for young livestock producers. Since the Acadian communities showed little interest in these efforts, the Committee decided to take on the task of setting up the clubs. It was in 1945, therefore, that the President, J.-Edmond Arsenault, sent around a circular to Acadian farmers asking for their support:

> It is an aspect of our agricultural organization that has been neglected for too long. Instead of moving ahead we have regressed alarmingly while our sister province New Brunswick and other provinces in the country have made very commendable progress. [...]
>
> The Agriculture Committee of the Saint Thomas Aquinas Society wishes to promote new interest amongst our youth in this type of agricultural activity designed to improve the state of our farming.
>
> We are requesting, therefore, that you take an interest in this question and that you discuss it with your neighbours in order to convince them of the need for this type of organization.
>
> You are no doubt aware that matters relating to our young farmers are far too neglected. We have no organization capable of helping them with their training or informing them about crop and livestock management. And yet these form the very basis of our agriculture. (TR)[10]

The efforts of the Committee were relatively productive: several clubs for young beef and poultry producers were organized in the parishes of Rustico, Mont Carmel and Egmont Bay. Some of the clubs were active for several years[11]. The Agriculture Committee also took on the task of providing study groups, schools and producers with farming publications and encouraged Acadian farmers to subscribe to agricultural papers. The Committee also raised the question of applying the necessary pressure in order to get the Department of Agriculture to appoint a francophone agricultural representative who would handle information and organization in the Acadian areas of the Island. There was not one agronomist in the government capable of communicating in French, which of course did not facilitate the formation and development of circles for young producers in the Acadian parishes where the young people spoke little English[12]. It was not until the 1960s that some services were obtained in French.

The Agriculture Committee considered other projects but, due to a lack of personnel and little interest on the part of the farmers, their accomplishments remained limited in scope. Numerous agricultural institutes and clubs petered out during the 1940s, 50s and 60s. The cheese factory in Abram's Village closed its doors in 1952 and joined several other cheese factories in Prince County to form the Amalgamated Dairies Ltd. The factory in Tignish closed down in 1961.

Despite all this, various self-help groups were created during the same period. A circle of farmers was formed in Rustico with the aim of jointly purchasing agricultural machinery so that about a dozen farmers could share the same tractor and other equipment. This provided a practical solution to the high cost of machinery[13]. In 1953 the parish of Egmont Bay saw the formation of a circle of Cheviot sheep producers which lasted for about ten years[14]. The Acadian Farmers' Co-operative, organized in the same region in 1955, enabled farmers to unite in order to market potatoes, operate a flour mill, and buy agricultural equipment and other items like lime, chemical fertilizer and feed. This co-operative was dissolved in 1978 mainly because of the limited number of farmers[15].

The drop in the number of Acadian farmers had a direct effect on the Egmont Bay and Mont Carmel Agricultural Exhibition. When the Fair was founded, participation was restricted to exhibitors from these two parishes, but in order to survive it was gradually expanded to include all of Prince County. Today the majority of entries in the cattle exhibits are no longer submitted by Acadians. Nevertheless, farmers of French origin can now be compared favourably with any other farmer on the Island and elsewhere; such was not the case a few generations ago.

The Prince Edward Island Development Plan of 1969 had a profound effect on Acadian farmers and on the entire agricultural community on the Island. Numerous small farms were sold to the government or to other farmers who wanted to expand their operations. In addition, large tracts of land formerly belonging to Acadians passed into the hands of foreign landowners.

While agriculture still formed the basis of the Island economy, it must be said that the impoverished Acadian farmers were able to contribute little to the radical changes that the industry underwent after the Second World War. It became particularly obvious during the 1960s that the Acadians had slipped into a marginal position in agriculture. To be on the fringes of agricultural production signified a major cultural transformation. One has but to think of the great speeches at the National Conventions at the end of the nineteenth century to recall the key position the Acadian farmer once held.

FISHING

Nowadays the fishing industry is without doubt the most important economic activity for Island Acadians. It forms the basis of the economy around Tignish, Palmer Road, Egmont Bay, Mont Carmel and North Rustico and provides employment for a considerable number of fishermen, fishhands and male and female factory workers. The fishing industry has also created jobs in trucking, boatbuilding and the sale of gasoline. Of all the co-operatives formed in the 1920s and 30s that we examined earlier, only two still existed in 1980: one in Tignish and another in Abram's Village. Both of these are large enterprises and constitute the biggest employers in their respective communities.

As in the past, most of the work is seasonal and does not last more than six months. For the rest of the year those who do not manage to find another job—the majority, in other words—can draw unemployment insurance which gives them a regular income during the off-season. The fisherman is no longer forced to leave his family and the Island after the fishing season in order to find another source of income. One should note, however, that this period of unemployment is not an off-season from the point of view of work to be done. During the fall and winter months fishermen perform various tasks including making and mending fishing gear, maintenance work on their property, cutting firewood, community work or taking retraining courses. As for the women, they constitute an important part of the workforce. It should be emphasized that especially since the 1960s, women make a substantial contribution to the family income.

The Development Plan for the province had a considerable impact on the fishermen, as it did on farmers. Various measures were taken to prevent over-fishing, to increase the income of fishermen and to modernize the industry. Programs were thus implemented to limit the number of fishermen and to improve harbour installations and processing plants. Fishermen were given access to training courses in their trade and could benefit from sizeable subsidies that enabled them to modernize their equipment and even to build new boats.

Since the 1940s, the Island fishing industry has become much more diversified. Lobster is still the main product but tuna, redfish, scallop and plaice have also become very profitable. In 1979 the commercial value of the principal species was as follows[16]:

lobster	$18,073,895
cod	2,002,742
scallops	817,082
redfish	787,835
oysters	762,517
hake	704,527
tuna	566,830
mackerel	544,985
plaice	425,307
winter flounder	256,613
herring	246,285

Many fishermen also gather Irish moss. This industry began on the Island around 1940[17] and has become relatively important today. The Irish moss harvest was valued at $2,688,903 in 1980[18].

A MORE DIVERSIFIED ECONOMY

The economy in Acadian communities started becoming diversified primarily in the 1960s. Nowadays Acadians earn their living from various activities and no longer just from farming and fishing. A large number are employed by small businesses such as construction, transportation, auto repair and maintenance, restaurants, the retail trade and others. Tourism has also developed in several areas, but particularly in North Rustico (located on the edge of the National Park) and Mont Carmel where the Acadian Pioneer Village (built in 1967) is situated.

The co-operative movement begun in the 1930s is still very much alive amongst the Island Acadians. Nearly every Acadian community has a credit union and a Co-op store. In the Tignish area and in the Evangeline region (i.e. Egmont Bay, Mont Carmel and Wellington) there are also co-operatives for the fisheries, forestry, tourism and health. They all constitute an important economic asset and a source of employment.

When the roads were paved in the 1960s, the great improvement in transportation meant that people could find jobs outside their communities without having to move. Many workers and professionals were able to be employed more than twenty miles away from their home.

The increase in the level of education among Acadians obviously contributed to the diversification of the economy. More and more Acadian men and women were entering the professions and their numbers were slowly increasing in the civil service.

The emigration of Acadian youth to other centres in Canada is still a fact of life, as it is for all young Islanders. The restricted number of job opportunites on the Island forces them to look elsewhere, mainly in the large urban centres of the country.

Wharf and plant belonging to the Acadian Fishermen's Co-operative in Abram's Village.
Georges Arsenault.

Changes In The Church

The Acadian community on the Island has always been concerned with the absence of French-language priests in the Acadian and francophone areas. The bishop was petitioned on this matter on four different occasions between 1946 and 1965[19]. In each case, he was requested to remedy numerous distressing injustices which included: a lack of religious services in French in parishes with a large number of Acadians; unilingual English-language priests serving in Acadian parishes; Acadian priests appointed to totally English-language parishes; and the virtual absence of Acadian priests in the ecclesiastical hierarchy. In the memorandum of 1954, the bishop was informed that the presence of priests who could only speak English was having a harmful effect on the religious instruction of the Acadians:

> ...there are many mothers of families in several of the parishes of the Diocese for whom a sermon or an instruction in English means very little. Many of these women have learned their catechism and their prayers in French. Even for well-educated people it becomes very difficult to use another language than their own mother tongue in the performance of their religious devotions. Many Acadian mothers find themselves handicapped in their efforts to train their children in their religious duties. We can assure Your Excellency that there are a great many such cases in several Acadian parishes.[20]

Although the situation did improve somewhat over the years, it must be said that even in 1965 the Acadians still had many justifiable complaints. In the parishes with a majority or a high concentration of Acadians, the number of priests who only spoke English was still just as high. The Saint Thomas Aquinas Society met with the bishop of Charlottetown in 1965 to present a memorandum containing virtually the same grievances and requests that had been made in the past. The prelate was reminded of the fact that, since its foundation, the Saint Thomas Aquinas Society had helped sponsor eighteen priests, nine of whom were attached to the diocese of Charlottetown, but that it was not always Acadians who benefited from their ministry. The situation is described in the following passage from the memorandum:

> Although the aim of the Saint Thomas Aquinas Society was to create an Acadian clergy that would be called upon to minister to Acadian parishes, its members

> are often disappointed to discover that this is not what happens. They are unable to listen to a prayer or a sermon in French in their own churches and yet Acadian priests are sent to serve in English parishes. We believe that our complaint is legitimate. (TR)[21]

At the end of the 1960s and during the 1970s, there was finally more allowance made for French in the diocese. Not only did some Acadian parishes receive an Acadian pastor for the first time in fifty years, but also several diocesan services were offered in French. We examine these in the section on the consequences of Vatican II.

RELIGIOUS INSTRUCTION AND OTHER RELIGIOUS ACTIVITIES

In most Acadian communities throughout the province, at least until consolidation, religious instruction took place in the classroom even though public schools on the Island were offically non-denominational. This was possible because Acadians went to district schools that were attended almost entirely by Catholics. The catechism was taught either before or after the school hours set by the Department of Education or, if all the pupils were Catholic, during school hours. In the latter case, prayers could be said also during the course of the school day and the crucifix and religious pictures could be hung in classrooms. The occasional complaint against these practices, made to the Department of Education by Protestant taxpayers, was usually sent back to the district school board in order to avoid any political controversy[22].

These practices were disrupted somewhat by the educational reforms that began in the early 1960s because, more often than in the past, a single school now housed pupils of various denominations. Today religious instruction is therefore given outside regular classes, except in almost entirely Catholic districts like the Evangeline district (Unit 5) where it is still part of the school curriculum.

During the 1950s, clubs for young Catholics were formed in several parishes. They were run by chaplains and continued operating until the beginning of the 1970s. The young people who were enrolled in these groups organized a variety of educational, cultural and recreational activities. In Egmont Bay, the Youth Club was particularly active under the leadership of Father Philippe Cloutier, assistant priest in the parish. The club took part in Catholic rallies, public speaking contests and hockey leagues. It also organized field trips, bowling leagues, night classes, study groups on religious topics and current events, and sponsored money-making activities such as an annual lobster supper[23].

The temperance movement which had constituted such an important socio-religious trend throughout the nineteenth century faded rapidly in the early years of the twentieth century. This decline in popularity coincided with the law on prohibition passed by the provincial legislature in 1900 and enforced throughout the Island in 1906[24]. Prohibition lasted on Prince Edward Island until 1948 without, however, eliminating alcoholism.

After lapsing for almost fifty years, a new temperance movement was started in several Acadian parishes. The *Mouvement Lacordaire*, a French-Canadian organization with the motto "God is first served" (TR), set about promoting abstinence. A "Lacordaire" or a "Jeanne d'Arc", as the male and female members of the movement were called, had to promise not to consume any alcoholic beverages. The movement was first set up in Egmont Bay in 1951 on the initiative of Father Charles Gallant[25]. Later it spread to Mont Carmel and Tignish and operated successfully on the Island for about fifteen years. During the more active period, the members in each parish district met once a month and also fairly regularly for larger gatherings in the parish hall. These meetings included speeches or lectures on various topics which often gave rise to discussions related primarily to temperance and religion. Some form of entertainment usually ended the session.

The Lacordaire movement had petered out by the end of the 1960s as attitudes changed with regard to alcoholic beverages. People preferred moderation to total abstinence. It should be noted that it was only at the beginning of the 1960s that clubs, restaurants and bars on the Island were able to obtain a licence to sell alcohol. Consumption of alcoholic beverages in moderation gradually became socially acceptable.

THE CONSEQUENCES OF VATICAN II

The twentieth century represents an era of developments in science and technology and profound cultural transformations. Urbanization, the development of mass media and the consumer society constitute the main factors in the social upheaval which has taken place particularly since the Second World War. Confronted with a modern world in constant evolution, the Catholic Church saw an urgent need to take on a new direction in order to adapt and to better communicate its message of Christianity. It was in this spirit that, in 1962, Pope John XXIII convoked the Second Vatican Ecumenical Council. Bishops from all over the world spent three years defining a new direction for their Church.

The consequences of Vatican II in the Catholic world were both numerous and considerable. Age-old religious traditions were suddenly changed or abolished, the catechism and the presentation of the sacraments completely altered, the role of the layperson in the Church made greater, and, finally, the Catholic Church became open to the idea of unity among all Christians.

This upheaval had significant impact on the average practicing Catholic. First of all, religion took on a new meaning. The God that had been feared for so long now became a God of love and liberation; in fact, a religion of fear and authority became a religion of love and trust. The ceremonies of worship were changed to facilitate communication and greater participation on the part of the congregation: Latin was replaced by the vernacular as the language for all religious services, and both laymen and women were encouraged to take an active part in the ceremonies. The Church became less authoritarian, no longer imposing periods of penitence and fasting such as Lent, but rather urging the faithful to choose their own form of worship. Vatican II stressed the participation of lay people in parish administration and pastoral work. The Second Vatican Council brought about innumerable changes that affected virtually every aspect of the religious life of every Catholic.

The Island Acadians adapted to these profound transformations without too much difficulty. However, their religious practices and observances changed dramatically, as did those of Catholics throughout North America. Many people no longer went to Mass regularly and no longer observed certain forms of worship; civil and mixed marriages became more frequent and, with the practice of birth control, families became smaller; nuns deserted their convents, many priests returned to secular life and fewer and fewer individuals felt a calling for the Church. However, since the Acadians lived in primarily rural parishes, the change in religious practices was less radical, or at least took place more slowly than in urban communities. It was not only the Second Vatican Council that produced cultural transformations, but also many new social and moral values that were to become synonymous with a modern society in a state of flux.

The recommendations of the Council brought about changes in the orientation and administration of the Diocese of Charlottetown. Several new commissions were set up including a Presbytery Council, a Diocesan Mission Council, an Ecumenical Commission and an Office for Religious Instruction. The Acadian community was represented on these various commissions.

In order to ensure that francophone Catholics receive services pertaining to religious and pastoral instruction in their own language at the diocesan level, the *Centre d'éducation chrétienne* (Christian Education Centre) was founded in 1972 on the request of the Acadian clergy in Prince County. The Centre offered various services in French such as catechism, classes for the preparation of marriage, family orientation and several other Christian training and education programs. The Centre also helped promote movements like Marriage Encounter and A.L.P.E.C., a program in liturgical animation through various forms of expression and communication. Priests and nuns were recruited to form the personnel of the Centre[26]. The board of directors was composed principally of lay people representing the Acadian communities.

The Christian Education Centre was set up in the Convent in Miscouche but later moved to the *Centre Goéland* in Cape Egmont. This centre was built in 1972 to fulfil several needs. In particular it was to provide space for the Boy Scout and the Girl Guide Movements which were started in the Evangeline region in 1972 under the leadership of Father Eloi Arsenault. The Centre Goéland is also used by other groups including *Jeunesse Acadienne* and the Tisou Cultural Camps and for training sessions organized by the Christian Education Centre.

Religion represents a very real and important element in the life of the Acadians on Prince Edward Island, although its influence has comparatively diminished. It is difficult to assess what place religion will occupy in the lives of future generations brought up according to the principles of the Second Vatican Council. If the present trend continues, the Acadian community, like any other Catholic community in the country, will be faced with a scarcity of priests and nuns since the calling for the Church has become increasingly rare. Undoubtedly lay people will have to assume a much greater role in the life of the Church. It may become necessary for Acadian parishes to reorganize in order to share the services of a less numerous clergy.

EDUCATION

CONSOLIDATED SCHOOLS

Two world wars and the economic depression of the 1930s left little opportunity for the province to make many improvements in its educational system. Being both a poor and rural province, the Island lacked the necessary financial resources for an economic recovery. There was, among other things, an urgent need for better schools and for more qualified and better paid teachers. This required a change in thinking since, traditionally, a good education was not regarded as a necessity. According to popular beliefs, any young person who intended to farm, to fish or do housework would be quite capable of getting along in life if he or she could read, write, and add and subtract a bit. Obviously this type of reasoning did not further the cause of education, especially since many children of school age were kept at home to help with work on the farm.

After the Second World War, governments were better able to implement social programs, several of which were directly related to educational matters. The family allowance, established in 1946, probably did more for public education than any other program[27]. In order to receive a monthly allowance, parents had to prove that their children of school age (fifteen years old or younger) were attending school regularly. The benefits were discontinued if the pupil was absent too often without a valid excuse. To control school attendance more closely, the Minister of Education appointed, during the same year, an officer in charge of school attendance[28]. According to Inspector François-E. Doiron's report also dating from 1946, these measures worked miracles:

Evangeline Regional High School in 1960.
Francis Blanchard Collection.

> The appointment of an Attendance Officer and the granting of Family Allowance, I believe, has been a forward step in education in this province. It is pleasing to note a very marked improvement in attendance in this inspectorate under the new system. In fact some of the schools are now overcrowded and hardly able to accommodate the increased number of pupils in attendance. It is true there are still some children of school age not going to school and trying to circumvent the work of the Attendance Officer, but as time goes on I believe the children will gradually become accustomed to attend regularly as they begin to realize that they cannot absent themselves from school with impunity as they have done in the past.[29]

The provincial government inaugurated a program of subsidies for the construction and renovation of schools in 1947[30]. The program was welcomed enthusiastically in the school districts. Throughout the Island, taxpayers were able to take advantage of this government support in order to make improvements to their old schools or to construct new ones.

Ever since the turn of the century, administrators in Public Education had been considering a program to consolidate small rural schools, thus eliminating the poor performance in schools where one teacher was forced to teach between twelve and fifty pupils ranging from Grades 1 to 10. Under these conditions it was difficult to provide Island students with varied and good quality teaching.

In 1958 the provincial government took the first step towards the consolidation of schools. The Legislature adopted a bill which paved the way for the creation of regional schools at the secondary level, that is Grades 9 to 12. This legislation encouraged small adjoining school districts to collaborate in the establishment of secondary schools. As a result of this law, numerous regional high schools were created all over the Island. The consolidation of elementary schools began in 1965[31].

We have already examined the economic changes brought about by the Prince Edward Island Development Plan of 1969. The Plan also made provisions for a major reorganization of the educational system designed to improve the quality of teaching, to double the percentage of pupils who completed Grade 12, and generally to provide Islanders with a flexible structure that could be adapted to handle both short-term problems and long-term needs[32]. A substantial contribution from the federal government enabled this restructuring to take place. The 217 school boards were regrouped into five administrative units in 1972[33]. As a result, the remaining small rural schools closed their doors and pupils at the elementary, intermediate and secondary levels enrolled in consolidated schools. This massive reorganization enabled more variety to be introduced into the curriculum and the quality of teaching to be improved.

It was at the end of the 1960s that important changes were made at the post-secondary level. The Catholic college, St. Dunstan's, and Prince of Wales College were amalgamated in 1969 to form the University of Prince Edward Island which, as a provincial university, was financed mainly by government. Holland College for vocational and industrial arts was founded the same year[34]. In collaboration with the federal Department of Employment and Immigration, these two institutions organized a very diversified program for retraining and continuing education.

ACADIAN SCHOOLS AND TEACHING IN FRENCH

With the arrival of family allowances and government subsidies for the improvement or construction of schools, Acadians, like other Islanders, became increasingly interested in education. However, studies carried out at the beginning of the 1950s, showed that Acadian children were leaving school at a very early stage, namely between Grades 6 and 9[35]. A committee of the Acadian Teachers' Association was instructed in 1950 to examine the teaching of French in Acadian schools. It recommended that parents be made aware of the importance of education:

> The first problem, upon which all others hinge, is to wake up our people and make them understand how important it is to send their children to school. How can we solve this problem? It would appear that the only solution is an intensive campaign carried out not only by teachers, but also by the clergy and other groups and individuals who know the value of education. To borrow a commercial expression: "We have to sell the importance of education". (TR)[36]

The problem of teaching in French was becoming more and more acute. There was still a scarcity of qualified francophone teachers which meant that many Acadian schools were forced to hire English-speaking teachers. In addition, the Department of Education had no program for teaching French. The Acadian Teachers' Association thus took the initiative and formed a committee to prepare such a program. It was distributed to the Acadian schools in 1952. A major problem still remained, however. Since the program was not recognized by the Department of Education, it was not compulsory and teachers did not always use it.

It should be noted that the Education Committee of the Saint Thomas Aquinas Society, formed during the 1940s, united with a similar committee in the Acadian Teachers' Association to avoid any duplication. The resulting joint committee took charge of the program for teaching French and the French competitions in the Acadian schools. In addition to continuing its program of loans and scholarships, the Saint Thomas Aquinas Society launched a student bursary program in 1953. It was designed to help get well-trained, licenced teachers for the Acadian schools. One of the conditions for receiving a bursary stipulated that the student agree to take summer courses in Education given in French[37]. The Saint Thomas Aquinas Society continued other projects which included setting up French libraries in the Acadian schools, making financial contributions for the French competitions and buying a subscription to the newspaper *L'Évangéline* for every Acadian school.

The directors of the Society also discussed the possibility of founding a central French school at the secondary level that would alleviate the shortage of French language educational facilities. The aim was to attract boys since there were very few in the higher grades[38]. This particular project did not come to complete fruition, but it did lead to the creation in 1960 of the Evangeline Regional High School in Abram's Village. Thanks to the initiative of Father Jean-François Buote, Euclide Arsenault and Ulric Poirier and supported by numerous educators, the Acadian school districts in the parishes of Mont Carmel, Egmont Bay and Wellington rallied together to build one of the first regional secondary schools on the Island. A French atmosphere prevailed in the school, located in a homogeneous region. The regular English curriculum set by the Department of Education was taught along with additional courses in French Grammar and Literature. Administrative and school activities took place almost entirely in French.

The direction of the school and part of the teaching load was entrusted to teaching sisters from the Acadian religious order, *Notre-Dame du Sacré-Coeur* in Moncton. They had come to the Island the previous year to teach in several of the schools in the Evangeline District. The sisters were asked specifically to promote French and the Christian spirit, a mission they carried out in Prince Edward Island for almost twenty years[39].

Outside the Evangeline Region, Acadian students attended various high schools which were established after 1960. Obviously English dominated in these schools and French was only taught as a second language.

An important step in teacher training was taken in 1959 when scholarships were made available for Acadian students from the Island to attend the normal school, *Notre-Dame-des-Flots*, on the Magdalen Islands. This represented an historic event because it was the first time future teachers from Acadian communities on Prince Edward Island could take Education courses entirely in French. The school was run by the sisters of the Congregation of Notre Dame. It was the Superior of the Convent in Miscouche, Sister Sainte-Charité (Eléosa Arsenault), who took the initiative to obtain these scholarships which were funded by her Order, the Department of Education in Quebec and the Saint Thomas Aquinas Society[40]. Over a period of about ten years approximately thirty young women benefited from these scholarships. Most of them came back to the Island to teach and are still carrying out their duties.

The creation in 1969 of a French-language teachers' college on the campus of the University of Moncton constituted a turning-point in Acadian education in the Maritime Provinces. The teachers' college has subsequently become the Faculty of Education which provides a high standard of training in French for any student who intends to take up teaching.

ADVANCES AND SETBACKS

After twenty-three years as inspector of Acadian schools, François-E. Doiron retired in 1962 and was replaced by J.-Albert Gallant. After his first visit to the thirty-five "Acadian" classes, the new inspector discovered that in seventeen of these classes all the teaching was done in English. Inspector Gallant also discovered that the knowledge of French varied considerably from one school to another. He recommended that the schools be divided into two categories with different French programs. As a result of his recommendation, the Acadian schools in the parishes of Egmont Bay, Mont Carmel and Wellington were grouped to form Section A in which French continued to be taught as a first language. Section B comprised the Acadian schools in the parishes of Tignish, Palmer Road, Bloomfield, Miscouche, North and South Rustico, and Hope River where the majority of the pupils could no longer speak French. A curriculum was set up establishing French as a second language, even though there were many pupils whose mother tongue was still French[41]. A few years later (1966) a study carried out in the schools of both Sections A and B showed that only 50.6 percent of the pupils of Acadian origin understood and spoke French[42].

During the 1960s the Department of Education showed more awareness than ever of the need for French education. In announcing

Delegates at the 1966 Convention of the Acadian Teachers' Association of P.E.I. held in Abram's Village.
Musée Acadien.

policy changes in his Department pertaining to education for Acadians, Gordon Bennett, the Minister of Education stated publicly that "there are no second class Islanders. The people of this province join other Canadians across Canada in our efforts to ensure that Canadians of either founding group may, wherever feasible, have instruction in their maternal tongue[43]." However, this new and more open-minded policy indicating both understanding and good will only seemed aimed at the Evangeline Region where the "dosage" of French was increased, little by little, in the school curriculums.

The schools in the Evangeline Region, regrouped in 1963 under one school board (the first of its kind on the Island), were thus given "unoffically" a special status. The Minister of Education recognized the distinctive cultural nature of the region and the primary role that schools must play in the preservation of the French-Acadian culture. When the government decided in 1972 to consolidate all the small school boards into large administrative units, the Evangeline School Unit, because of its special status, was left intact. It became Unit 5 with French as the language for both teaching and administration.

The reorganization of the school system on the Island affected the education of Acadians differently according to the region they lived in. On the one hand, the Evangeline Unit was protected and everything done to ensure a good standard of teaching in French. On the other hand, the so-called Acadian schools in the other areas of the province found themselves in the middle of large school units. As the smaller schools were gradually closed down, the Acadian students made their way to consolidated schools where French was taught only as a second language starting in Grade 3, or sometimes even as late as Grade 7.

The restructuring of the educational system brought about other changes. The position of Inspector for Acadian Schools was eliminated and replaced by the position of French Curriculum Advisor within the Department of Education. Superintendents are now attached to school units. The Evangeline Unit thus has a francophone superintendent, but his jurisdiction does not extend beyond the limits of the Unit. The reorganization of the school system made it more difficult for the Acadian Teachers' Association to meet since the teachers could not obtain leave in order to attend the meetings[44]. Hence, the Association held its last conference in 1971. To fill the gap, the teachers in the Evangeline Unit formed their own organization in 1975.

Growing Assimilation

After the Second World War, Acadians and their communities were becoming anglicized at an alarming rate. According to the census of 1951, there were 15,477 people of French origin on the Island but only 8,477 (or about fifty-eight percent) declared French as their mother tongue. Twenty years later, in 1971, the situation had deteriorated considerably. Of the 15,325 people of French origin, 7,365 (or about forty-eight percent) learned French as their mother tongue. Only 4,405 of these people declared that they could speak French fluently[45]. Already in 1956 the Inspector for Acadian Schools, François-E. Doiron, had deplored the ever-increasing rate of assimilation:

> As time goes by it is becoming increasingly difficult to preserve the French language in our province and there is no doubt that French is losing ground at an alarming rate. This is particularly distressing to those of us who have pride in our French origin and would like to preserve our language and the French traditions.
>
> More and more Acadians are giving up their language, and in several of our large French parishes English has been adopted as the language in general use, with French spoken by a few of the older people. Therefore, our only hope for the future lies in trying to teach as much French as possible in the schools.[46]

There were many factors contributing to this anglicization. French was taught on a limited basis in many schools, even if Acadians were in the majority. There was a shortage of qualified francophone teachers. Several Acadian parishes had anglophone priests for a long time. With the arrival of television, much more English was introduced into the home. Urbanization caused an increase in the number of marriages between francophones and anglophones. In order to find work, more and more Acadians had to move to Summerside and Charlottetown where the English-speaking environment made it difficult for families to preserve French, particularly since there were no French schools for their children.

It should also be emphasized that preserving the French culture was not made any easier by the fact that the language occupied an inferior status on the Island and in the country as a whole. Very often French was not highly regarded. In the homogeneous Acadian districts and parishes, French was still the language used in public meetings, religious functions and even in the workplace. In mixed parishes, however, English was spoken most of the time for any public business in the church, at school, at work or in community organizations even if Acadians constituted the majority. French was thus reduced to a language spoken in the privacy of the home or among friends. It is not hard to understand the feeling of inferiority many Acadians felt with regard to French, and even more so with regard to the Acadian dialect which was often ridiculed. It is not surprising, therefore, that many people associated their inferior socio-economic status with their Acadian origin and the French language. Thus they purposefully chose assimilation for themselves and their children as a means for social advancement.

Despite the strong trend towards anglicization, Acadian organizations such as the Mutual Assumption Society, the Acadian Teachers' Association and the Saint Thomas Aquinas Society continued to struggle for the preservation and growth of the French language and Acadian culture on the Island. In 1951, most of the Acadian groups in the province met at the third National Acadian Congress held in Egmont Bay. The aim was to assess the state of French life on Prince Edward Island as the president of the Congress, J.-Edmond Arsenault, explained in his opening speech:

> The primary aim of this convention is to study our problems [. . .] Factual reports will bring to light all our accomplishments, problems we have not yet solved, and the conditions under which we are working for the survival of the Acadians.[47]

This type of large gathering was more useful for stimulating Acadian pride than for actually finding concrete solutions to the problem of survival. The next congress took place in Rustico in 1955 as part of the "celebrations" for the bicentenary of the expulsion of the Acadians. This congress was essentially a patriotic and religious event. Numerous speakers reminded the Acadians of their forefathers' tragic fate and of their own duty to preserve intact the values cherished by their courageous ancestors. The Acadian Historical Society of Prince Edward Island was formed as a result of the interest in Acadian history generated during this bicentennial year. Nine years later this historical society set up the Acadian Museum in Miscouche.

Until the 1940s the Saint Thomas Aquinas Society had concentrated its efforts on fundraising to finance post-secondary education for young Acadians. The Mutual Assumption Society and the Acadian Teachers' Association looked after other projects related to Acadian life on the Island. Gradually, however, the Saint Thomas Aquinas Society increased the scope of its activities to include all aspects of French education. The Society also took an interest in the economic sector and had some success in the area of agricultural education and training. In addition, the Society tried to introduce the French language newspaper, *L'Évangéline*, into Acadian homes and to encourage a greater use of French in the convents and churches located in Acadian parishes.

It should be stressed that there was nothing unusual about the linguistic and cultural situation of Island Acadians. All French-Canadian groups living outside of Quebec encountered similar problems. Even at a national level, the French language and French Canadians were always alloted a very minimal part in any government institution. It was not until the 1960s that the federal government decided to address the issue. In 1963 the Royal Commission on Bilingualism and Biculturalism (B and B Commission) was set up under the joint presidency of André Laurendeau and Davidson Dunton. The Commission travelled throughout Canada in order to hear complaints and suggestions. The members of the Commission very quickly discovered not only the flagrant inequalities between English and French Canadians, but also the serious threat of assimilation faced by French Canadians living outside of Quebec.

When the Commissioners came to the Atlantic region the Saint Thomas Aquinas Society presented a well-documented report on behalf of the Acadian community on Prince Edward Island. The following five recommendations summarize the main concerns of the Island Acadians represented by the Society:

1) that a French normal school be established in order for Acadian teachers to complete their studies in education.
2) that the Department of Education adopt a special curriculum for the teaching of French in the Acadian regions of the province.

J.-Henri Blanchard Centre in Summerside where the offices of the Saint Thomas Aquinas Society and of the newspaper *La Voix Acadienne* are located. *Georges Arsenault.*

3) that all Acadians on Prince Edward Island have access to French language radio and television.
4) that bilingual individuals be hired in provincial and federal agencies.
5) that a senator be appointed to represent Island Acadians in Ottawa. (TR)[48]

After the enquiry was completed, the B and B Commission made recommendations to the federal government for major changes aimed at putting French and English on an equal footing. The result was the Official Languages Act passed by Parliament in 1969. This law was to have profound repercussions throughout the entire country. At last, times were propitious for French Canadians everywhere—especially for francophones, in a minority situation, whose cultural survival was obviously at great risk.

Great Strides

Once the Official Languages Act was passed, the government set up programs to develop a bilingual country. These programs, administered by the Secretary of State, had a notable effect on the federal civil service, arts and culture, school instruction in the official languages, and French language minority groups. All these programs affected the Acadians on Prince Edward Island in one way or another, although it was the program for the support of French minorities that had the greatest impact. It was called the Social Action Directorate and was designed to provide French minority groups with the necessary tools for their cultural growth. Funds and technical assistance were granted to representative organizations to help them meet their objectives. Youth movements and projects involving cultural and social activities also benefited from the same program.

The Saint Thomas Aquinas Society was recognized by the Secretary of State as the official organ of the Acadian community on Prince Edward Island and the organization with which it would collaborate in order to implement the program for socio-cultural action. The Society thus received grants that enabled it to maintain permanent administrative headquarters and to expand its activities. Up to that point the work had always been done by volunteers. The Society set out immediately to make the Acadian public aware of the need to preserve and support French life in the province. According to the philosophy of the Secretary of State in the area of social and cultural development, this was considered to be an extremely important approach:

> Activities that revitalize groups will enable the minority to fight against apathy and indifference, the main causes of assimilation. (TR)[49]

The Saint Thomas Aquinas Society hired its first cultural animateur in 1970. One year later, permanent headquarters were opened. The resurgence stimulated by this unprecedented support on the part of the government had been long-awaited in some Acadian circles. The Saint Thomas Aquinas Society, with the help of its cultural animateur, Antoine Richard, visited all the Acadian communities on the Island in order to involve as many people as possible in the developmental work that needed to be done. The results of these efforts were soon to appear: two French socio-cultural clubs were formed, one in the Tignish-Palmer Road area (Ti-Pa Cultural Club) and another one in Charlottetown (Port Lajoie Cultural Centre); the Acadian youth camp (Tisou) was founded in 1971; the newspaper *La Voix Acadienne* in 1975; and *Jeunesse Acadienne* in 1976. The Saint Thomas Aquinas Society increased its membership and was able to involve more young people in its activities.

Education was still the most important area of concern since the survival of the French language and the Acadian culture depended a great deal on the education the young people received. The Education Committee of the Saint Thomas Aquinas Society worked hard to convince not only Acadians but also English-speaking Islanders of the importance of French-language education. Seminars, workshops, enquiries, public awareness and promotional campaigns, and other activities were organized to encourage Acadian parents to demand French language education for their children. In 1974, the Saint Thomas Aquinas Society convinced all the school districts to take advantage of the financial help available from the Secretary of State and hire a French co-ordinator. The French Immersion Program was started and French-language teaching was improved in schools throughout the Island as a result.

After consulting its members in 1977, the Saint Thomas Aquinas Society drew up a global development plan for the Acadian community on the Island[50]. It was a five-year plan of action which covered educational, social, cultural, political and economic matters. After first seeking ways to implement the plan, the Society began expanding its services and activities so that by 1979 it had a staff of nine and was comprised of a board of directors, an executive and six committees[51].

The Saint Thomas Aquinas Society now assumed, more than ever, the role of a political pressure group. By various means including the press, petitions, requests, and meetings with the Premier and the members of his Cabinet, the Society demanded that the provincial government establish a policy for the development of the Acadian communities and government services in French, and that the School Act be amended to legalize the creation and existence of homogeneous French schools. The provincial government agreed, at least in part, to some of these demands. In 1977, for example, the Executive Council of the Island government set up a committee for the development of the Acadian communities. The "Acadian Committee", made up of representatives from the government and the Acadian community, was to act as an advisory committee for the provincial government. In addition, the School Act was amended in 1980 giving access to French-language education where numbers warrant it.

The Saint Thomas Aquinas Society is a member of several national and regional organizations working in similar areas. These organizations provide the Society with necessary resources, stimulation and support. The National Acadian Society operates at a regional level and the Federation of Francophones Outside Quebec and the French-Canadian Cultural Federation at a national level.

Throughout the 1970s, the Acadian community on Prince Edward Island showed signs of an extraordinary revival. Nevertheless, the process of anglicization and cultural assimilation which started over a century ago continues to take its toll. Today, over fifty percent of Island Acadians can only speak English. Numerous Acadian communities are almost entirely English-speaking. The English language is making its way into more and more homes—even in the Evangeline region where French traditions are the most alive and where the population is the most uniformly Acadian.

As in the past, the preservation of French life on the Island promises to be difficult. However, many people remain optimistic and still desire to live as French Acadians on their Island. Yet they do not want to live on the fringes of society. They wish to contribute to both the province and the country while respecting their history, their culture and their language.

NOTES AND REFERENCES

I. Under The French Regime: 1720–1758

1. Andrew Hill Clark. *Acadia: The Geography of Early Nova Scotia to 1760*. Madison: The University of Wisconsin Press, 1968, pp. 72–73.
2. *Ibid.*, p. 101.
3. See table given by Muriel K. Roy in "Peuplement et croissance démographique en Acadie" in *Les Acadiens des Maritimes*. Edited by Jean Daigle. Moncton: Centre d'études acadiennes, 1980, p. 144.
4. J.-Henri Blanchard. *Histoire des Acadiens de l'Île du Prince-Édouard*. Summerside: Société Saint Thomas d'Aquin, 1927, p. 8.
5. Le Conseil de la Marine, le 5 juin 1717. *Archives des Colonies*, C11B, vol. 2, pp. 110–111.
6. "Lettres patentes de concession de l'isle St. Jean et de celle de Miscou, situées dans le Golphe St. Laurent, en faveur de M. le Comte de St. Pierre, au mois d'août, 1719." *Archives de la Marine*, C11C, vol. 8. New letters patent in 1720 included the Magdalen Islands in the concession. See also C11C, vol. 8.
7. J.-Henri Blanchard. *op. cit.*, p. 11.
8. D.C. Harvey. *The French Regime in Prince Edward Island*. New York: AMS Press, 1970 (first edition, 1926), p. 64.
9. "De Pensens au Ministre, 31 octobre 1728," *Archives des Colonies*, C11B, vol. 10, pp. 157–164.
10. *Ibid.*
11. J.-Henri Blanchard. *op. cit.*, p. 14.
12. *Ibid.*, p. 15.
13. For a study on Jean-Pierre Roma, see: Jill MacLean. *Jean-Pierre Roma of the Company of the East of Isle St. Jean*, Charlottetown: P.E.I. Heritage Foundation, 1977.
14. Concerning Duvivier's expedition and the Acadians' reluctance, see Bernard Pothier. *Course à l'Accadie. Journal de Campagne de François Du Pont Duvivier en 1744*, Moncton: Editions d'Acadie, 1982, 195 pages.
15. Blanchard. *op. cit.*, p. 17.
16. Harvey, *op. cit.*, p. 111.
17. *Ibid.*, p. 116.
18. *Ibid.*, p. 119.
19. "De Pensens au Ministre, 31 octobre 1728," *Archives des Colonies*, C11B, vol. 10, p. 162.
20. "De Pensens au Ministre, 22 octobre 1729," *Archives des Colonies*, C11B, vol. 10, p. 233.
21. "De Pensens au Ministre, 30 novembre 1730," *Archives des Colonies*, C11B, vol. 11, pp. 95–97.
22. Harvey. *op. cit.*, p. 97.
23. *Ibid.*, p. 101.
24. "Duchambon au Ministre, 2 octobre 1737," *Archives des Colonies*, C11B, vol. 19, pp. 157–161.
25. Harvey. *op. cit.*, p. 132.
26. A. H. Clark. *Three Centuries and the Island*. Toronto: University of Toronto Press, 1959, p. 32.
27. *Ibid.*
28. Blanchard. *op. cit.*, p. 23.

29. Harvey. *op. cit.*, pp. 146–147.
30. *Ibid.*, p. 182.
31. "Vaudreuil au Ministre, 7 août 1756," *Archives des Colonies*, C11A, vol. 101, p. 85.
32. Clark. *op. cit.*, p. 198.
33. On this topic, see Ernest Martin. *Les Exilés acadiens en France au XVIIIe siècle et leur établissement en Poitou*. Paris: Hachette, 1936, 333 pages; Naomi Griffiths. "The Acadians who had a problem in France", *National Geographic*, vol. 101, no. 4 (Aug./Sept., 1981), pp. 40–45.
34. Charles de la Morandière. *Histoire de la pêche française de la morue dans l'Amérique septentrionale*, tome II. Paris: G. P. Maisonneuve et Larose, 1962, pp. 520 and 691.
35. *Ibid.*
36. *Ibid.*, pp. 519–520.
37. *Ibid.*, p. 692.
38. "Requête du comte de Saint-Pierre ou comte de Toulouse, Amiral de France, mars 1722," *Archives des Colonies*, C11B, vol. 6.
39. *Ibid.*
40. "Réponse à la requête du comte de Saint-Pierre, le 10 mars 1722." *Archives des Colonies*, C11B, vol 6. p. 6.
41. *Archives des Colonies*, G1 466, no. 36.
42. "Saint-Ovide de Brouillan au Ministre des Colonies, 20 novembre 1726," *Archives des Colonies*, C11B, vol. 8, p. 55.
43. "De Pensens au Ministre des Colonies, 20 septembre 1727," *Archives des Colonies*, C11B, vol. 9, p. 252.
44. *Ibid.*, 31 octobre 1728, *Archives des Colonies*, C11B, vol. 10, p. 157.
45. "Poitier Dubuisson au Ministre, 12 septembre 1731," *Archives des Colonies*, C11B, vol. 12, p. 178.
46. "Lenormant de Mezy au Ministre, 16 novembre 1732," *Archives des Colonies*, vol. 13, p. 79.
47. "De Pensens au Ministre, 31 octobre 1728," *Archives des Colonies*, C11B, vol. 10, p. 157.
48. "De Pensens au Conseil de la Marine, 5 mars 1732," *Archives des Colonies*, C11B, vol. 12, p. 195.
49. "Voyage d'inspection du Sieur de la Roque. Recensement. 1752," *Rapport concernant les Archives canadiennes pour l'année 1905*. Ottawa: Imprimeur Du Roi, vol. II, p. 127.
50. *Ibid.*, p. 132.
51. *Ibid.*, p. 143.
52. *Ibid.*, p. 148.
53. "Le Voyage de Franquet aux Îles Royale et Saint-Jean," *Rapport de l'Archiviste de la province de Québec pour 1923–24*, p. 131.
54. *Ibid.*, p. 133.
55. Clark. *op. cit.*, p. 35.
56. Blanchard. *op. cit.*, pp. 22–23.
57. Clark. *op. cit.*, p. 37.
58. Harvey. *op. cit.*, p. 195.
59. "Voyage d'inspection du sieur de la Roque. Recensement, 1752," p. 148.
60. "Prévost au Ministre, 31 octobre 1753," *Archives des Colonies*, C11B, vol. 33, fol. 279.
61. "Daillebout au Ministre, 7 novembre 1753," *Archives des Colonies*, C11B, vol. 33, fol. 95.

62. "Prévost au Ministre," *loc. cit.*
63. Harvey. *op. cit.*, p. 99.
64. Blanchard. *op. cit.*, p. 15.
65. *Ibid.*, p. 22.
66. Clark. *op. cit.*, p. 36.
67. "Voyages d'inspection du sieur de la Roque...," *op. cit.*, p. 149.
68. "Prévost au Ministre, 27 novembre 1752," *Archives des Colonies*, C11B, vol. 32, fol. 220.
69. Léon Thériault. "L'Acadianisation de l'Église catholique en Acadie, 1763–1953", in Jean Daigle. *Les Acadiens des Maritimes, op. cit.*, p. 194.
70. Wilfred Pineau. *Le Clergé français dans l'Île du Prince-Édouard 1721– 1821*. Québec: Les Éditions Ferland, 1967, pp. 14–15.
71. John C. Macmillan. *The Early History of the Catholic Church in Prince Edward Island 1721–1835*. Québec: 1905, p. 12.
72. *Ibid.*, p. 17.
73. "De Pensens au Ministre, 27 avril 1733," *Archives des Colonies*, C11B, vol. 14, p. 377.
74. Harvey. *op. cit.*, p. 204.
75. "Le Voyage de Franquet aux îles Royale et Saint-Jean," *loc. cit.*, p. 134.
76. "Prévost au Ministre, 31 octobre 1753," *Archives des Colonies*, C11B, vol. 33, pp. 279–287.
77. "Le Voyage de Franquet aux îles Royale et Saint-Jean," p. 121.
78. Pineau. *op. cit.*, p. 146.
79. "Prévost au Ministre, 31 octobre 1753," *Archives des Colonies*, C11B, vol. 33, p. 279–287.
80. "Mémoire à présenter à la Cour sur la nécessité absolue et pressante de déterminer et de fixer les limites entre la France et l'Angleterre dans l'Acadie...," (1753). *Documents pour servir à l'histoire de l'île Saint-Jean et des pays voisins sous la domination Française*. Collection compiled by Pierre Margry, no. 4, p. 135. Moncton: Centres d'études acadiennes.

II. The First Century After The Expulsion: 1758–1860

1. "Le journal des visites pastorales de Mgr Joseph-Octave Plessis (Evêque de Québec) en Acadie, 1811, 1812, 1815", *Les Cahiers*, La Société historique acadienne, vol. 11, No. 1, 2, 3, p. 81.
2. Duncan Campbell. *History of Prince Edward Island*. Charlottetown: Bremner Brothers, 1875, p. 5.
3. *Ibid.*, pp. 5 and 9.
4. A. B. Warburton. A *History of Prince Edward Island*. St. John: Barnes, 1923, pp. 146–147.
5. Clark. *Three Centuries and the Island. op. cit.*, p. 161.
6. Father Patrice Gallant. *Michel Haché-Gallant et ses descendants*. vol. 2, Sayabec, P.Q., 1970, pp. 22, 23, 29.
7. Georges Arsenault. *Deux branches de l'arbre généalogique de la famille Arsenault*. 1972, mimeographed manuscript, pp. 2–3.
8. J.-Henri Blanchard. *Rustico: une paroisse acadienne à l'Île du Prince Edouard* s. l., 1937, pp. 64–66.

9. Notes by Father Patrice Gallant. "Les Acadiens à Miquelon", dossier I, manuscript, Moncton: Centre d'études acadiennes; Blanchard. *op. cit.*, p. 58.
10. Warburton. *op. cit.*, p. 147.
11. "Le Journal des visites de Mgr Joseph-Octave Plessis", *loc. cit.*, p. 81.
12. "Callbeck to Germain, 20 May, 1776", *Colonial Office*, 227/2, pp. 84–85.
13. Paul Surette. *Memramkouke, Petcoudiac et la Reconstruction de l'Acadie 1763–1806. Histoire des Trois-Rivières*. Memramcook: Société historique de la vallée de Memramcook, 1981, pp. 42–46.
14. "Fanning to Portland, 30 September 1794", *Colonial Office*, 226/15, p. 531.
15. Clark. *op. cit.*, p. 50.
16. *The Colonial Herald*. 2 March, 1844, p. 3.
17. *Journal of Prince Edward Island House of Assembly*. 1850, p. 24. See also *Abstract of the Proceedings of Land Commissionners' Court, Held During the Summer of 1860....* 1862, pp. 54–55.
18. Naomi Griffiths. *The Acadians: Creation of a People*. Toronto: McGraw-Hill Ryerson Limited, 1973, pp. 73–74.
19. *Abstract of the Proceedings...*, *op. cit.*, pp. 150–151.
20. "Petition of French Inhabitants of Fortune Bay to Fanning", 4 June 1787, *Colonial Office* 226/11.
21. Patrice Gallant. *op. cit.*, pp. 118–119. See also the document published by the author which gives a report of the meeting of the Cape Breton Council on 9 May, 1788 during which Baptiste LeBlanc and George LeBlanc were questioned.
22. *Executive Council Minutes (St. John's Island)*. Vol. 1, 17 September 1787, p. 174.
23. "Fanning to Even Nepean", 4 October 1784, *Colonial Office*. 226/11, pp. 154–157.
24. Gallant. *op. cit.*. The spokesmen, Baptiste et George LeBlanc were among those who had presented a petition to Fanning the previous year. The properties referred to here are the ones the government of the colony confiscated from absentee landlords who did not occupy their concessions.
25. With regard to this trial, see the different interpretations: "Narrative relative to Prince Edward Island by J. Hill, proprietor", c. 1801, *Colonial Office*. 226/17, pp. 278–280. *Abstract of the Proceedings of Land... 1860*. *op. cit.*, pp. 150–151. Rev. Alfred Burke. *Catholic Parishes of Prince Edward Island*. Manuscript at the Centre d'études acadiennes. See section on Rollo Bay Parish.
26. Burke. *op. cit.*
27. Blanchard. *Rustico: une paroisse acadienne....op. cit.*, p. 30.
28. "Cécile à Plessis, le 22 janvier 1822", *Archives de l'Archidiocèse de Québec* (A.A.Q.) 310, C.N. I: 78.
29. "Cécile à Plessis, le 1 septembre 1822", A.A.Q. 310, C.N. I: 82.
30. "MacEachern à Plessis, le 8 septembre 1829", A.A.Q. 310, C.N. I: 86.
31. Warburton. *op. cit.*, p. 153. The author writes: "Some French fishermen had houses on Malpeque Point, where some of the castaways found shelter." Blanchard, in *Album-Souvenir. Paroisse St-Philippe et St-Jacques 1812–1962*, s. 1., 1962, p. 12, writes that it "is almost impossible to know exactly where these people settled. It was probably on the original properties in Lots 13 and 14." (TR) He does not give a source.
32. John Stewart. *An Account of Prince Edward Island*. London: 1806, pp. 167–168.
33. *Ibid.*
34. Patterson had already taken six Acadian farmers from Princetown (Malpeque) to court in 1780 for outstanding debts. They signed notes payable to order

on January 4, 1875. There is nothing to indicate that the money in this case is related to previous debts. See: *Supreme Court of Judicature*, 13 August 1780, Public Archives of P.E.I., R.G. 6, *Court Case Papers* 1780.

35. "Narrative relative to Prince Edward Island by J. Hill, proprietor," *loc. cit.*, pp. 278–280.
36. "MacEachern à Plessis, le 5 novembre 1805", A.A.Q., 310, C.N. I: 34.
37. "Mission of S.S. Phillip and James, Egmont Bay", in Burke, *op. cit.* Father Burke states that Compton made the offer in 1813. Most of his information comes from oral sources. In his correspondence, Bishop Plessis states that the offer was made to the Acadians in 1812, the year of his pastoral visit. See "Plessis à Beaubien, le 18 mai 1812", A.A.Q. 211A, vol. 8, No. 267.
38. "MacEachern à Plessis, le 22 octobre 1813", A.A.Q., 310, C.N. I: 46.
39. Georges Arsenault. *Complaintes acadiennes de l'Île-du-Prince-Edouard*, Montréal: Leméac, 1980, pp. 95–96. From the collection of P.P. Arsenault, ms. 92.
40. "Plessis à Beaubien, le 27 novembre 1815", A.A.Q., 211A, vol. 8, No. 511.
41. Blanchard. *Histoire des Acadiens de l'Île du Prince Edouard*, *op. cit.*, p. 105. See also the history of this property up to 1978 in *La Voix Acadienne*, 4 January 1978.
42. Until the middle of the nineteenth century, the parish of Tignish also included the parish of Palmer Road.
43. "Beaubien à Plessis, le 13 septembre 1817", A.A.Q., 310 C.N. I: 63.
44. "Plessis à Beaubien, le 16 octobre 1817", A.A.Q., vol. 9, No. 268.
45. "Cécile à Plessis, le 22 janvier 1822", A.A.Q. 310, C.N. I: 78.
46. "MacEachern à Plessis, le 8 septembre 1823", A.A.Q. 310, C.N. I: 86.
47. *Abstract of the Proceedings of Land. . .1860*, *op. cit.*, p. 50.
48. *L'Impartial*, 2 August 1894, p. 3. Article on Hubert Gaudet, one of the leaders of the resistance.
49. *Ibid.*, pp. 39–40. See also "Un chapitre des troubles à Tignish. L'année des 'constables'", by Gilbert Buote in *L'Impartial*, 3 March 1904, p. 7. The article was reprinted in *La Petite Souvenance*, Vol. 1 No. 1 (May 1978), pp. 14–18.
50. *Royal Gazette*, 9 July 1844, p. 4.
51. *Abstract of the Proceedings of Land. . . 1860*, *op. cit.*, p. 55. See the report presented to the Crown by the Legislative Assembly of the colony in 1850.
52. *Royal Gazette*, 8 March 1852, p. 230.
53. *Ibid.*, 3 May 1852, p. 264.
54. E. Rameau. *La France aux colonies: études sur le développement de la race française hors de l'Europe: les français en Amérique; Acadiens et Canadiens*, Paris: A. Jouby, 1859, p. 111.
55. Warburton, *op. cit.*, p. 147. The Acadians in Rustico, Tracadie, Bay Fortune and Malpeque own boats whereas the fifteen families in St. Peters Harbour did not.
56. "Patterson to the Earl of Hillsborough, 24 octobre 1770", *Colonial Office*, Vol. 1, p. 13.
57. John McGregor. *British America*. Vol. I, London, 1832, p. 332.
58. D. A. MacKinnon. "Fisheries" in *Past and Present of Prince Edward Island*. Charlottetown, 1905, p. 168.
59. Hugh Murray. *An Historical and Descriptive Account of British America*. Vol. II, Edinburgh: Oliver and Boyd, 1839, p. 269.
60. Patrick C.T. White, ed., *Lord Selkirk's Diary 1803–1804: A Journal of His Travels in British North America and the Northeastern United States*. Toronto: 1958, pp. 40–41.

61. *Ibid.*
62. John McGregor. *Historical and Descriptive Sketches of the Maritime Colonies of British America*, London, 1828, p. 74.
63. S.S. Hill. A *Short Account of Prince Edward Island.* London: Medden and Co., 1839, p. 7.
64. *Ibid.*, p. 18.
65. *Ibid.*, p. 21.
66. "Voyage de Célestin Robichaud à l'île du Prince Edouard en 1825", *Les Cahiers*, La Société historique acadienne, Vol. 6, No. 1 (March 1975), p. 45.
67. John Mollison. "Prince County", *Past and Present of Prince Edward Island. op. cit.*, p. 91.
68. *Journal of the House of Assembly of Prince Edward Island*, 1853, appendix R. The table does not identifiy these foreign countries. The term does not, however, include Great Britain or the British West Indies.
69. Marvin Moore. "The Island and Reciprocity Treaty of 1854", Harry Baglole, ed., *Exploring Island History.* Belfast: Ragweed Press, 1977, p. 159.
70. Mollison. *op. cit.*
71. *Abstract of the Proceeding of Land Commissionners' Court... 1860. op. cit.*, Testimony of Nicholas Conroy, p. 51.
72. "Patterson to Hillsborough, 24 October 1977." *Colonial Office* Vol. 1, p. 13.
73. "Petition distressed Inhabitants Island of St. John's, 20th August 1782 [Grand Rustico]". Moncton: Centre d'études acadiennes, 1.36–7.
74. These leases can be consulted at the Public Archives of P.E.I. They were signed on 1 May 1787. The Acadians in question included: John Gallant, Joseph Gallant, Alexey Duyrong [Alexis Doiron], Bartlet Mews [Barthélemy Muise], Simon Gallant, James Peters [Jacques Pitre], Francis Blanshard [François Blanchard], Lewis Gallant [Louis], John Peters senior [Jean Pitre], John Peters junior, Fearmin Martin [Firmin].
75. John McGregor. *Historical and Descriptive.... op. cit.*, p. 74.
76. Elinor Vass. "The Agricultural Societies of Prince Edward Island", *The Island Magazine*, No. 7 (Fall-Winter 1979), p. 32.
77. *Ibid.*, p. 34.
78. John McGregor. *British America*, Vol. 1, *op. cit.*, p. 324.
79. John McGregor. *Historical and Descriptive Sketches....op. cit.*, pp. 74–75. *Information to Emigrants. An Account of the Island of Prince Edward*, London, 1819.
80. John Lawson. *Letters on Prince Edward Island.* Charlottetown: George T. Haszard, 1851, p. 38.
81. *Abstract of the Proceeding of Land Commissionners' Court... 1860. op. cit.*, p. 231. Testimony of Henry J. Cundall.
82. "Voyage de Célestin Robichaud...", *op. cit.*, p.45.
83. "Indenture between Harry Compton and the Tenants of St. Eleanors Village, March 1st, 1807", Public Archives of P.E.I., Conveyance Register, liber 16, folio 45.
84. *The Examiner*, 24 November 1856, p. 79.
85. Clark. *Three Centuries and the Island. op. cit.*, pp. 74 and 104.
86. "Voyage de Célestin Robichaud...", *op. cit.*, p. 45.
87. Joseph Bouchette. *The British Dominions in North America.* London: 1831, p. 122.
88. Clark. *op. cit.*, pp. 41 et 63.
89. "Holland to Hillsborough, 28 November 1764," Public Archives of P.E.I., 2324 8a.

90. McGregor. *British America*. Vol. 1, p. 323.
91. Clark. *op. cit.*, p. 69.
92. "Voyage de Célestin Robichaud...", *op. cit.*, p. 45.
93. Clark. *op. cit.*, p. 76.
94. *Ibid.*, pp. 77 and 112.
95. "Indenture between Harry Compton and the Tenants of St. Eleanors...", *op. cit.*
96. Lawson. *op. cit.*, p. 39.
97. Georges Arsenault. *Courir la Chandeleur.* Moncton: Editions d'Acadie, 1982, p. 116.
98. Léon Thériault. "L'Acadianisation de l'Église catholique en Acadie, 1763–1953", in Jean Daigle, ed., *Les Acadiens des Maritimes. op. cit.*, p. 297.
99. John Garner. "The Enfranchisement of Roman Catholics in the Maritimes", *The Canadian Historical Review*, Vol. 34, No. 9, 1953, p. 203.
100. *Ibid.*, p. 205.
101. *Ibid.*, pp. 210–213.
102. Thériault. *op. cit.*, p. 297.
103. *Ibid.*, pp. 310–311.
104. Quoted in Pineau. *Le Clergé français dans l'Île du Prince-Edouard 1721–1821. op. cit.*, p. 41.
105. Thériault. *op. cit.*, p. 297.
106. Quoted in Pineau. *op. cit.*, p. 52.
107. *Ibid.*, p. 52.
108. Pineau. *op. cit.*, pp. 57–58.
109. *Ibid.*, p. 53.
110. *Mémoire sur les missions de la Nouvelle-Ecosse, du Cap-Breton et de l'Île-du-Prince-Édouard de 1760 à 1820....* Québec: C. Darveau, 1895, p. 50. "Ledru à l'Évêque de Québec, le 1er juin 1787". *Archives de l'Archidiocèse de Québec* (A.A.Q.), 311, III-5. Father William Phelan, an Irish priest in Arichat (N.S.), received permission to serve the Acadian regions, but the Acadians in Malpeque do not appear to have appreciated him. They preferred to bring in, at their own expense, Father LeRoux from Memramcook. He stayed with them on several occasions between 1786 and 1788. Finally, after insisting, the Island Acadians were visited by Father Ledru (in charge of the missions in St. Mary's Bay, N.S.) towards the end of 1786.
111. Macmillan. *op. cit.*, pp. 74 and 89.
112. "Plessis à MacEachern, le 23 juillet 1798." A.A.Q., 211A, III-64.
113. Pineau. *op. cit.*, pp. 68–69.
114. *Ibid.*, A third French priest, Father Gabriel Champion, arrived on the Island in the autumn of 1800. He spent the winter in Bay Fortune but was sent by the bishop to Cape Breton in the spring.
115. *Ibid.*, p. 95.
116. *Ibid.*, p. 109.
117. "Cécile à Plessis, le 10 octobre 1821." A.A.Q., 310, C.N. I: 79.
118. "Cécile à Plessis, le 24 mai 1819." A.A.Q., 310, C.N. I: 74.
119. *Ibid.* and Macmillan. *op. cit.*, p. 206.
120. "MacEachern à Plessis, le 17 décembre 1825," A.A.Q. 310 C.N. I: 96. "Cécile à Plessis, le 20 mai 1820," A.A.Q. 310 C.N. I: 75. "Cécile à Plessis, le 1er mai 1821," A.A.Q. 310 C.N. I: 78.
121. Pineau. *op. cit.*, pp. 134–140.

122. Rev. John C. Macmillan. *The History of the Catholic Church in Prince Edward Island from 1835 till 1891*. Québec: L'Evénement Printing Co., 1913, pp. 35, 67, 77. They were Fathers Nazaire-Charles Boudreault, Cajétan Miville et Mathurin Dabareul.
123. "Peter McIntyre à (J.O. Paré), le 29 septembre 1857." *Archives de la Chancellerie de l'Archidiocèse de Montréal* (A.C.A.M.), 255.103, 857–1.
124. "Aubré à (J.O. Paré), le 2 juin 1858." A.C.A.M., 255.103, 858–2.
125. "De Calonne à Plessis, le 14 août 1800." Centre d'études acadiennes, 22. 2–6 (copy).
126. "Plessis à de Calonne, le 4 octobre 1800." A.A.Q., 211A, III: 220.
127. "Beaubien à Mgr Plessis, le 3 octobre 1812." A.A.Q., 310 C.N. I: 39.
128. "Cécile à Mgr Plessis, le 10 octobre 1818." A.A.Q., 310 C.N. I: 68.
129. J.-Henri Blanchard. "L'instruction chez les Acadiens de l'Île-du-Prince-Édouard", *Compte rendu: La Convention Nationale Acadienne de l'Île-du-Prince-Édouard*, 1951, p. 31.
130. "Secretary of State Portland to Governor Fanning, 20 July 1800." Colonial Office series 226, vol. 16, pp. 106–107.
131. "Beaubien à Mgr Plessis, le 15 novembre 1814." A.A.Q., 310 C.N. I: 48.
132. "Beaubien à Mgr Plessis, le 3 janvier 1816." A.A.Q., 310 C.N. I: 53.
133. *The Examiner*, 6 April 1857, p. (153).
134. "Ant. Gagnon à Mgr Plessis, le 2 mai 1821." A.A.Q. 311 NB C.N. 5–54. Father Gagnon, the missionary from Memramcook, gives a biographical sketch of Dominique Charles Auffray. He says that Auffray taught in Tignish from 1816 to 1819. Gilbert Buote states in his history of Cascumpec that a "Dominique Auffry" taught there for several years. See *L'Impartial*, 17 March 1904, p. 3.
135. John McGregor. *op. cit.*, pp. 201–202.
136. D.C. Harvey, ed., *Journeys to the Island of St. John or Prince Edward Island 1775–1832*. Toronto: MacMillan, 1955, p. 178.
137. S.N. Robertson. "The Public School System", *Past and Present of Prince Edward Island. op. cit.*, p. 364a.
138. Harvey. *op. cit.*
139. Robertson. *op. cit.*, p. 365a.
140. *Assembly Journal*, P.E.I., 1838, Appendix B.
141. *Assembly Journal*, P.E.I., 1842, Appendix D., p. 11.
142. *Acts of the General Assembly of P.E.I.*, 1852, pp. 92, 96.
143. Ian Ross Robertson. "The Bible Question in Prince Edward Island from 1856 to 1860", *Acadiensis*, Vol. V, No. 2 (Spring 1976) p. 5.
144. *Assembly Journal*, P.E.I., 1831. See: "Copy of the Warrant Book, from 1st February 1830 to 31st January 1831".
145. *Laws of Prince Edward Island 1825–1833*, p. 209.
146. *Assembly Journal*, P.E.I., 1834, pp. 22–23.
147. John Richard Bott was from the Isle of Jersey. See: "John Richard Bott (1792–1862) and his Descendants", *History of Saint Anthony Parish 1803–1980, Bloomfield*. Bloomfield Historical Society (1980), p. 66. Pierre Dollard, who also signed his name Petre Dallar, lived in Tracadie (N.S.) at least between 1817 and 1828 before moving to P.E.I. His nationality is uncertain. See the notes on the Dallaire family at the Centre d'études acadiennes, Université de Moncton.
148. *Assembly Journal*, P.E.I., 1845, Appendix H, p. 48.

149. *Ibid.*, p. 41.
150. An amendement to the School Act in 1844 stipulated that a teacher in an Acadian school who did not have certification from the School Board could still receive the annual stipend of 5 pounds if he attested that he was of good character and had taught at least twenty school children for one year. *Acts of the General Assembly of P.E.I.*, 1844, p. 1087.
151. *Acts of the General Assembly of P.E.I.*, 1847, p. 182.
152. *Assembly Journal*, P.E.I., 1847, Appendix F.
153. *Acts of the General Assembly of P.E.I.*, 1854, pp. 55–56.
154. *Assembly Journal*, P.E.I., 1855, Appendix M.
155. *Assembly Journal*, P.E.I., 1847, Appendix F. "The Catholic Clergyman resident at Tignish, to whose influence and zealous efforts for their improvement much of this change is to be attributed, has stated to me his opinion that the Acadian Schools will, in a few years be qualified to rank among the District Schools of the Island."
156. "Perrey (Poirier) à Cazeau, le 30 mai 1845," A.A.Q. 310 C.N. II-114.
157. "MacDonald à Cazeau, le 19 août 1848," A.A.Q. 310 C.N. II: 45.
158. "Perrey (Poirier) à Cazeau, le 27 juillet 1846, A.A.Q. 310 C.N. II-116.
159. *Assembly Journal*, P.E.I., 1843, Appendix F, p. 25. It is difficult to determine precisely the size of the Acadian population on the Island for this period. Joseph Bouchette, in *The British Dominions in North America* (Vol. II, p. 178) gives an estimate of 4,000 around 1830. The historian, J.-Henri Blanchard, states that the Acadian population was estimated at approximately 9,000 in 1860 (*Histoire des Acadiens de l'Île-du-Prince-Édouard*, p. 59).
160. *Assembly Journal*, P.E.I., 1855, Appendix M.
161. *Assembly Journal*, P.E.I., 1850, "Report of the Visitor of District Schools for Prince County for the year 1849".
162. *Assembly Journal*, P.E.I., 1843, Appendix B, p. 24.
163. *Ibid.*
164. *Assembly Journal*, P.E.I., 1851, Appendix R.
165. *Assembly Journal*, P.E.I., 1838, Appendix B.
166. See: Georges Arsenault. *L'Education chez les Acadiens de l'Île-du-Prince-Édouard*. Summerside: Société Saint Thomas d'Aquin, 1982, pp. 11–19.
167. John McGregor. *British America*. *op. cit.*, pp. 198–199.
168. S. S. Hill. *op. cit.*, p. 7.
169. *Ibid.*, pp. 6 and 21.
170. Bouchette. *The British Dominions in North America*. *op. cit.*, p. 178.
171. McGregor. *British America*. *op. cit.*, p. 198.
172. *Executive Council Minutes (St. John's Island)*, 6 June 1792, p. 290.
173. *Colonial Office*. 226/21, pp. 529–536.
174. *The Summerside Progress*, 1 June 1868, p. 1.

III. A Period Of Transition: 1860–1890

1. "Rapport de M. Poirier sur la situation particulière des Acadiens dans la Confédération", in J.-J.-B. Chouinard, *Fête Nationale des Canadiens-français célébrée à Québec en 1880*.... Québec: l'Imprimerie A. Côté et Cie, 1881, p. 448.

2. *The Summerside Journal*, 14 April 1870, p. 2.
3. See the speech given by Stanislas Poirier at the first national convention of the Acadians and published by Ferdinand J. Robichaud *Conventions Nationales des Acadiens*, Shédiac, 1970, p. 79.
4. *Le Moniteur Acadien*, 29 April 1880, p. 1; 10 June 1880, p. 2.
5. *Ibid.*, 20 November 1884, p. 2.
6. *The Summerside Progress*, 1 June 1868, p. 1; 15 June 1868, p. 1.
7. *Le Moniteur Acadien*, 20 May 1880, p. 2.
8. Blanchard. *Histoire des Acadiens de l'Île du Prince-Édouard. op. cit.*, p. 59.
9. Muriel K. Roy. "Peuplement et croissance démographique en Acadie", in Jean Daigle, ed., *Les Acadiens des Maritimes. op. cit.*, pp. 180 and 197. This was the first federal census after the Island entered Confederation in 1873.
10. *L'Eglise catholique à l'Île-du-Prince-Édouard 1720–1979*. Charlottetown: La Corporation épiscopale catholique romaine, 1979. See Chapter IV, "L'épiscopat le plus long" by Rev. Dr Wendell P.H. MacIntyre, pp. 77–111.
11. The priests from Quebec were: George-Antoine Belcourt, Joseph Quévillon, André Roy, G.A. Picotte, J.-S. Turbide, Cajétan Miville, F.X. Delangie and Azade Trudel although he was ordained on the Island.
12. The priests in question were: Charles-Nazaire-Antoine Boudreault and Stanislaus-A. Boudreault.
13. They included the Frenchman, Gérard de Finance and the Belgian, Félix-Von Blerk.
14. The priests of Scottish origin included: Fathers Dugald M. MacDonald, Ronald B. MacDonald, John A. MacDonald and R.P. MacPhee.
15. *The Summerside Progress*, 1 June 1868, p. 1.
16. "Landry à Rameau, le 20 mai 1867." Centre d'études acadiennes, 2.1–8.
17. Centre d'études acadiennes, Georges Arsenault Collection, tape 1175. Informant: M. Charles M. Arsenault.
18. "Père N.-C.-A. Boudreault à Mgr Peter McIntyre, le 27 janvier 1888." *Archives du diocèse de Charlottetown*. Boudreault does not give the exact date for these events. He merely states that they took place after 1879 when he became the priest at Miscouche and was responsible for the Mont Carmel mission. Blind and retired, Father Poirier was still living in Mont Carmel. He published an announcement in the *Moniteur Acadien*, 23 September 1875, "urgently requesting that any persons having claims against him present them as soon as possible in order that he may settle them and that any persons owing him anything settle forthwith." (TR)
19. Father Anselme Chiasson. "Le clergé et le réveil acadien (1864–1960)", *Revue de l'Université de Moncton*, Vol. II, No. 1 (Feb. 1978), pp. 43–46.
20. Quoted in Robidoux. *Conventions Nationales des Acadiens, op. cit.*, p. 7.
21. Macmillan. *The History of the Catholic Church in Prince Edward Island from 1835 till 1891. op, cit.*, pp. 79–81.
22. "Belcourt à Cazeau, le 28 septembre 1860," A.A.Q., C.N. II: 82.
23. "Belcourt à Cazeau, le 31 janvier 1864," A.A.Q., C.N. II: 89.
24. "Belcourt à Rameau, le 3 avril 1863," Centre d'études acadiennes, 2.1–5.
25. "Belcourt à Rameau, le 12 mai 1867," Centre d'études acadiennes, 2.1–9.
26. Cécile Gallant. "L'Engagement social de Georges-Antoine Belcourt, curé de Rustico, 1859–1869", *Les Cahiers*, La Société historique acadienne, Vol. II, No.4 (December 1980), p. 327.

27. See the account books of the Institut catholique de Rustico for 1875 to 1938 (?), at the Museum of the Farmers' Bank of Rustico. They are also available on microfilm at the Centre d'études acadiennes.
28. Quoted in translation in *L'Eglise catholique à l'Île-du-Prince-Édouard 1720–1979, op. cit.*, p. 90.
29. *Le Moniteur Acadien*, 24 January 1878, p. 2.
30. *Ibid.*
31. *History of Saint Anthony Parish 1803–1980, op. cit.*, p. 44.
32. Macmillan. *op. cit.*, pp. 456–457.
33. *The Protector and Christian Witness*, 3 February 1858, p. 2. *The Protestant and Evangelical Witness*, 24 September 1859, p. 2.
34. *The Islander*, 13 March 1863, p. 3.
35. *Acts of the General Assembly of P.E.I.*, 1860, pp. 60–61.
36. Ian Ross Robertson. "Party Politics and Religious Controversialism in Prince Edward Island from 1860 to 1863", *Acadiensis*, Vol. VII, No. 2 (Spring 1978), p. 52.
37. *Assembly Journal*, P.E.I., 1864, Appendix N.
38. *Assembly Debates*, P.E.I., 4 April 1864, p. 50.
39. *The Summerside Progress*, 13 May 1867, p. 2. Statement made by the Honourable Joseph-Octave Arsenault at the Legislative Assembly.
40. Ian Ross Robertson. *Religion, Politics, and Education in Prince Edward Island from 1856 to 1877*, M.A. thesis, McGill University, 1968, p. 169. The bill does not make any reference at all to either the language question or religion.
41. *Assembly Journal*, P.E.I., 1868, p. 60.
42. *Report of the Parliamentary Committee appointed to Investigate and Report upon the manner in what the Education Law has been and is being carried on in the Public Educational Establishments of the Island*, (1867), Public Archives of P.E.I., R.G. 10, Vol. 29, p. (7).
43. Ian Ross Robertson. *op. cit.*, Note B. "The French Acadian Schools and the Appeals of Bishop MacIntyre", pp. 317–322.
44. *Annual Report of the Board of Education... for 1877, 1878*, p. 14. However, the Board of Education did authorize as of 1877 the *Histoire du Canada* and a French Grammar book (Michard) in public schools. (P.A.P.E.I., R.G. 10: *Minutes of Meetings of the Board of Education for P.E.I.*, vol. 5, 5 December 1877.) The textbooks do not appear to have been used very much.
45. "Belcourt à Rameau de Saint-Père, le 12 mai 1867," Centre d'études acadiennes, 2. 1–8.
46. "Model School" was the term given to a school where future teachers did their practice teaching. There was a "Model School" associated with the Normal School in Charlottetown where the students received their teacher training. Father Belcourt does not indicate in his correspondence whether his school had a class of children for practice teaching.
47. Blanchard. *Histoire des Acadiens de l'Île-du-Prince-Édouard, op. cit.*, p. 94.
48. "Belcourt à Rameau de Saint-Père, le 12 mai 1867," Centre d'études acadiennes, 2. 1–8.
49. Blanchard. *Rustico, une paroisse acadienne. op. cit.*, pp. 47–48.
50. "Quévillon à Bourget, le 8 juin 1863." *Archives de la Chancellerie de l'Archidiocèse de Montréal*, 255. 103.
51. *Annales du Couvent de Miscouche*. See also: *La Petite Souvenance*, Vol. 1, No. 2,

p. 21, "La fondation du Couvent de Miscouche: Un extrait des annales du couvent".

52. *Annales du Couvent de Miscouche*, 6 July 1865.
53. *Ibid.*, 19 November 1864.
54. *The Summerside Progress*, 16 July 1866, p. 3.
55. *Annales du Couvent de Miscouche*, le 10 March 1871.
56. *Ibid.*, 8 January 1872.
57. *Ibid.*, 6 July 1865 and 10 March 1871. See also: *The Summerside Progress*, 22 February 1869, p. 2. Father Miville was the priest in Egmont Bay.
58. *Le Moniteur Acadien*, le 30 July 1869, p. 3.
59. Father Quévillon also wanted to set up a teaching establishment in Mont Carmel. In 1868 he helped the parishioners construct a building designed as a college for boys. But for various reasons, partly financial, he was unable to complete the project. (See: Macmillan. *The Catholic Church in Prince Edward Island from 1835 to 1891*, *op. cit.*, p. 293. *The Summerside Progress*, 12 October 1868, p. 2.) Father Azade Trudel, the priest in Egmont Bay, also wanted to establish a convent in his parish where boys could receive their secondary education. A hall was thus built around 1868, but the convent was never built. (*The Examiner*, 28 September 1868; *Le Moniteur Acadien*, 30 October 1868, p. 2.) Oral tradition has it that the bishop refused to authorize the project because he had not been consulted.
60. *Assembly Journal*, P.E.I., 1886, Appendix A, p. 57.
61. *Assembly Journal*, P.E.I., 1883, Appendix B, p. X.
62. *Reports of the Visitors of Schools. . .for 1875*. Charlottetown: 1876, p. 55.
63. *Assembly Journal*, P.E.I. 1887, Appendix A, p. 41.
64. *Report of The Visitor of Schools for Prince County*, 1873, p. 60.
65. *Le Moniteur Acadien*, 20 November 1884, p. 2.
66. *Reports of the Visitors of Schools. . .for 1875*, Charlottetown: 1876, p. 56.
67. *Ibid.* and *Assembly Journal*, P.E.I., 1864, Appendix X.
68. *Assembly Journal*, P.E.I., 1861, Appendix W.
69. *The Examiner*, 22 May 1876, p. 1. "The Education Law. Report of Investigation Committee."
70. On the 19th of January 1882, the Board of Education authorized the use of the "Graduated Series of French Readers" in public schools (P.A.P.E.I., R.G. 10, *Minutes of Meetings of the Board of Education for P.E. Island*, Vol. 5, 1877–1892). According to several sources this was the Montpetit series. Gilbert Buote states that he was "the first person to submit the Montpetit series for the approval of the provincial Board of Education in 1879, and with the help of the Superintendent of Schools, Mr. Donald Montgomery, succeeded in introducing these books into our French schools" (*L'Impartial Illustré*, 1899, p. 60.). André Doiron, a former teacher in the Acadian schools on the Island, wrote in *L'Impartial* in 1902: "Around 1884, after the revolutionary fever had passed, so to speak, several very dedicated men of whom you, Mr. Editor, are perhaps the sole survivor, went to the Board of Education to demand that the books in the Montpetit series be adopted. The aim was to fill the gap for the fourth and fifth French books (I should say "half French") in the series from Nova Scotia. [. . .] The efforts of these men bore fruit. The Superintendent responded favourably to their request and not long after the Montpetit series was adopted it was used throughout our schools. Only the speller from Nova Scotia is being

used in our schools because teachers find it more suitable for introducing English to young pupils." (*L'Impartial*, 27 February 1902, p. 2.) Joseph-Octave Arsenault is also given credit for having the series adopted. (*Le Moniteur Acadien*, 6 August 1886, p. 2.) J.-Henri Blanchard is thus mistaken when he states that the series was introduced in 1891. (Blanchard, *Histoire des Acadiens de l'Île-du-Prince-Édouard, op. cit.*, p. 63.)

71. *Assembly Journal*, P.E.I., 1886, Appendix A, p. 57.
72. *Le Moniteur Acadien*, 20 December 1884, p. 2.
73. Robidoux. *Conventions Nationales des Acadiens, op. cit.*, p. 155.
74. *Le Moniteur Acadien*, 19 November 1874, p. 2.
75. *Ibid.*, 1 June 1876, p. 2.
76. *Ibid.*, 18 April 1878, p. 1.
77. *Ibid.*, 19 November 1874, p. 2.
78. *Le Moniteur Acadien*, 1 June 1876, p. 2.
79. *Le Moniteur Acadien*, 12 August 1880, p. 2.
80. "Belcourt à Rameau, le 4 janvier 1863; le 3 août 1863", Centre d'études acadiennes, 2.1–5. *The Vindicator*, 27 February 1863, "The Hon. Mr. Yeo".
81. See in particular: *Abstract of the Proceedings of Land Commissioners' Court... 1860, op. cit.*
82. *The Examiner*, 14 June 1858, p. 198. *The Islander*, 2 July 1858, p. 2; 23 July 1858, p. 2; 6 August 1858, p. 2. *The Examiner*, 9 August 1858, p. 2; 16 August 1858, p. 3; 21 March 1859, p. 2.
83. *The Examiner*, 21 February 1859, p. 2.
84. *Ibid.*, 14 March 1859, p. 2. The Liberal candidates were Nicholas Conroy, Charles McCarthy and P. Doyle.
85. Francis Gallant from Tignish was elected in 1875 in a by-election to fill the seat left vacant by Stanislas Perry after he was elected to the House of Commons. Gallant was defeated in 1876.
86. *Summerside Journal*, 21 February 1867, p. 2.
87. With regard to the accusations against Perry, see: *Le Moniteur Acadien*, 29 August 1878, p. 2 ("L'élection du Comté de Prince"). 22 April 1887, p. 2 (letters signed "Acadien" and "Un fermier"). *L'Impartial*, 12 October 1893, p. 2 (letter to the editor signed "Vindex"). 4 June 1896, p. 2 (article entitled "Assemblée enthousiaste"). 28 May 1896, p. 2 ("Perry et les écoles françaises").
88. *The Examiner*, 5 May 1890, p. 2.
89. *The Daily Examiner*, 1 March 1898, p. 6.
90. Published in translation in *Le Moniteur Acadien*, 17 December 1897, p. 2.
91. Wayne E. MacKinnon. *The Life of the Party. A History of the Liberal Party in Prince Edward Island*. Charlottetown: P.E.I. Liberal Party, 1973. See chapters III to V.
92. *The Vindicator*, 3 April 1863, p. 2.
93. "Belcourt à Cazeau, le 9 mai 1865," A.A.Q. 310, C.N. II: 94.
94. *Summerside Journal*, 21 February 1867, p. 2.
95. *Ibid.*
96. *Ibid.*, 24 February 1870, p. 2.
97. *The Islander*, 25 March 1870, p. 2.
98. *Le Moniteur Acadien*, 11 February 1870, p. 1.
99. *Summerside Journal*, 14 April 1870, p. 2. See quote on p. 2.
100. *The Examiner*, 6 March 1871, p. 2.
101. *Ibid.*, 15 May 1871, p. 1.

102. *L'Impartial*, 7 December 1893, p. 2.
103. *Abstract of the Proceedings of Land Commissionners' Court, Held During the Summer of 1860...*, 1862, p. 103.
104. "Belcourt à Cazeau, le 4 mars 1860," A.A.Q. 310, C.N. II: 55.
105. "Belcourt à Rameau, le 3 décembre 1861," Centre d'études acadiennes 2.1–3.
106. With regard to the efforts of Father Belcourt in the area of colonization, see Cécile Gallant: "L'Engagement social de George-Antoine Belcourt, curé de Rustico, 1859–1869", *Les Cahiers*, La Société historique acadienne, Vol. 11, No.4 (December 1980), pp. 317–325. See also Georges Arsenault: *Histoire de l'émigration chez les Acadiens de l'Île-du-Prince-Édouard*. Summerside: Société Saint Thomas d'Aquin, 1980, pp. 15–24.
107. Blanchard. *Rustico: une paroisse acadienne, op. cit.*, pp. 48–49.
108. Cécile Gallant. *loc. cit.*, pp. 325–328.
109. John T. Croteau. "The Farmers' Bank of Rustico: An Episode in Acadian History", *The Island Magazine*, No. 4 (Spring–Summer 1978), p. 4.
110. *Ibid.*, pp. 7–8.
111. *Ibid.*, p. 8.
112. Cécile Gallant. *Le Mouvement coopératif chez les Acadiens de la région Evangéline 1862–1982*, Wellington, le Conseil Coopératif de l'Î.-P.-É., 1982, p. 28.
113. *Le Moniteur Acadien*, 28 October 1880, p. 2.
114. Gallant. *op. cit.*
115. *The Examiner*, 13 April 1868, p. 2.
116. Croteau. *op. cit.*, pp. 128–129.
117. *Ibid.*
118. *Ibid.*, p. 130.
119. Robidoux. *Conventions Nationales des Acadiens. op. cit.*, p. 123.
120. *The Summerside Progress*, 1 June 1868, p. 1.
121. *Le Moniteur Acadien*, 1 June 1876, p. 2.
122. *Ibid.*, 19 November 1874, p. 2.
123. *L'Évangéline*, 28 August 1890, p. 2.
124. *The Prince Edward Island Agriculturist*, 11 March 1886, p. 1.
125. *Ibid.*, 12 May 1890, p.6.
126. A.H. Clark. *Three Centuries and the Island. op. cit.*, p. 175.
127. *Summerside Journal*, 29 August 1867, p. 2.
128. *The Summerside Progress*, 5 August 1867, p. 4.
129. *The Prince Edward Island Agriculturist*, 3 October 1887, p. 4.
130. *The Summerside Progress*, 18 May 1868, p. 2.
131. *The History of Saint Anthony, 1803–1890. op. cit.*, p. 23.
132. *Le Moniteur Acadien*, 18 November 1880.
133. *L'Évangéline*, 23 November 1887, p. 2.
134. *The Summerside Progress*, 8 October 1866, p. 1. (letter to the editor from Jas. H. Fitzgerald, entitled "Flax").
135. *The Prince Edward Island Agriculturist*, 7 April 1887, p. 1.
136. *Recensement du Canada 1880–81*, Vol. III, Ottawa, 1883, pp. 136–137. Corn production in Lot 15 represented approximately one third of the total production in the province.
137. Clark. *op. cit.*, p. 112.
138. Clark. *op. cit.*, p. 182.
139. *The Pioneer*, 20 October 1880, p. 2.

140. *Clark. op. cit.*, p. 186.
141. *Ibid.*, p. 198.
142. *Ibid.*, p. 204.
143. *Le Moniteur Acadien*, 22 October 1885, p. 2. The three main products exported from the Island that year were oats ($443,165), eggs ($160,901) and lobster ($151,583).
144. *Le Moniteur Acadien*, 7 December 1886, p. 2. Buote exported more than 80,000 dozen eggs during the summer of 1880.
145. *The Prince Edward Island Agriculturist*, 22 October 1885, p. 2.
146. *The Summerside Progress*, 10 September 1866, p. 2.
147. *Summerside Journal*, 26 September 1867, p. 2.
148. *Ibid.*, 21 May 1868, p. 2.
149. "Lieutenant-Governor to Secretary of State. Part VI. On Manufactures, Fisheries and Coal, Appendix O." *P.E.I. Legislative Assembly Journal, 1872.*
150. "Annual Report on the Fisheries of Prince Edward Island", *Sessional Papers, Marine and Fisheries*, Vol. X, No. 5, 1877. Appendix 16, p. 292.
151. *Alberton Pioneer*, 10 July 1878, p. 2.
152. *Sessional Papers*, 1879, No. 3, Appendix 16, pp. 288–289.
153. *Fishing: A Part of the Island Heritage*. Charlottetown: Department of Fisheries, s.d., p. 2.
154. *Sessional Papers of Canada*, 1885, No. 9, pp. 247–248. Apart from the 88 plants in operation, 12 factories did not open that year.
155. *Ibid.*
156. *Documents de la Session du Parlement du Canada*, 1884, Vol. 5, No. 7, p. 176.
157. *Sessional Papers*, 1885, No. 9, p. 247.
158. *Past and Present of Prince Edward Island, op. cit.*, p. 381.
159. *Sessional Papers*, 1885, *op. cit.* The Acadians in New Brunswick were Bruno Poirier, Geo. P. LeBlanc, Peter M. Poirier and Samuel Petitpas.
160. "Rapport des commissaires: Pêcheries de homard et d'huîtres du Canada. 1887". Annexe No. 1, *Documents de la Session*, Vol. 8, 1888, No. 6A, pp. 28–34.
161. *Ibid.*, pp. 32–33.
162. *Le Moniteur Acadien*, 21 August 1891.
163. *Documents de la Session*, 1880–81, Vol. 6, No. 11, Annex 11, p. 232.
164. *Sessional Papers*, 1890, Vol. 23, No. 17, Appendix 5, p. 162.
165. *Le Moniteur Acadien*, 12 August 1880.
166. *The Daily Examiner*, 2 November 1881, p. 1.
167. *Le Moniteur Acadien*, 23 July 1886, p. 3.
168. *Ibid.*, 20 May 1884.
169. *Documents de la Session*, 1880, Vol. 6, No. 9, Annex 15, pp. 259–260.
170. *Documents de la Session*, 1882, Vol. 4, No. 5, Supplement No. 2, Annex 5, p. 188.
171. "Rapport des commissaires. Pêcheries de homard et d'huîtres du Canada. 1887", *op. cit.* See submissions on P.E.I., pp. 28–34.
172. *Documents de la Session*, 1882, Vol. 4, No. 5, Supplement No. 2, Annex 5, p. 182.
173. *Le Moniteur Acadien*, 10 August 1882, p. 3.
174. *Le Moniteur Acadien*, 23 September 1875, p. 2.
175. *Ibid.*, 10 January 1878, p. 2.
176. The Island delegates were: Joseph-Octave Arsenault, Etienne-E. Gallant and U.-C. Trudelle from Egmont Bay; Stanislas-F. Perry from Tignish; Gilbert DesRoches from Miscouche; Paul Thibodeau, Eustache Gallant, Firmin Gallant and

Laurent Gallant from Rustico. *Le Moniteur Acadien*, 24 June 1880, p. 2.
177. *Le Moniteur Acadien*, 10 June 1880, p. 2.
178. Chouinard. *Fête Nationale des Canadiens français. op. cit.*, p. 445.
179. Robidoux. *Conventions Nationales des Acadiens. op. cit.*, p. 9.
180. *Ibid.*, p. 178.
181. *Le Moniteur Acadien*, 9 October 1884, p. 2.
182. *Le Moniteur Acadien*, 20 November 1884, p. 2. *The Examiner*, 6 December 1886.

IV. A Period Of Successful Initiatives: 1890–1945

1. *L'Impartial*, 22 June 1893, p.1.
2. See Gabrielle LeBlanc and Diane Lecouffe (editors), *Inventaire de L'Impartial*. Summerside: Société Saint-Thomas d'Aquin, 1980, 110 p.
3. Placed in an awkward position, the Acadian priests did not openly support the project although they could see that it would be a great asset for the Acadians. As members of the clergy in the diocese of Charlottetown, they felt obliged to give their full and open support to St. Dunstan's, the diocesan college, although little importance was given there to the teaching of French. In the light of this position, some laymen favoured a compromise that would allow the creation of a chair of French at St. Dunstan's. This was suggested by Sylvain, an anonymous contributor to *L'Impartial* who nevertheless left the final decision in the hands of the clergy: "I am far from wishing to be stubborn with regard to cooperating with St. Dunstan's. The last word belongs to our Island priests. Once they have reached a decision on the matter, we have but to follow their leadership. . ." (TR) (*L'Impartial*, 20 December 1906, p. 4.)
4. *L'Évangéline*, 10 April 1947, p. 4.
5. Father Charles Gallant. "La Société L'Assomption", *Compte rendu. La Convention Nationale des Acadiens de l'Île-du-Prince-Édouard*, 1951, p. 49.
6. Minutes of 9 December 1933, Beaubien (Rustico) branch of the *Société l'Assomption*. Deposited in the Musée Belcourt. They can also be consulted on microfilm at the Centre d'études acadiennes.
7. *L'Évangéline*, 22 July 1932, p. 1.
8. Blanchard. *Histoire des Acadiens de l'Île-du-Prince-Édouard, op. cit.*, p. 62.
9. *Ibid.*, [p. 2].
10. J.-Henri Blanchard. *Acadiens de l'Île-du-Prince-Édouard*. Charlottetown, 1956, p. 136.
11. Public Archives of P.E.I., R.G. 10, *Minutes of Meetings of the Board of Education for P.E. Island*, Vol. 5, April 23, 1892.
12. Joseph-Octave Arsenault's position was occupied by Joseph Blanchard, Marin Gallant, J.-Sylvère DesRoches, Pierre Gallant, J.-Wilfred Arsenault, François-E. Doiron and J.-Albert Gallant. The position was transformed when the school system was reorganized in 1972. Inspector Gallant became French pedagogical consultant for the Department of Education.
13. *L'Impartial*, 3 August 1893, p. 2.
14. Article 2 of the Constitution of the Association. For the text of this document, see: *Extraits des Conventions de l'Association des Instituteurs Acadiens de l'Île-du-Prince-Édouard, 1893–1969*, compiled by J.-Albert Gallant. After 1910, the feminine form of teacher, "institutrices", was usually added to the name of the Association.

15. *Ibid.*, p. 2.
16. *L'Impartial*, 25 April 1895, p. 2.
17. *Extraits des Conventions...*, *op. cit.*, p. 9.
18. Minutes for the 1930 annual conference of the *Association des instituteurs acadiens de l'Î.-P.-É.*. The minutes of the Association are on microfilm at the Centre d'études acadiennes.
19. Minutes for the 1910 annual conference of the *Association des instituteurs acadiens de l'Î.-P.-É.* Alexandre-J. Savoie. *Un siècle de revendications scolaires au Nouveau-Brunswick 1871–1971*. Vol. I *Du français en compte-gouttes 1871–1936*. Edmundston: Alexandre-J. Savoie, 1978, p. 184.
20. P.E.I. *Annual Report of the Public Schools*, *1907*, pp. XXVI A and XXVII.
21. In collaboration, *Histoire de la Société Saint-Thomas d'Aquin de l'Île-du-Prince-Édouard 1919–1979*. Summerside: Société Saint-Thomas d'Aquin, 1979, p. 8.
22. J.-Henri Blanchard. *Les Acadiens de l'Île Saint-Jean* (lecture given at the 1920 pedagogical conference of the Acadian Teachers Association held in Miscouche; "thanks to the good will of our leaders" (TR), a free copy copy of the lecture was distributed to all the Acadian families in the province), Mont-Carmel, 1921, pp. 25–26.
23. *Histoire de la Société Saint-Thomas d'Aquin...*, *op. cit.*, p. 11.
24. Father Jean-F. Buote, "L'oeuvre de la Société Saint-Thomas d'Aquin", *Compte rendu. La Convention Nationale Acadienne de l'Île-du-Prince-Édouard*, *op. cit.*, p. 46.
25. The young man in question was Monseigneur Jean-François Buote, ordained in 1938.
26. J.-Henri Blanchard, "L'Enseignement du Français dans les Écoles publiques de l'Île-du-Prince-Édouard", *Deuxième Congrès de la Langue française au Canada, Mémoires*, Vol. III, Québec, 1938, p. 229.
27. Autobiographical notes by J.-Henri Blanchard, Centre d'études acadiennes, 22.2–4.
28. Father Jean-F. Buote, *loc. cit.*, p. 46.
29. *Histoire de la Société Saint-Thomas d'Aquin*, *op. cit.*, p. 22.
30. P.E.I. *Annual Report of the Public Schools for 1899*, Appendix C, p. 65.
31. *L'Évangéline*, 28 July 1932, p. 2.
32. J.-Henri Blanchard, "Les écoles acadiennes de l'Île-du-Prince-Édouard", *Relations*, No. 18, June 1942, p. 157.
33. Blanchard, "L'Enseignement du Français dans les Ecoles publiques de l'Île-du-Prince-Édouard", *op. cit.*, p. 225.
34. *Assembly Journal*, P.E.I., 1902, Appendix C. p. 25–D.
35. Blanchard. *Histoire des Acadiens de l'Île-du-Prince-Édouard*, *op. cit.*, p. 64.
36. *Annual Report of the Department of Education*, 1936, p. 14.
37. *Assembly Journal*, P.E.I., 1888, Appendix A, p. XXVII.
38. P.E.I. *Annual Report of the Public Schools for 1916*, p. 12.
39. Blanchard, "L'Enseignement du Français dans les Écoles publiques de l'Île du Prince-Édouard", *loc. cit.*, p. 226.
40. Minutes of the 1907 annual conference of the *Association des instituteurs acadiens de l'Î.-P.-É.*
41. P.E.I. *Annual Report of the Public Schools*, 1908, p. XXIII.
42. P.E.I. *Annual Report of the Public Schools for 1897*, p. 53.
43. Blanchard, *loc. cit.*, p. 225.

44. Minutes of the 1938 conference of the *Association des instituteurs acadiens de l'Î.-P.-É.*
45. *Annual Report of the Department of Education*, 1940, Inspectorate No. 2, F.E. Doiron, pp. 17–18.
46. *L'Impartial*, 8 March 1894, p. 2.
47. *L'Impartial*, 5 March 1896, p. 6; 9 January 1896, p. 3; 6 February 1896, p. 4; 25 April 1895, p. 3; 8 November 1894, p. 3.
48. *P.E.I. Annual Report of the Public Schools*, 1898, p. 56; 1928, p. 59. These courses were given in 1898 in Urbainville and St. Chrysostome. There were offered in 1928 in the districts of Tignish, St. Nicholas, Mont Carmel, Abram Village, Urbainville, Cape Egmont and St. Andrews.
49. Gallant. *Le Mouvement coopératif chez les Acadiens de la région Évangéline (1862–1982), op. cit.*, p. 130.
50. J.T. Croteau. *Adult Education in P.E.I. A Survey.* 1936, P.E.I. Collection, Robertson Library, U.P.E.I., Vertical File. See also: Cécile Gallant, *op. cit.*, pp. 129–139.
51. Léon Thériault, "L'Acadianisation de l'Église catholique en Acadie, 1763–1953", *Les Acadiens des Maritimes, op. cit.*, p. 329.
52. Raymond Huel, "The Irish French Conflict in Catholic Episcopal Nominations: The Western Sees and the Struggle for Domination Within the Church", *The Canadian Catholic Historical Association Study Sessions*, Vol. 42, 1975, p. 52.
53. *L'Évangéline*, 23 October 1924, p. 8.
54. J.-Henri Blanchard, "L'Enseignement du Français dans les Écoles publiques de l'Île-du-Prince-Édouard", *Deuxième Congrès de la Langue française au Canada, Mémoires, op. cit.*, p. 229.
55. Insert in a parish register of Notre-Dame-de-Mont-Carmel.
56. It is difficult to establish the number of Island Acadian women who entered religious congregations between 1890 and 1945. The historian, J.-Henri Blanchard, estimated that prior to 1964, there were more than 200 who took the veil in 22 congregations. Blanchard, *The Acadians of Prince Edward Island, 1720–1964, op. cit.*, pp. 117–118.
57. Marguérite Michaud, "Mère Évangéline Gallant", *La Petite Souvenance*, No. 8 (December 1982), pp. 11–13.
58. *L'Impartial*, 20 July 1893, p. 2; 19 October 1893, p. 3.
59. *L'Église catholique à l'Île-du-Prince-Édouard 1720–1979, op. cit.*, p. 144.
60. Madame Emmanuel-J. (Madeleine) Gallant, "Les Associations féminines", *Compte rendu. La Convention Nationale Acadienne de l'Île-du-Prince-Édouard, 1951*, pp. 61. The precise date of the founding of the *Dames du Sanctuaire* is not known. Madame Gallant states that it was in 1939. *L'Évangéline* published a report of the meeting of the *Dames du Sanctuaire* in Abram's Village on 23 December 1936. According to *L'Évangéline* of 11 March 1935, the Women's Institute was still operating in the district in 1935.
61. Madame Emmanuel-J. Gallant. *op. cit.*, pp. 61–62.
62. *History of Saint Anthony Parish 1803–1980, op. cit.*, p. 172.
63. Pascal Poirier. *Le Parler franco-acadien et ses origines*. Québec: Imprimerie Franciscaine Missionnaire, 1928, p. 223.
64. *The Examiner*, 5 July 1887.
65. Centre d'études acadiennes, Eunice Arsenault Collection, ms. No.21.
66. Prayer which the author learnt from his mother in Abram's Village.
67. Centre d'études acadiennes, Eunice Arsenault Collection, ms. No. 2.

68. Sister Saint Hildebert, c.n.d., *L'Ame Acadienne*, (manuscript), c. 1941, p. 164. Manuscript deposited at the *Société Saint-Thomas d'Aquin*. A copy is available on microfilm at the Centre d'études acadiennes.
69. Centre d'études acadiennes, Georges Arsenault Collection, ms. No. 10.
70. The New Year's paternal blessing was known in Acadia; several testamonies indicate that the tradition was practiced in some Island families until the beginning of the twentieth century. Among others, see the Georges Arsenault Collection, tape 751.
71. *L'Impartial*, 15 February 1894, p. 2
72. *L'Impartial*, 22 June 1893, p. 1.
73. *Ibid.*, 10 November 1908, p. 2. J.-Henri Blanchard, "Histoire de *L'Impartial*", published in *L'Évangéline*, 10 April 1947, p. 4. According to Blanchard, the switch in political allegiance was made to save the newspaper which was in serious financial difficulty.
74. *L'Impartial*, 24 November 1904, p. 4.
75. *Ibid.*, 10 November 1904, p. 4.
76. *Ibid.*, 3 August 1893, p. 3.
77. Quoted in *L'Impartial*, 28 February 1895, p. 2.
78. *Ibid.*
79. Blanchard. *Histoire des Acadiens de l'Île-du-Prince-Édouard*, *op. cit.*, p. 58.
80. *Ibid.*, p. 57.
81. *P.E.I. Department of Agriculture Annual Report*, 1906, p. 31.
82. J. C. Ready, "Agriculture", *Past and Present of Prince Edward Island*, *op. cit.*, p. 159.
83. Lorne C. Callbeck, "Economic and Social Developments Since Confederation", *Canada's Smallest Province. A History of Prince Edward Island*, Charlottetown: The P.E. Island 1973 Centennial Commission, 1973, p. 348.
84. *Ibid.*
85. *L'Impartial*, 6 April 1905, p. 4.
86. The Agricultural Historians. *History and Development of the Dairy Industry in Prince Edward Island*, s. 1. [1978], p. 26.
87. *L'Impartial*, 23 April 1896, p. 5.
88. *Ibid.*, 16 June 1898, p. 4.
89. The Agricultural Historians, *op, cit.*, p. 23; and *P.E.I. Department of Agriculture. Annual Report 1914*, p. 3.
90. Muriel K. Roy, "Peuplement et croissance démographique en Acadie", *Les Acadiens des Maritimes*, *op. cit.*, p. 197.
91. Georges Arsenault. *Histoire de l'émigration chez les Acadiens de l'Île-du-Prince-Édouard*. Summerside: Société Saint-Thomas d'Aquin, 1980, pp. 27–29.
92. *L'Impartial*, 5 September 1895, p. 3.
93. *Ibid.*, 6 February 1896, p. 6.
94. *Ibid.*, 21 and 28 October 1897, p. 5.
95. *Ibid.*, 16 September 1897, p. 2.
96. *L'Évangéline*, 1 August 1932, p. 2.
97. *Ibid.*, 26 July 1932, p. 3.
98. *Ibid.*, 25 July 1932, p. 2.
99. *L'Impartial*, 17 October 1907, p. 3.
100. *Ibid.*, 10 March 1898, p. 5.
101. *Ibid.*, 17 August 1899, p. 5; 16 February 1899, p. 5; 28 March 1901, p. 4.
102. *Ibid.*, 17 August 1899, p. 5.

103. *Ibid.*, 28 February 1901, p. 4.
104. *Ibid.*, 9 March 1899, p. 5.
105. J. S. Clark, "Farmers' Institutes: Or Schools for the People", *The Prince Edward Island Magazine*, Vol. 3, No. 3 (May 1901), p. 86.
106. P.E.I. *Department of Agriculture. Annual Report*, 1901, p. 4.
107. See the reports of the Institutes published in the annual reports of the provincial Department of Agriculture.
108. P.E.I. *Department of Agriculture. Annual Report 1907*, p. 21.
109. *L'Impartial*, 22 December 1908, p. 3.
110. *Year Book, Province of Prince Edward Island, 1915*, Charlottetown: 1916, p. 75.
111. Cyrus-P. Gallant, "Nos Expositions Agricoles", *Compte rendu. La Convention Nationale Acadienne de l'Île-du-Prince-Édouard*, *op. cit.*, pp. 22–23.
112. *L'Évangéline*, 1 December 1927.
113. David E. Weale, "The Mud Diggers", *The Island Magazine*, No. 5 (Fall-Winter 1978), p. 30.
114. J.-Edmond Arsenault, "Les Acadiens et l'Agriculture de l'Île-du-Prince-Édouard", *Culture*, Vol. VII, 1946, p. 221.
115. P.E.I. *Department of Agriculture. Annual Report*, 1916, p. 41. See also the *Annual Report*, 1917, pp. 34–35.
116. Clark. *op. cit.*, p. 166.
117. *Ibid.*, p. 170.
118. J.-Edmond Arsenault, "Les Acadiens de l'Île-du-Prince-Édouard", *Action Nationale*, XXXI, May 1948, pp. 366–367. Mr. Arsenault does not give the source for his statistics. He did, however, inform the author during an interview that these figures were based on the 1941 census and his own field research.
119. *L'Évangéline*, 8 December 1915, p. 6.
120. Clark. *op. cit.*, p. 256.
121. J.-Edmond Arsenault. *loc. cit.*
122. Jean Chaussade. *La Pêche et les pêcheurs des Provinces Maritimes du Canada*. Montréal: les Presses de l'Université de Montréal, 1983, pp. 226–230.
123. *L'Impartial*, 21 May 1896, p. 3.
124. Jean Chaussade *op. cit.*, pp. 224–225.
125. *L'Impartial*, 9 September 1897, p. 2.
126. Félix Gallant, "Les pêcheurs de Baie-Egmont", published as an appendix in Cécile Gallant and Georges Arsenault, *Histoire de la pêche chez les Acadiens de l'Île-du-Prince-Édouard*, Summerside: Société Saint-Thomas d'Aquin, 1980, p. 38.
127. Cécile Gallant. *Le Mouvement coopératif chez les Acadiens de la région Évangéline (1862–1982)*, *op. cit.*, p. 106.
128. *Ibid.*
129. Thomas Pineau's Testimony at the "Lobster Fishery Commission, Quebec and Maritime Provinces", *Sessional Papers of the Parliament of Canada*, Vol. XLIV, No. 13, 1910, p. 325.
130. Bertram A. Blaquiere, *What Fishermen Can Do. The Story of North Rustico*, The Adult Education League of P.E.I., [1939], pp. 4–5.
131. Gary Webster, "Cooperation, Co-operatives and Credit Unions: Their Place in Island History", in Harry Baglole, ed., *Exploring Island History*, *op. cit.*, pp. 184–185.
132. *Report of the Royal Commission Investigating the Fisheries of the Maritime Provinces and of the Magdalen Islands*. Ottawa, 1928.

133. See section entitled "Adult Education".
134. Minutes of the *Association des instituteurs acadiens de l'Île-du-Prince-Édouard*, 25–26 August 1909.
135. "Discours prononcé à Church Point, N.-E., le 15 août 1907, par l'Hon. Sénateur Poirier", in Ferdinand Robidoux, *Conventions Nationales des Acadiens, op. cit.*, p. 272.
136. Percentage based on the statistics in the 1921 census published by J.-Henri Blanchard in *Histoire des Acadiens de l'Île-du-Prince-Édouard, op. cit.*, p. 81.
137. Muriel K. Roy, "Peuplement et croissance démographique en Acadie", in Jean Daigle, ed., *Les Acadiens des Maritimes, op. cit.*, p. 197.

V. The Post-war Period: 1945–1980

1. William Janssen, "Agriculture in Transition", in Smitheram, Milne and Dasgupta, *The Garden Transformed, Prince Edward Island 1945–1980*, Charlottetown: Ragweed Press, 1982, pp. 115–129.
2. Verner Smitheram, "Development and the Debate over School Consolidation", in Smitheram, Milne and Dasgupta, *op. cit.*, p. 181.
3. Smitheram, Milne and Dasgupta, *op. cit.*, p. 245.
4. *Ibid.*, pp. 172–174.
5. The St. Thomas Aquinas Society met with the Minister of Regional Economic Expansion and the Premier of the province in 1980 to request that the third phase of the Plan include a program of development related specifically to the Acadian communities. As a result of this meeting, the Minister set up a program of one million dollars, spread over a period of three years (1981–1984), for economic development in the French-Acadian communities on the Island.
6. Clark. *Three Centuries and the Island, op. cit.*, p. 134.
7. *Prince Edward Island, Canada. A Good Place to Farm*, Department of Agriculture, 1980, p. 2.
8. *Ibid.*, p.5.
9. *La Société Saint-Thomas d'Aquin de l'Île-du-Prince-Édouard. 1919–1979*, Summerside: Société Saint-Thomas d'Aquin, 1979, p.37.
10. A circular letter of Agricultural Committee of the St. Thomas Aquinas Society, 15 October 1945. Archives de la Société Saint-Thomas d'Aquin.
11. Léo J.-T. Arsenault, "Les organisations agricoles et les Cercles de Jeunes Eleveurs", *Compte rendu. La Convention Nationale Acadienne de l'Île-du-Prince-Édouard, op. cit.*, p. 55.
12. *Ibid.*
13. Charles M. Arsenault, "Les Organisations Coopératives agricoles", *Compte rendu. La Convention Nationale Acadienne de l'Île. . ., op. cit.*, p. 21.
14. *Album-Souvenir. 150e anniversaire. Paroisse St-Philippe et St-Jacques*, 1962, pp. 44–45.
15. For the history of this cooperative see: Cécile Gallant, *Le Mouvement coopératif chez les Acadiens de la région Évangéline (1862–1982), op. cit.*, pp. 199–210.
16. *Annual Report*, Department of Fisheries, Prince Edward Island for the year ended March 31st 1980, p. 14.
17. J.T. Croteau. *Cradled in the Waves*, Toronto: Ryerson Press, 1951, p. 91.
18. *Annual Report*, Department of Fisheries, *op. cit.*

19. Acadian delegations met with Bishop James Boyle in 1946 and 1954, and with Bishop Malcolm MacEachern in 1955 and 1965. Copies of the 1954, 1955 and 1965 reports exist in the Archives of the St. Thomas Aquinas Society.
20. "Communication of the Acadians of the Diocese to Rt. Rev. Msgr. James Boyle, D.D., Bishop of Charlottetown", March 10, 1954. Archives of the St. Thomas Aquinas Society.
21. "Mémoire de la Société Saint-Thomas d'Aquin à Son Excellence Monseigneur Malcolm MacEachern...", 1965, p. 14.
22. "J.-Henri Blanchard à R.P. Léopold Taillon, le 23 janvier 1957". Centre d'études acadiennes., 22.2–1.
23. *Album-Souvenir. 150e anniversaire. Paroisse St-Philippe et St-Jacques*, *op. cit.*, p. 65.
24. Marlene-Russel Clark, "Island Politics", *Canada's Smallest Province: A History of Prince Edward Island*, *op. cit.*, p. 320.
25. *Album-Souvenir. 150e anniversaire. Paroisse St-Philippe et St-Jacques*, *op. cit.*, p. 63.
26. Sisters from the congregation of the *Soeurs Servantes du Saint Coeur de Marie* (Beauport, Québec) came in 1976 to help with pastoral development in the region.
27. J.G. Lees (ed.). *An Educational Quo-Vadis, Development of Education in the Atlantic Provinces and Future Trends*, Toronto: Ryerson, 1969, p. 95.
28. *Ibid.*
29. *P.E.I. Department of Education Annual Report 1945–46*, p. (78).
30. *P.E.I. Department of Education Annual Report*, 1947, p. 3.
31. J. Charles Campbell, "School Consolidation: Seventy Years of Evolution", *The Abegweit Review*, Vol. 2, No. 2, (Fall 1975) p. 9.
32. *Le Plan de développement de l'Île-du-Prince-Édouard*, Ottawa: Ministère de l'Expansion économique régionale, 1969, p. 50.
33. *P.E.I. Department of Education Annual Report*, 1973, p. 103.
34. *Ibid.*
35. Report of the committee established to examine the French language in Acadian schools on the Island (1952), Centre d'études acadiennes 22.2–3.
36. *Ibid.*
37. "Plan d'aide financière destiné à procurer des instituteurs mieux qualifiés pour enseigner dans nos écoles dites acadiennes", 1 April 1953. Archives de la Société Saint-Thomas d'Aquin.
38. Minutes of the Board meeting of the St. Thomas Aquinas Society, 4 May 1955, 5 October 1955, 13 June 1956, 28 November 1956.
39. *La Voix Acadienne*, 19 December 1979.
40. Annual report of the Secretary General of the St. Thomas Aquinas Society, 30 September 1959.
41. *Le Bulletin*, Société Saint-Thomas d'Aquin, February 1963.
42. *P.E.I. Department of Education Annual Report*, 1966, p. 36.
43. *Le Bulletin*, Société Saint-Thomas d'Aquin, December 1968.
44. Minutes of the Educational Committee of the St. Thomas Aquinas Society, 27 May 1973.
45. Muriel K. Roy, "Peuplement et croissance démographique en Acadie", *Les Acadiens des Maritimes*, *op. cit.*, p. 171.
46. *P.E.I. Department of Education Annual Report 1955–56*, p. 52.
47. *Compte rendu. La Convention Nationale Acadienne de l'Île-du-Prince-Édouard*, 1951, pp. 6–7.

48. Annual Report of the Secretary General of the St. Thomas Aquinas Society, J.-Edmond Arsenault, 1964–65. Archives of the St. Thomas Aquinas Society.
49. "Programme d'action socio-culturelle du Secrétariat d'Etat", Archives de la Société Saint-Thomas d'Aquin.
50. *Les Héritiers de Lord Durham. Société Saint-Thomas d'Aquin*, Summerside, 1977.
51. *Rapport annuel des activités de l'année 1978–79 de la S.S.T.A. par le secrétaire administratif, Alcide Bernard*. Archives of the St. Thomas Aquinas Society.

SELECTIVE BIBLIOGRAPHY

We have concentrated on publications that have been quoted, and archival collections that were consulted. For more precise information, see ***Notes and References.***

VOLUMES

Agricultural Historians (The), *History and Development of the Dairy Industry in Prince Edward Island*, s.l., (1978), 104 p.

Album-Souvenir, Paroisse St-Phillippe et Saint-Jacques 1812 - 1962, s.l., 1962, 87 p.

Arsenault, Georges, *Complaintes acadiennes de l'Île-du-Prince-Édouard*, Montréal, Leméac, 1980, 261 p.

____ , *Courir la Chandeleur*, Moncton, Éditions d'Acadie, 1982, 116 p.

____ , *L'Agriculture chez les Acadiens de l'Île-du-Prince-Édouard. 1720–1980*, Summerside, la Société Saint-Thomas d'Aquin (S.S.T.A.), 1981, 69 p.

____ , *L'Éducation chez les Acadiens de l'Île-du-Prince-Édouard. 1720–1980*, Summerside, S.S.T.A., 1982, 85 p.

____ , *Histoire de l'émigration chez les Acadiens de l'Île-du-Prince-Édouard*, Summerside, S.S.T.A., 1980, 42 p.

____ , *Initiation à l'histoire acadienne de l'Île-du-Prince-Édouard*, Summerside, S.S.T.A., 1984, 110 p.

____ , *La Religion et les Acadiens à l'Île-du-Prince-Édouard. 1720–1980*, Summerside, S.S.T.A., 1983, 102 p.

Arsenault, Georges and Cécile Gallant, *Histoire de la pêche chez les Acadiens de l'Île-du-Prince-Édouard*, Summerside, S.S.T.A., 1980, 52 p.

Baglole, Harry, editor, *Exploring Island History*, Belfast, Ragweed Press, 1977, xi-310 p.

Blacquiere, Bertram A., *What Fishermen Can Do. The Story of North Rustico*, The Adult Education League of Prince Edward Island, (1939), 21 p.

Blanchard, J.-Henri, *The Acadians of Prince Edward Island 1720–1964*, Charlottetown, Blanchard, 1964, 151 p.

____ , *Acadiens de l'Île-du-Prince-Édouard*, Charlottetown, Blanchard, 1956, 143 p.

____ , *Les Acadiens de l'Île Saint-Jean*, Mont-Carmel, 1921, 27 p.

____ , *Histoire des Acadiens de l'Île-du-Prince-Édouard*, Moncton, Blanchard, 1927, 120 p.

____ , *Rustico—une paroisse acadienne de l'Île-du-Prince-Édouard*, Blanchard, 1937, 126 p.

Bolger, Francis W.P., editor, *Canada's Smallest Province. A History of Prince Edward Island*, Charlottetown, The P.E.I. 1973 Centennial Commission, 1973, 403 p.

Bouchette, Joseph, *The British Dominions in North America*, Volume II, London, 1831, xi-296-(176) p.

Campbell, Duncan, *History of Prince Edward Island*, Charlottetown, Bremner Brothers, 1875, vii-224 p.

Chaussade, Jean, *La Pêche et les pêcheurs des Provinces Maritimes du Canada*, Montréal, Presses de l'Université de Montréal, 1983, 304 p.

Chouinard, J.-J.-B., *Fête Nationale des Canadiens-français*, Québec, L'Imprimerie A. Côté et Cie, 1881, xiv-631 p.

Clark, Andrew Hill, *Acadia, The Geography of Early Nova Scotia to 1760*, Madison, University of Wisconsin Press, 1968, xx-450 p.

____ , *Three Centuries and the Island*, Toronto, University of Toronto Press, 1959, xiii-287 p.

Compte rendu, La Convention Nationale Acadienne de l'Île-du-Prince-Édouard, 1951, 96 p.

Croteau, J.T., *Cradled in the Waves: The Story of a People's Cooperative Achievement in Economic Betterment on Prince Edward Island*, Toronto, Ryerson Press, 1951, ix-149 p.

Daigle, Jean, editor, *Les Acadiens des Maritimes : études thématiques*, Moncton, Centre d'études acadiennes, 1980, 691 p.

L'Église catholique à l'Île-du-Prince-Édouard 1720–1979, Charlottetown, la Corporation épiscopale catholique romaine, 1979, 158-(41) p.

Gallant, Cécile, *Le Mouvement coopératif chez les Acadiens de la région Évangéline 1862–1982*, Wellington, le Conseil Coopératif de l'Île-du-Prince-Édouard, 1982, 283 p.

Gallant, J.-Albert, *Extraits des Conventions de l'Association des Instituteurs Acadiens de l'Île-du-Prince-Édouard, 1893–1969*, s.l.n.d., 26 p.

Gallant, Patrice, *Michel Haché-Gallant et ses descendants*, Volume II, Sayabec, Gallant, 1970, 143 p.

Griffiths, Naomi, *The Acadians: Creation of a People*, Toronto, McGraw-Hill Ryerson Ltd., 1973, xiii-94 p.

Harvey, D.C., *The French Regime in Prince Edward Island*, New York, AMS Press, 1970 (original publication, 1926), xi-265 p.

____, editor, *Journeys to the Island of St. John or Prince Edward Island 1775–1832*. Toronto, MacMillan, 1955, 213 p.

Les Héritiers de Lord Durham, Société Saint-Thomas d'Aquin, Summerside, S.S.T.A., 1977, 43 p.

Hill, S.S., *A Short Account of Prince Edward Island*, London, Medden and Co., 1839, vi-90-iii p.

Histoire de la Société Saint-Thomas d'Aquin de l'Île-du-Prince-Édouard 1919–1979, Summerside, S.S.T.A., 1979, 103 p.

History of Saint Anthony Parish 1803–1980, Bloomfield, Bloomfield Historical Society, 1980, 256 p.

L'Impartial Illustré, Tignish, 1899, 64-(24) p.

Information to Emigrants. An Account of the Island of Prince Edward, London, James Asperne, (1819), 20 p.

Journal (Le) des visites pastorales de Mgr Joseph-Octave Plessis (Évêque de Québec) en Acadie, 1811, 1812, 1815, Moncton, La Société historique acadienne, 1980, 311 p.

La Morandière, Charles de, *Histoire de la pêche française de la morue dans l'Amérique septentrionale, des origines à 1789*, Paris, G.P. Maisonneuve et Larose, 1962, 2 volumes, xviii-1023 p.

La Roque, sieur de, *Voyage d'inspection du Sieur de la Roque, Recensement, 1752*, from *Rapport concernant les Archives canadiennes pour l'année 1905*, Ottawa, King's Printer, Volume II, 169 p.

Lawson, John, *Letters on Prince Edward Island*, Charlottetown, George T. Haszard, 1851, (82) p.

LeBlanc, Gabrielle et Diane Lecouffe, compilers, *Inventaire de l'Impartial*, Summerside, S.S.T.A., 1980, 110 p.

Lees, J.G., editor, *An Educational Quo-Vadis: Development of Education in the Atlantic Provinces and Future Trends*, Toronto, Ryerson Press, 1969, 118 p.

MacKinnon, D.A. and A.B. Warburton, editors, *Past and Present of Prince Edward Island*, Charlottetown, B.F. Bowen & Co., (1905), 304, (305a)-400a, 305-731 p.

MacKinnon, Wayne E., *The Life of the Party. A History of the Liberal Party in Prince Edward Island*, Charlottetown, P.E.I. Liberal Party, 1973, 153 p.

MacLean, Jill, *Jean-Pierre Roma of the Company of the East of Isle St. Jean*, Charlottetown, P.E.I. Heritage Foundation, 1977, 46 p.

Macmillan, Rev. John C., *The Early History of the Catholic Church in Prince Edward Island 1721–1835*, Québec, L'Evenement Printing, 1905, xi-304 p.

_____ , *The History of the Catholic Church in Prince Edward Island from 1835 till 1891*, Québec, L'Evenement Printing, 1913, xv-486 p.

Martin, Ernest, *Les Exilés acadiens en France au XVIIIe siècle et leur établissement en Poitou*, Paris, Hachette, 1936, 333 p.

McGregor, John, *British America*, 2 volumes, London, 1832, 605 p.

_____ , *Historical and Descriptive Sketches of the Maritime Colonies of British America*, London, 1828, v-266 p.

Mémoire sur les missions de la Nouvelle-Écosse, du Cap-Breton et de l'Île-du-Prince-Édouard de 1760 à 1820..., Québec, C. Darveau, 1895, 269 p.

Murray, Hugh, *An Historical and Descriptive Account of British America*, Volume II, Edinburgh, Oliver and Boyd, 1839, 356 p.

Pineau, Wilfred, *Le Clergé français dans l'Île-du-Prince-Édouard. 1721–1821*, Québec, Les Éditions Ferland, 1967, 157 p.

Poirier, Pascal, *Le Parler franco-acadien et ses origines*, Québec, Imprimerie Franciscaine Missionnaire, 1928, 339 p.

Pothier, Bernard, *Course à l'Accadie. Journal de Campagne de François Du Pont Duvivier en 1744*, Moncton, Éditions d'Acadie, 1982, 195 p.

Rameau, E., *La France aux colonies : études sur le développement de la race française hors de l'Europe : les Français en Amérique; Acadiens et Canadiens*, Paris, A. Jouby, 1859, xxxix-160-355 p.

Robertson, Ian Ross, *Religion, Politics and Education in Prince Edward Island from 1856 to 1877*, M.A. thesis, McGill University, 1968, 169 p.

Robidoux, Ferdinand J., *Conventions Nationales des Acadiens*, Shédiac, Imprimerie du Moniteur Acadien, xxix-281 p.

Savoie, Alexandre-J., *Un siècle de revendications scolaires au Nouveau-Brunswick 1871–1971. Volume 1, Du français au compte-gouttes 1871–1936*, Edmundston, Savoie, 1978, 255 p.

Smitheram, Milne & Dasgupta, *The Garden Transformed. Prince Edward Island, 1945–1980*, Charlottetown, Ragweed Press, 1982, 271 p.

Stewart, John, *An Account of Prince Edward Island*, London, Printed by W. Winchester, 1806, xiii-304 p.

Surette, Paul, *Memramkouke, Petcoudiac et la Reconstruction de l'Acadie 1763–1806. Histoire des Trois-Rivières*, Memramcook, Société historique de la vallée de Memramcook, 1981, 192 p.

Warburton, A.B., A *History of Prince Edward Island*, St. John, Barnes & Co. Ltd., 1923, xv-494 p.

White, Patrick C.T., *Lord Selkirk's Diary 1803–1804: A Journal of His Travels in British North America and the Northeastern United States*, Toronto, The Champlain Society, 1958, 359-xvi p.

Articles

Arsenault, Georges, "The Acadian Experience in Prince Edward Island", *Les Cahiers*, vol. 14, no. 2 (June 1983), pp. 59-72.

____ , "La Colonisation et les Acadiens de l'Île-du-Prince-Édouard à l'époque des premières Conventions nationales acadiennes", *Les Cahiers*, vol. 16, no. 1 (Jan.-March 1985), pp. 19-30.

____ , "Le Dilemme des Acadiens de l'Île-du-Prince-Édouard au 19e siècle", *Acadiensis*, vol. XIV, no. 2 (Spring 1985), pp. 29-45.

____ , "Historique de l'École Régionale Évangéline", *La Petite Souvenance*, no. 8 (December 1982), pp. 14-20.

____ , "The Miscouche Convention, 1884", *The Island Magazine*, no. 15 (Spring-Summer 1984), pp. 14-19.

____ , "La Société des Dames du Sanctuaire", *La Petite Souvenance*, no. 12 (June 1985), pp. 17-22.

Arsenault, J.-Edmond, "Les Acadiens de l'Île-du-Prince-Édouard", *Action Nationale.* XXXI (May 1948), pp. 362–372

____ , "Les Acadiens et l'Agriculture de l'Île-du-Prince-Édouard", *Culture*, Volume VII, 1946, pp. 220-222.

Blanchard, J.-Henri, "Les Écoles acadiennes de l'Île-du-Prince-Édouard", *Relations*, no. 18 (June 1942), pp. 156-158.

____ , "L'Enseignement du français dans les écoles publiques de l'Île-du-Prince-Édouard", *Deuxième Congrès de la Langue française au Canada. Mémoires*, Volume III, Québec, 1938, pp. 221-230.

Buote, Gilbert, "Un chapitre des troubles à Tignish. L'année des 'constables'", *La Petite Souvenance*, vol. 1, no. 1 (May 1978), pp. 14-18.

Campbell, J. Charles, "School Consolidation: Seventy Years of Evolution", *The Abegweit Review*, vol. 2, no. 2, (Fall 1975), pp. 2-10.

Chiasson, Père Anselme, "Le Clergé et le réveil acadien (1864–1960)", *Revue de l'Université de Moncton*, vol. 11, no. 1 (February 1978), pp. 29-46.

Clark, J.S., "Farmers' Institutes—Or Schools for the People", *The Prince Edward Island Magazine*, vol. 3, no. 3 (May 1901), pp. 86-89.

Croteau, John T., "The Acadian Grain Banks of Prince Edward Island", *Agricultural History*, vol. 29, 1955, pp. 127-130.

——, "The Farmers' Bank of Rustico: An Episode in Acadian History", *The Island Magazine*, no. 4, (Spring-Summer 1978), pp. 3-8.

Gallant, Cécile, "L'Engagement social de Georges-Antoine Belcourt, curé de Rustico, 1859–1869", *Les Cahiers*, vol. 11, no. 4 (December 1980), pp. 316-339.

——, "L'Oeuvre de J.-Henri Blanchard", *La Petite Souvenance*, no. 14 (June 1986), pp. 12-17.

Garner, John, "The Enfranchisement of Roman Catholics in the Maritimes", *The Canadian Historical Review*, vol. 34, no. 3, 1953, pp. 203-218.

Griffiths, Naomi, "The Acadians who had a problem in France", *National Geographic*, vol. 101, no. 4 (Aug./Sept. 1981), pp. 40-45.

Huel, Raymond, "The Irish French Conflict in Catholic Episcopal Nominations: The Western Sees and the Struggle for Domination Within the Church", *The Canadian Catholic Historical Association Study Sessions*, vol. 42, 1975, pp. 51-70.

Michaud, Marguerite, "Mère Évangéline Gallant", *La Petite Souvenance*, no. 8 (December 1982), p. 11-13.

Robertson, Ian Ross, "The Bible Question in Prince Edward Island from 1856 to 1860", *Acadiensis*, vol. V, no. 2 (Spring 1976), pp. 3-25.

——, "Party Politics and Religious Controversialism in Prince Edward Island from 1860 to 1863", *Acadiensis*, vol. VII, no. 2 (Spring 1978), pp. 29-59.

Vass, Elinor, "The Agricultural Societies of Prince Edward Island", *The Island Magazine*, no. 7 (Fall-Winter 1979), pp. 31-37.

"Le Voyage de Franquet aux Îles Royale et Saint-Jean", *Rapport de l'Archiviste de la province de Québec pour 1923–24*, Ls.-A. Proulx, King's Printer, 1924, pp. 111-137.

"Voyage de Célestin Robichaud à l'Île-du-Prince-Édouard en 1825", *Les Cahiers*, vol. 6, no. 1 (March 1975), pp. 43-47.

Weale, David E., "The Mud Diggers", *The Island Magazine*, no. 5 (Fall-Winter 1978), pp. 22-30.

Government Publications

Prince Edward Island

Abstract of the Proceedings of Land Commissioners' Court, Held During the Summer of 1860, to inquire into the difficulties relative to the rights of landowners and tenants in Prince Edward Island, Charlottetown, 1862.

Acts of the General Assembly of Prince Edward Island.

Annual Reports of the Department of Education.

Assembly Debates.

Department of Agriculture Annual Reports.

Department of Fisheries Annual Reports.

Journal of Prince Edward Island House of Assembly.

Laws of Prince Edward Island. 1825–1833.

Report of Proceedings before the Commissioners appointed under the Provisions of "The Land Purchase Act, 1875".

Year Book, Province of Prince Edward Island, 1915, Charlottetown, 1916.

Canada

Documents de la Session du Parlement du Canada.

Recensement du Canada 1880–81, Volume 3, Ottawa, 1883.

Report of the Royal Commission Investigating the Fisheries of the Maritime Provinces and of the Magdalen Islands, Ottawa, 1928.

Plan de développement de l'Île-du-Prince-Édouard. (Le), Ottawa, ministère de l'Expansion économique régionale, 1969, 92 p.

Newspapers

Alberton Pioneer.

The Colonial Herald (Charlottetown).

L'Évangéline (Weymouth and Moncton).

The Examiner (Charlottetown)

L'Impartial (Tignish).

The Islander (Charlottetown).

Le Moniteur Acadien (Shédiac).

The Pioneer (Summerside).

The Prince Edward Island Agriculturalist (Summerside).

The Protector and Christian Witness (Charlottetown).

The Protestant and Evangelical Witness (Charlottetown).

Royal Gazette (Charlottetown).

The Summerside Journal.

The Summerside Progress.

The Vindicator (Charlottetown).

La Voix Acadienne (Summerside).

ARCHIVES

Archives de la Chancellerie de l'Archidiocèse de Montréal.
- Correspondence, Series 255.

Archives de l'Archidiocèse de Québec.
- Correspondence from the Missionaries and the Bishop of Québec, Series 211A, 310 and 311. Documents on microfilm.

Archives des Colonies (France).
- Series $C^{11}A$, $C^{11}B$, $C^{11}C$, $G^{1}466$. Documents on microfilm at the Centre d'études acadiennes.

Archives du Diocèse de Charlottetown.
- Correspondence.

Centre d'études acadiennes (Moncton).
- Fonds Placide-Gaudet (1), Edme-Rameau-de-Saint-Père (2), J.-Henri-Blanchard (22).
- Folklore collections, Eunice Arsenault and Georges Arsenault.
- Burke, Rev. Alfred, *Catholic Parishes of Prince Edward Island*, manuscript.
- Gallant, Patrice, "Les Acadiens à Miquelon", file, manuscript.
- Saint-Hildebert, Soeur, *L'Âme Acadienne*, manuscript, (c. 1941), 363 p. (on microfilm).
- Minutes: P.E.I. Acadian Teachers' Association, Annual Congress, 1893-1963 (on microfilm). Beaubien Office (Rustico) of the Assumption Society (on microfilm).

Colonial Office (London).
- Correspondence and other documents, Series 226 and 227. On microfilm.

Public Archives of Prince Edward Island (Charlottetown).
- Executive Council Minutes (St. John's Island), Volume I.
- Minutes of Meetings of the Board of Education for P.E.I. 1877–1892, Record group 10.
- Court Case Papers 1780, Supreme Court of Judicature, Record group 6.
- "Report of the Parliamentary Committee appointed to Investigate and Report upon the manner in what the Education Law has been and is being carried on in the Public Educational Establishments of the Island", (1867), Record group 10.
- Conveyance Registers.

La Société Saint-Thomas d'Aquin.
- Minutes of meetings, *Le Bulletin*, correspondence.

INDEX